PENGUIN BOOKS

CHINESE SHADOWS

Pierre Ryckmans, who writes under the pseudonym Simon Leys, was born in Brussels in 1935. Although he holds doctorates in law and in the history of art and archaeology from the University of Louvain, his predominant interests are the language and culture of China, which he calls "the country I love more than my own." During more than twenty years devoted to Sinology, he has given courses in art history at the Chinese University of Hong Kong, served as cultural attaché at the Belgian Embassy in Peking, and taught Chinese language and literature at the Australian National University in Canberra, his current post. In 1971 Dr. Ryckmans published *La Vie et l'oeuvre de Su Renshan, rebelle, peintre et fou,* a study of an eccentric nineteenth-century Chinese painter that won the prestigious Stanislaus-Julien Prize from the Institut de France. He has also published three volumes of translations from the Chinese as well as works of his own on Chinese subjects—among the latter *Les Habits neufs du Président Mao,* which John K. Fairbank in the *New York Times* described as "one of the most caustic exposés by a Sinologist of the Cultural Revolution's basically anti-intellectual attack on China's cultural heritage." Dr. Ryckmans is married to a Chinese woman, Han-fang, to whom the present book is dedicated.

Thus, if a foreigner could be found today who, though admitted to the Chinese banquet, would not hesitate to rant in our name against the present state of China, him I would call a truly honest man, a truly admirable man!

—Lu Hsün

The pamphlet ought to be the literary form of an age like our own; we live in a time when political passions run high, channels of free expression are dwindling, and organized lying exists on a scale never before known. For plugging the holes of history, the pamphlet is the ideal form.

—George Orwell

CHINESE SHADOWS
CHINESE SHADOWS

by Simon Leys

PENGUIN BOOKS

Penguin Books Ltd, Harmondsworth,
Middlesex, England
Penguin Books, 625 Madison Avenue,
New York, New York 10022, U.S.A.
Penguin Books Australia Ltd, Ringwood,
Victoria, Australia
Penguin Books Canada Limited, 2801 John Street,
Markham, Ontario, Canada L3R 1B4
Penguin Books (N.Z.) Ltd, 182–190 Wairau Road,
Auckland 10, New Zealand

First published in France under the title *Ombres Chinoises* 1974
First published in the United States of America by
The Viking Press 1977
Published in Penguin Books 1978
Reprinted 1978 (twice)

LIBRARY OF CONGRESS CATALOGING IN PUBLICATION DATA
Ryckmans, Pierre.
Chinese shadows.
Translation of Ombres chinoises.
Bibliography: p. 211.
Includes index.
1. China—Description and travel—1949–
2. Ryckmans, Pierre. I. Title.
DS711.R9313 1978   915.1'04'5   77-15419
ISBN 0 14 00.4787 5

Printed in the United States of America by
Offset Paperback Mfrs., Inc., Dallas, Pennsylvania
Set in Linotype Caledonia

ACKNOWLEDGMENTS
Atheneum Publishers: From *Hope Against Hope* by Nadezhda Mandelstam, translated by
Max Hayward. Copyright © Atheneum Publishers, 1970. Reprinted by permission of
the publishers.

Brandt & Brandt, A. M. Heath & Co. Ltd, Mrs. Sonia Brownell Orwell and Martin Secker
& Warburg: From *Nineteen Eighty-Four* by George Orwell. Copyright 1949 by Harcourt,
Brace & World, Inc., copyright renewed © Sonia Brownell Orwell. 1976. Reprinted by
permission.

Harcourt Brace Jovanovich, Inc.: From "Some Thoughts on the Common Toad," Volume
IV, from "Inside the Whale," Volume 1, from *The Collected Essays, Journalism and
Letters of George Orwell*. Reprinted by permission.

to Han-fang

Contents

A Note from the Author

Nothing prepared me to become involved in contemporary political polemics. My scholarly research revolved around topics generally remote from foreign affairs. My own political stand, deeply felt but not coherently formulated, can be summarized as a basic adhesion to socialism—the humanistic, anti-totalitarian brand of socialism exemplified by Orwell, for instance—combined with a spontaneous if somewhat muddled sympathy for anarchism.

My interest in China was triggered by a visit I made to the young People's Republic when I was 19. This experience did not merely arouse a burst of juvenile enthusiasm: it was the starting point of a lifetime's exclusive vocation. For 20 years my life and work has been entirely devoted to the study of China, her language, and her culture. Ten of those years I spent continuously in the Far East (Singapore, Taiwan, and Hong Kong), where I found among the Chinese my dearest friends and most inspiring teachers, and where I met my wife, to whom I feel I owe almost everything.

Until 1966 Chinese politics did not loom large in my preoccupations, and I confidently extended to the Maoist regime the same sympathy I felt for all things Chinese, without giving it more specific thought. But the Cultural Revolution, which I observed from beginning to end from the vantage point of Hong Kong, forced me out of this comfortable ignorance. At first, I had the highest expectations for the Revolution with its stirring mobilization of youthful revolutionary fervor. But soon, alas and inevitably, it showed its real nature: neither revolutionary nor cultural, the movement ended up in ruthless military repression and the apotheosis of a semi-fascist, Lin Piao. Yet while it was going on, the Cultural Revolution, through both the official press and the organs of the various rebel-revolutionary groups, provided an unprecedented flow of information on the inner workings of the Maoist regime. Living among Chinese and on the very doorstep of China, subjected daily to a flood of fascinating political literature, orthodox and heretical, straight from the People's Republic, meeting young rebels and Red Guards who had just escaped from the military-bureaucratic repression, it was impossible to remain aloof from the political turmoil.

For four years I spent most of my time collecting and analyzing Chinese documents relating to the Cultural Revolution. To my increasing dismay and horror, I realized that in the West, news media kept the public almost entirely ignorant of the evidence available to anyone who could read Chinese. As for professional China-watchers, they already knew most of the facts I was compiling, but, with no particular commitment to the Chinese people, they were content to feed their employers the required amount of information, and seemed to have no compulsion to come out publicly and put themselves in the uncomfortable position of being a a witness to the truth. At first I myself was reluctant to speak out: not being a political scientist, I felt ill-qualified to write on political issues. Also, I foresaw to some degree the anger which my ill-timed and unfashionable utterances would provoke amongst the largely pro-Maoist Western intelligentsia. Most of all, I was frankly terrified of the idea that in reprisal, the Maoist authorities would bar me forever from the country I love more than my own. (Thus does the People's Republic blackmail into silence countless witnesses who happen to know too much about China.) Nevertheless, the indignation I felt when I saw how information on China was deliberately censored in the West compelled me to write and publish an account of the Cultural Revolution: *Les Habits neufs du Président Mao*. The book did raise a storm, yet it is one of the very few early studies of the Cultural Revolution that has stood the test of time: not only was the accuracy of my analysis confirmed by subsequent events, but the book even proved prophetic in its prognosis (one year before Lin Piao's fall) of a latent conflict between Mao and his heir-designate.

In order to keep open the possibility of visiting China again, I wrote *Les Habit neufs du Président Mao* under the pseudonym Simon Leys, Leys being a common Flemish surname which also alludes to V. Segalen's posthumous masterpiece *René Leys*. Thanks to this device I was able to return twice more to China, first on diplomatic assignment for a half a year in 1972, and then again in 1973 for a shorter visit. [*Chinese Shadows* is the result of these personal experiences.]

My love for China and her people was if anything increased by those last encounters. Yet I feel that however considerable the achievements of the present regime, we should not forget, if we have any respect for the Chinese and their culture, what price the people have paid for those accomplishments. Most of the praise bestowed on Mao and his bureaucrats by Westerners comes from people who feel only contempt for Chinese people and who are ignorant of Chinese culture. Is it not time, then, for someone who owes China all that he treasures most in his life to stand up and criticize Maoism on behalf of those who taught him so much? We must acknowledge the considerable material improvements in many areas of Chinese life since 1948, but at the same time it is a fantastic imposture to present the regime as socialist and revolutionary when in fact it is essentially totalitarian and feudal-bureaucratic.

In Europe the Maoist faithful, incensed by my sacrilege, zealously tracked down my real identity and dutifully denounced me to the Peking authorities. My pen name thus lost its original function, but I have continued to use it for my political and polemical essays. My only wish is that writers with better qualifications than I will soon take my place and deal with these political issues, so that Leys can retire and Ryckmans can quietly return to the plowing of his own old field.

1976   Simon Leys

Foreword

In politics more than in anything else, the beginning of everything lies in moral indignation.

—*Milovan Djilas*

This short book is the result of a six-month stay in China which I made in 1972.

The pages that follow may be criticized for being disjointed and negative, and the criticism would be valid had I wished to give a general accounting of the People's Republic. But my aim was not to question the achievements of the Mao–Liu regime,[1] which if not always so revolutionary as their Western supporters would claim, are still considerable in several fields. There is no question of describing them once again; this has already been done in the West by distinguished professionals who are much better qualified than I. I am thinking of the works of Han Suyin (not her first book, written when Chiang Kai-shek was at the height of his power and still full of praise for the Generalissimo and the Madamissima, but her more recent works), the books and articles by Edgar Snow, the writings of John King Fairbank (published in 1972 in *Foreign Affairs*),[2] and so on. My little book, far from having the impudent ambition to rival them, even less to dispute them, aims at being their modest complement, adding only some shadows without which even the most luminous portrait lacks depth, offering a few notes—in counterpoint, as it

1. When in fact—if not in name—Liu Shao-ch'i's policy is applied in almost all fields, when nine-tenths of his men are back in the saddle, it would be unfair not to associate the name of the former head of state with Mao's.

2. Since included in his *China Perceived* (New York, 1974).

were—about some details that have been omitted for one reason or another by those prestigious witnesses. As the Chinese maxim says, "In a thousand observations, the wise may make one that is foolish and the fool one that is wise." Let us simply say that I am offering here the modest contribution of the fool to the pertinent remarks of the wise.

Some people will no doubt also reproach me for treating grave matters lightly. This reproach is also well founded. I can only paint shadows, and is it not in their very nature to be weightless? The good souls who deplore the skimpiness or levity of these pages should know that it irritated me even more. I maintain that under the conditions in which foreign residents and visitors now live in the People's Republic of China, it is impossible to write anything but frivolities, and those who think they can do something serious when reporting their Chinese experiences, or who pretend they describe Chinese realities when they are in fact describing the Chinese shadow play produced for them by Maoist authorities, either deceive their readers or, worse, delude themselves.

As for me, the only advantage I derived from my knowledge of the language and from a fairly long experience of Chinese life prior to my 1972 visit was that I could better measure with what efficacy the Maoist authorities are now able to prevent all natural human contacts, however brief, between foreigners and the Chinese people.

Being effectively cut off from the only important reality— the daily life of the Chinese people—the foreigner who wants to talk about "China" can do one of only two things: he can copy down the official slogans (which he gets either in "interviews" or in propaganda leaflets distributed freely in twelve languages), or he can try desperately to glean the crumbs of the reality denied to him, and to patch together as best he can a series of unrelated vignettes. Since doing the first would have meant reduplicating the work of Le Monde/New China[3] or emulating

3. Le Monde used to be, many years ago, a prestigious French newspaper. Lately, however, it has been reduced to the status of a daily supple-

famous living ideologues, I have chosen the second, frivolous as it seems.

"Why the hell did you go back to China?" I was asked in Paris by one of my elders in Sinology—a scholar whom I like and respect. I confess that his question astounded me. Is there a Sinologist alive who does not feel in exile when he is away from China? Another one—a dear friend—said to me: "Your book *Les Habits neufs du Président Mao* was a pretty piece, but I hope you'll waste no more time with Chinese affairs. Leave that to journalists, and come back to your work on the classics." Such advice reminds me that, alas, "Sinology" rhymes with "Assyriology" or even "entomology." God knows how much simpler life would be if only China of the past claimed our attention! How easy it would be to keep silent on the living, suffering China, and at that price to keep open the possibility of seeing once again that beloved country—but I fear that such a silence would be the silence Lu Hsün was talking about in his famous remark: "John Stuart Mill said that dictatorship makes people cynical; he did not realize that there would be republics to make them mute."[4]

1973   Simon Leys

---

ment to a monthly called *La Nouvelle Chine*, the informal organ of the Chinese Embassy in Paris, edited by the same journalists.
4. *Lu Hsün ch'üan-chi* (Peking, 1963), III, 396. One should not be surprised to find so many quotations from Lu Hsün (1881–1936), China's greatest modern writer, in my book. Chairman Mao, who consecrated himself as intellectual master of contemporary China, was once of the opinion that his works were of burning relevance. I have just read through them all again, and I am of the same opinion. Lu Hsün fought relentlessly for the cause of enlightenment, social revolution, human dignity, and intellectual freedom. A fierce enemy of the Kuomintang dictatorship, after his death his memory was manipulated by the Maoists who tried to annex him posthumously to their camp by means of various falsifications.

Foreword to the English-Language Edition

In handbooks on Chinese traditional painting, an advice commonly given to the artist who wishes to learn to paint trees is to sketch them in winter, for then, without the seductive yet confused and blurry effect of their leafy masses, through their stark nudity they can best reveal their inner structure and specific character. These sketches of the People's Republic of China were made at the end of one of its most rigorous political winters. Faint stirrings of a timid spring were beginning to make themselves felt, here and there, but this did not much alter the drab outline of the scenery.

I have no doubt that a superficial observer visiting China this year might discover a certain amount of *quantitative* discrepancies between his experiences and mine: since I wrote this book, things have evolved a bit—I mean, the free zone for foreigners around Peking may have been enlarged by a few miles, a few more museums, monuments, and temples may have reopened, a little more variety may have been introduced in the theaters, bookshops may display more books, and so forth. And on the whole the atmosphere may be more relaxed and pleasant. Yet these appearances could be quite misleading if the visitor were to take them for permanent features of the regime. Beneath this welcoming veneer lies, unchanged, a harsh and dour reality, the reality I saw before most of its present cosmetics had been applied—and foreigners who had stayed in Peking two or three years before me had seen it in the raw. It may be useful to know what China actually was like when I was there, since it can and will be like that again at any time. If you do not believe me, wait until next "winter," and you will find that my book deals not so much with the past as with the future.

Not that I claim for myself any prophetic insight: it is simply that totalitarian regimes have very little capacity for change, and the validity of whatever truths one may gather about them is bound to endure as long as the regimes themselves. (This applies even beyond ethnic and cultural frontiers: I was privileged to work in Peking with a man who had a long and thorough experience of Stalinist Russia, and despite his lack of any previous knowledge of China, he quickly felt at home with the Maoist regime.) Thus, most of what I wrote in these pages belongs to a category of observation that, bearing as it does on the basic, permanent nature of the system, should have a kind of timeless relevance; in this respect I consider as central the descriptions of the "class-struggle" (Chapter 8), of the bureaucracy (Chapter 5), of cultural policy (Chapter 6).

Other notations here and there may seem to be about less permanent features of China; yet I believe that the passage of time will not make them irrelevant. "Any fool may write a most valuable book by chance if he will tell us what he heard and saw with veracity," said Thomas Gray,[1] and indeed any faithful record kept by a resident of a foreign enclave under the Ch'ing dynasty, for instance, even if full of ephemeral trifles, would yield today a considerable measure of historical interest. Thus I feel that any attempt to update this candid account—like indicating what new embassies have been established in San-li-t'un since I left that ghastly diplomatic ghetto, or mentioning that K'ang Sheng and Chou En-lai and Mao Tse-tung have since died, or that Chairman Mao perpetrated another lousy poem and other equally worthy news items that are in your daily newspaper anyway—far from enhancing its interest would compromise its only asset, which is not that it provides a journalistic report of events but that it confesses a certain human experience, an ad-

---

1. In a letter to Horace Walpole about Boswell's *Account of Corsica*.

mittedly subjective yet genuine and deeply felt response to a phenomenon of world significance.

Confucius said—it is not very fashionable to quote Confucius nowadays, but this book, needless to say, does not concern itself with prevalent fashions—that real knowledge was to know the extent of one's ignorance (*Analects*, II, 17). A valiant academic journalist who visited China on one of those standard six-week tours (to be described here in Chapter 1) wrote a book of a fairly impressive size, which he had the guts to subtitle *The Real China*. I may not know the "real China" much better than he does; the main difference between him and me is that I know that I don't. And if I can help the reader to realize to what extent we do not know China, I shall have accomplished a tremendous feat. Actually my book could be entitled *The Unreal China*. Unreal in two senses: first, because it deals in part with the stage settings artificially created in China for the use of foreign visitors, second, because like most other books on the People's Republic it focuses not on the real life of real people (to which, alas! we have no access) but on the puppet theater of the Maoist gerontocrats, those wretched lead-and-cardboard bureaucrats who are mistaken for China's driving forces when they merely weigh on it as its fetters. (In a way, Mao himself has finally become as irrelevant to China's needs as Nixon to America's—which might explain why those two gentlemen grew so fond of each other.)

The pessimism that emanates from this book derives precisely from the essential unreality of its subject. But let this not mislead the reader: there is also a young, revolutionary China, repeatedly suppressed yet constantly struggling. Though invisible to us most of the time, it periodically bursts into the open with stupendous courage. To mention only two recent instances, I think of Li Yi-che's manifesto *On Democracy and Legality under Socialism*, which was defiantly posted on the walls of Kwangchow at the end of 1974, and of the spontaneous mass manifestation that exploded on April 5, 1976, in the heart of Peking denouncing "the feudal rule of the new Ch'in Shih-huang" (China's most dreaded tyrant, whose name has become a code word for Mao in the symbolic language of Chinese politics). On this "real China" we found our hopes: the future belongs to it.

1976   SIMON LEYS

1 Foreigners in the People's Republic

Throughout the ages, the Chinese have had only two ways of looking at foreigners: up to them as superior beings or down on them as wild animals. They have never been able to treat them as friends, to consider them as people like themselves.[1]

—*Lu Hsün*

As long as there is one paying ruffian in the audience, we shall not be sure of success, said the boss of the claque.

—*Paul Claudel*

Everyone has heard the story of the American journalist who like everyone else wrote a report on his travels in China. Trouble was—he hadn't been there. The hoax was uncovered, there was a scandal, and the poor fellow lost his job.

What is remarkable in this story is that the hoax was found out. Things being what they are, it seems to me that the feeblest hack should be able to write a report on China that would be lively, colorful, instructive, consistent, and convincing—all this without leaving his desk. Doesn't he have a hundred more or less identical models to guide him? And if professional scruple

---

1. *Lu Hsün ch'üan-chi* (Peking, 1963), I, 409. Like most of Lu Hsün's polemical utterances, this one, which was written in 1919 against the reigning orthodoxy, can well be applied to the Maoist bureaucracy today. However, it would be unfair to apply it more generally. Left to themselves, the Chinese people are the most friendly and hospitable people in the world.

got the better of him and he actually decided to look at China for himself, what more would he see that the others had missed? He would make the same tours with the same guides, sleep in the same hotels, visit the same institutions, meet the same people[2] who would tell him the same things; he would partake of the same banquets, where the same speeches would be heard—always conforming to an unvarying and unreal ritual, neither Western nor Chinese, belonging to an abstract world conceived by Maoist bureaucrats especially for foreign guests.

(A small classic example of this new ritual is the Used Razor Blade gambit, which crops up time and time again: the traveler leaves a used razor blade in his hotel room, and it is scrupulously returned to him at each stop on his trip; he can't get rid of it until he reaches Hong Kong. There is quite a stock of these touching and funny anecdotes; it would be amusing to collect them. Comparing them to the tales told by travelers a century ago, one finds that the image of virtuous, hard-working, and honest China given by today's pilgrims has something in common with the corrupt, lazy, pilfering China pictured by the Cook travelers of an earlier day: both versions are exotic, artificial, arbitrary.)

In the tours for foreign visitors, always superbly organized, anything that might be unpredictable, unexpected, spontaneous, or improvised is ruthlessly eliminated. Leisure, too: the visitors' programs are arranged to keep them on the go from dawn to late at night. In this life of forced labor in political tourism, it is technically possible to escape for fleeting moments, but this is not recommended: as will be seen below, it makes life more difficult for oneself as well as for one's keeper.

Yet most travelers who "do" China in this way, in three weeks, look back favorably on their experience. There is plenty of variety in the trips and the days are more than full. They

---

2. But not always in the same clothes: military men, who nowadays manage most of the large factories, are in mufti to greet common tourists; they only don their uniforms when their visitors already know who they really are.

think that if they did not accomplish more—well, it is because human beings are limited and a day has only twenty-four hours. But if they stayed longer, they would quickly find out how narrow, repetitive, and monotonous their experience was, how little they saw that was new; you don't have to take seven trips into the provinces, as I did, to discover this.

The Maoist authorities have accomplished a strange *tour de force*: they have managed to limit China—that immense and varied universe, for the exploration of which, however superficial, a lifetime is inadequate—to a narrow, incredibly constricted area. China has hundreds of cities; only about a dozen are open to ordinary foreigners. In each one, the foreigners are always put in the same hotel—usually a huge palace, set like a fortress in the middle of a vast garden, far away in a distant suburb. In these hotels, the guests enjoy a restaurant that offers the best cooking available in the province, a barbershop and hairdresser, a bookstore that sells luxury editions and art reproductions unavailable in the city itself, an auditorium where films are shown and where artists sometimes come to give special performances for the foreign guests. Needless to say, the local public is not admitted: watchmen at the gate check the identity of all Chinese visitors. In this way, the only contact the travelers have with the towns they "visit" is as they speed past along the boulevards, driving to factories and hospitals in the routine way.

If we see little of urban China, what of rural China! The countryside, which constitutes the true reality of China and where the destiny of the country is being decided, is a complete blank for us. Out of the tens of thousands of villages where more than 80 per cent of the Chinese people live, foreigners visit less than a dozen (and always the same ones); these are interesting in the limited way of agricultural pavilions at an international fair.

Since the vast Chinese world has thus been shrunk to the size of a pinhead, there don't have to be many foreign visitors in circulation for them to get the impression that they are all over the place, treading on each other's toes. Beyond space and time, a kind of Freemasonry springs up among them, the way it does among commuters on a shared little suburban tram line; thus one learns that French Senator F. sprained his ankle on the staircase of this monument; they show you the place where the Danish writer R. bought a shepherd's whistle and where the American newspaperman B. bought a walking stick; one travels in the limousine that carried the Italian lady M., ideologist of Maoism. This would be funny if it were Liechtenstein, but when one thinks of immense China being reduced to this puny size, to this cozy promiscuity of a small-town Rotary Club, sadness grips the heart.

The same treatment has been given to the Chinese population: out of eight hundred million Chinese, foreigners meet about sixty individuals. The literary world is represented by two or three writers, always the same, who take care of visiting men of letters; the same is true of scientists, scholars, and so on. It would seem that the thousands of foreigners who visit China each year all meet this inevitable handful of people, for whom greeting foreigners is a full-time job. But if by chance you knew some other personalities—artists, writers, or scholars—apart from those few pathetic mummies who have been cleared to be full-time public-relations men, you may well have to wait a long time to see them again. The chances you have of meeting someone are generally in inverse ratio to the gain you might enjoy from the encounter: for example, a senator from Texas or an Australian farmer is more likely to be allowed to meet a well-known archaeologist or a specialist in epigraphy—especially if he has not asked to—while it will be very hard for a specialist in those fields to enjoy the same privilege. If it appears that you are *less* ignorant than you decently should be about current changes in the political or cultural life of China, and if on top of that you know enough Chinese to be able to dispense with an interpreter, all your requests to meet various people, or just to know what has happened to them, will sink without a trace in the sands of a timid and fear-ridden bureaucracy.

"Friendship between peoples" is always exalted in China: the slogan is repeated in every speech, written in gigantic ideograms on every wall. But friendship between individuals is efficiently discouraged: the reader will find a number of instructive stories about this in the following pages. If the Maoist authorities, welcoming foreign visitors, run China like a restricted club, it is a *colonial* club, where meeting the "natives" is frowned upon. The only Chinese people one can talk to without getting into trouble are servants (personnel provided by the service section of the Ministry of Foreign Affairs), bureaucrats one meets at official gatherings, guides and interpreters provided by the government's travel agency, and "professional friends." These last are bureaucrats from the Foreign Office on temporary assignment to keep foreigners company; their names—they are few—come up time and again in the many accounts written by travelers who think, naïvely, that they had managed to make friends in China. As long as they are attached to you, you will find them talkative and pleasant, maybe even warm-hearted; but if you try to prolong the friendship beyond the term of their official mission, you risk disappointment.

If for most of the people traveling in China the trip is as neutral, aseptic, and predictable as if it had been planned by the Club Méditerranée, from time to time foreign residents learn with envious astonishment that so-and-so has been allowed some extraordinary expedition: a cruise on the Upper Yangtze, a visit to Lhasa, a safari in Yunnan! . . . If you meet the lucky pilgrim, do not expect extraordinary revelations: if he could make them, the privilege would not have been extended in the first place. Those who enjoy such luck are paid hacks, whose faculties of observation are so limited that they could as easily write their stuff before their departure, glancing through back issues of *China Reconstructs*, or they are people whose credulity or fanatical devotion to Maoism effectively protects them from reality. I shall give only one example, but a good one. Professor N., unlike most Western Maoists, is an authentic Sinologist; he is a first-class scholar, a delightful person, a man of integrity: but on anything relating to Maoist China, something clicks in his brain, instantaneously and completely blocking his critical judgment. He came back to China in 1972 and went on an amazing trip into remote provinces that are inaccessible to ordinary visitors. He returned with wonderful tales about the flourishing state of traditional culture and religions. But he puzzled me: in the interview he gave to a Hong Kong daily newspaper when he came out of China, he mixed descriptions that I could not verify (of places where I could not go) with descriptions of Peking landmarks that were familiar to me: for instance, he talked about the "remarkably well-preserved state of the famous Taoist Temple of the White Cloud," which, "with its precious collection of sacred books," is now "carefully protected." I had not had the chance, as Professor N. did, to visit Yunnan monasteries or Szechwan temples, but in Peking I lived ten minutes away by bicycle from the poor White Cloud, and I often sadly prowled about it. Someone who did not know Professor N. might suspect him of black humor: "carefully protected"—the White Cloud? I can believe it: it is used as an army barracks! (Later on I shall discuss in greater detail the sorry state of the Peking monuments.) Now some may argue that modern China can well do without its Taoist temples and that it is healthy for China to be rid of them. Without subscribing fully to this opinion, I am aware of the excellent arguments supporting it. It is not the transformation of temples into barracks that angers me, but the lies surrounding such an act, and the efforts made to disseminate those lies in the West by such means as these.

This kind of blindness comes the more easily to other foreign devotees, for the simple reason that in contradistinction to Professor N. their ignorance of China—its language, its past, and its present—is in direct proportion to their Maoist fervor; in a way, their ignorance makes the fervor possible. The most ambitious among them sometimes manage to decipher some Thought of Mao in the original, word by word, as if they were reading some Sumerian inscription, and this Chinese hobby entitles them to call themselves "Sinologists" (why not, after all? There is no patent on the label), though they would never dream of traveling in China without an interpreter. But they, like the more modest pilgrims, lack any curiosity about the concrete reality that is China. I know some who have come to China regularly for twenty years but have never, *never* taken a bus, or eaten a bowl of noodles at a corner stand, or shared a supper or an informal evening with a family of friends. Why take the bus, when a government car is always at their disposal? Why risk going to a "native" eating place, when every day they can enjoy a wonderful banquet paid for by the state? How could they share the intimacy of a family, when they meet only "professional friends" provided by the government? Having lived for six months in the Peking Hotel, which is the usual principal stopping place for most of these traveling salesmen of Maoism, I got to know them a little; they are nice people on the whole, and with some of them one can get along even when one is not of the same faith— on condition that one leaves China aside, since their abysmal ignorance and completely unconscious contempt for the country never cease to shock.

For example, the chairman of some international antifascist committee tells me at breakfast that he is leaving for the provinces the same afternoon.

"Wonderful! Where are you going?"

"Er, uh, well, you know, these Chinese names . . . [turning to his interpreter]—Wang, where are we going?"

"To Hangchow."

"Oh yes, to Hankow, I remember now."

Another party stalwart, who has come every year to Peking since 1949, eats only Western food. "Chinese cooking, you know, gives me diarrhea," this old "friend of China" explains. There is something symbolic in such a persistent allergy to the daily rice of eight hundred million Chinese. . . .

These docile visitors—who would never have the bad taste to venture alone in the streets to find out how people live, who never go anywhere without their guide and their interpreter, who meekly accept their cloistered existence in dismal palaces, blind and deaf to Chinese sights and sounds—fit superbly into the official plans. Their obedience is rewarded with free trips, which they repay by publishing articles or even books that pretend to describe China. In fact, these books are only a clever paste-up of what is published weekly in *Peking Review*, and in several languages, only changed into first-person direct discourse to give the illusion of a personal touch.

This is not hard to do. First you take the official version: "Under the direction of the Chinese Communist Party and enlightened by the Thought of Mao Tse-tung, the poor and middle-poor peasants of Lin-hsien district have waged a stubborn fight to overcome victoriously the sabotages of the counterrevolutionary revisionist line of the traitor Liu Shao-ch'i." Then you change it into direct discourse: "During my visit to Lin-hsien, I had the opportunity to talk to many peasants. One of them, a sturdy old farmer, his face deeply lined by the toil of years, told me: 'Yes, here we had to fight hard; the followers of Liu Shao-ch'i tried everything to sabotage our revolutionary spirit; but we got the better of them in the end. What could they do? [Here a gleam of malice appears in his eyes.] We, *we* were guided by the Party and by Chairman Mao, so who would have a chance against us?'" And so on.

Chinese authorities are especially grateful to the willing visitors for their lack of untimely curiosity about the political somersaults of the regime. Here, since the travelers know nothing, nothing surprises them. Liu Shao-ch'i, the head of state, right arm and successor-designate of Chairman Mao, suddenly becomes a traitor working for the restoration of capitalism. Ch'en Po-ta, confidential secretary to Chairman Mao and master ideologist of the Cultural Revolution, turns out to be a crook. Lin Piao, Chairman Mao's closest comrade in arms and his second heir-designate, is unmasked as an abominable plotter, assassin, and potential usurper. All these violent alterations leave our pilgrims unmoved. Ch'en and Lin, first accused of "leftism," are now indicted for "rightism." They played a major role in eliminating their sworn enemy, Liu Shao-ch'i, and they are now presented as his accomplices. The Cultural Revolution is paid lip service, but its main results are buried or denied and its promoters, one by one, are cast into outer darkness. The person of Liu Shao-ch'i is still reviled, but all his henchmen are back in power, and his policies are vigorously pursued again in all fields, the same "revisionist" policies which led to his downfall. These contradictions do not shake the faith of the believers but only strengthen it. *Credo quia absurdum.*

The blind docility with which these Western apologists of Maoism unconditionally follow the fluctuations of the Peking line sometimes embarrasses their employers; carried away by zeal, they sometimes miss a turn. In their eagerness to please the powers that be or those whom they believe to be in power (unfortunately it's a rather impermanent position), they sometimes "add paws to the snake,"[3] and thus detract from the credibility of their picture. At the time when Lin Piao's disgrace was well known throughout China, *Le Monde* explained ponderously that Lin still had the complete confidence of the Great Helmsman and that any other information could only be scurrilous calumnies propagated by CIA agents in Hong Kong.

But if they are sometimes a bit slow to realize that the wind has changed direction, they work doubly hard once they grasp which way it is blowing. Lu Hsün said, "Beat the dog, even after it has fallen in the water." They give that saying a new twist: "Never beat the dog *until* it has fallen in the water." Once they see the old heroes in the gutter, they make up for lost time in reviling them by doling out a double ration of insult. Thus, the most furious foes of Liu Shao-ch'i are those who described his

---

3. A reference to a Chinese proverb: in a competition to see who could draw a picture of a snake in the shortest time, the potential winner, trying to show off, destroyed his advantage by adding paws to his snake and thus it was a snake no longer.

China of the early 1960s as a kind of paradise: they suddenly discover *now* that China *then* suffered from famine and bureaucratic oppression, which of course were due to the sabotages of the all-powerful and all-present Liu. But anybody who might have been bold enough at the time to see the evidence of famine and oppression—and it was certainly obvious enough—would have been nothing but a lying detractor in the pay of the Americans. . . . This retrospective science practiced by the incense burners to Maoism can be seen most clearly in the Cultural Revolution: the way they discerned, after the event, the outrageous things that had remained invisible to them when they were actually happening is wondrous indeed.

We are all familiar with the magical hysteria of the Mao cult of 1966–70, with its incantations, amulets, and miracles. But even its most delirious manifestations did not shake the faithful: on the contrary, they became indignant when they saw the smirk of unbelief on the faces of those who observed their delirium. Only when new instructions were issued in 1971–72 did these enthusiasts begin to suspect "formalist deviations" or even "Lin Piaoist plots" in the madness they had supported so happily for four years. The bloody violence of the Cultural Revolution was known to all: one would have thought that confronted with the stark evidence our Maoists would have at least kept quiet. But no. Once again they accused all witnesses of lying—until . . . until Mao himself exonerated the witnesses, confiding to Edgar Snow in a well-remembered interview: "Foreign journalists have written about the excesses of the Cultural Revolution, but in fact they understated them." Meanwhile, for practical reasons, Mao found it necessary to disavow his former shock troops and to support their former enemies against them. It therefore also became necessary to argue that a so-called "extreme left" was guilty of a maximum number of crimes, for it was no longer useful and indeed was beginning to impede reconstruction of the military-bureaucratic machine, which alone could restore order in the country. Meekly, Maoist spokesmen in the West started talking about various atrocities that the "extreme left" had been guilty of during the Cultural Revolution, while conveniently forgetting the insults they had heaped on observers who had recorded the same facts at the time. Never, but never, did they dare to trust their own senses, to see for themselves the objective reality, but instead waited for the official version of what had happened before they uttered an opinion. If necessary, if such are the instructions, they will not waver in proclaiming that the deer they see is a horse, like the sycophants of Ch'in.[4]

"We have friends all over the world." This Thought of Chairman Mao can be seen on many walls. I do not know how much satisfaction the Chinese people derive from that idea, but the sight of those "friends" must leave them somewhat puzzled. I was certainly puzzled—when I lived in the Peking Hotel and had the opportunity to see them—for I could not understand the criteria used by the People's Republic in selecting its guests. It would appear that the elite of the guests are, as they were before 1949, under the old regime, the private friends of influential people—at that level ideological problems are not very important. I would put in that category two mysterious pianists—an American couple who were allowed an extraordinary trip across regions of China usually forbidden to foreigners. I do not know if such a privilege could be justified by their musical talents alone, for the only concert they gave in Peking, under the evocative title "From Bach to Rock and Back," was reserved to high cadres of the regime and foreigners were barred. What I do know is that, if the husband had the style of a fairground hustler in the Wild West, his wife was the daughter of a former bishop

4. A Chinese proverbial saying: the scheming prime minister of the second Ch'in emperor (3rd century B.C.), trying to determine who among the courtiers were his followers, pretended that a deer presented in court was actually a horse. All those who insisted it was a deer were later eradicated.

of Hankow who had been a friend of Chou En-lai in the 1920s.

Beyond these "private friendships," most visitors to China reflect "collective friendships," and these of course depend on the vicissitudes of international politics. Around October 1 (the Chinese National Day), Peking hotels are filled with foreign delegations, and the menus improve markedly for a few weeks. Rumanian officers in operetta costumes, covered with decorations, mingle with North Koreans with wooden faces and black suits who look like peasants going to Sunday Mass. The Vietnamese may be socialist and proletarian, but they are remarkable for their fragile grace; the Japanese are zealous flag-wavers and wear under their tangles of cameras and photographic equipment Mao signs as big as soup plates. In contrast with these disciplined units, the Africans, flamboyant and cheerfully noisy, offer a nice anarchic touch; they flummox their guides by asking for beer and women. Apart from these large groups, there are the small groups of improbable visitors: schoolteachers from Brittany, businessmen from Peru, railwaymen from New Zealand, progressive writers from Mauritius. . . . I nearly forgot the Americans, who are a separate species: newspapermen, hippies, politicians, professors, actors, congressmen—they come from all segments of society, but they all seem to swim in the same ecstatic stream. (The only American visitor whom I saw somewhat disappointed was one of the organizers of McGovern's presidential campaign; before the 1972 election he came to China in the hope of getting some support for or at least a show of interest in the Democratic candidate; he found that the Maoist authorities were stanch Nixonians.)[5]

Chinese from abroad who come back to visit the motherland are put in a special category. The Maoist authorities, with their

5. The ignorance of some of those visitors is truly astounding: the credulity with which they accepted some of the crudest anti-Communist clichés during the Cold War in part explains their surprise and enthusiasm today. I remember, for example, an important businessman who came to Peking with a small suitcase full of soap and toilet paper, convinced that such commodities were unknown in China.

fixation on classification, their obsession with hierarchy, arrange them in four different groups. At the top, you have the Chinese who have taken out foreign citizenship. They are the only ones we meet, because they stay in the same hotels and enjoy the same material privileges. But—*noblesse oblige*—these aristocrats also suffer from the same disabilities in their contacts with the people, including members of their own families. While they can usually see their parents in their homes (sometimes they may see them only in the hotels), they may not spend the night there. I know a Chinese artist with a European passport who came to see his old mother after a separation of twenty years. He spent his first night in China at her home. The next day, he was politely but firmly reminded that he could visit her during the day but that since he was legally a foreigner he had to sleep at his hotel.

The second class is made up of "compatriots from Taiwan" —in practice this means Taiwanese who live in Japan or the United States. This brand is in great demand because of its many political uses, but the stock is limited. The press talks about them, but you never really see them.

The third class, the Overseas Chinese, is more numerous. Usually they are well-to-do businessmen from Southeast Asia who enjoy the best of both worlds: patriotic pride in their mother country, wealth and ease in the country where they live. In the People's Republic they enjoy special hotels and restaurants: less expensive than those for foreigners, but out of bounds for the local population.

At the bottom one finds "compatriots from Hong Kong and Macao," most of whom come to China only to visit their relatives in Kwangtung province. This is really the largest group of all —on traditional festival days such as New Year's Day, the Feast of the Dead (Ch'ing-ming), and so on, they cross the frontier by the tens of thousands. And the procedure for that is very easy: only an identity card is required. Of course, they see only their family villages, but at least they enjoy direct and close contact with the Chinese in an everyday way, whereas the higher-class visitors, though they can travel on the wider tourst circuits, are insulated by the prophylactic measures that cut foreigners off from real Chinese life.

Chinese travelers are loquacious in inverse ratio to the amount of information they have. Those who have the luck to share the life of their relatives in Kwangtung shirk from being interviewed and will give their impressions only in private or under conditions of absolute anonymity. At the other end of the scale we find the university professors who have lived twenty years abroad; for those who teach in the United States, it is a must (especially since Nixon's visit to Peking) to have been to China at least once and to come back with enthusiastic tales about it: their academic prestige—sometimes their very livelihood—depends on it. To this pathetic need to be accepted in Peking so as to bolster their prestige in Chinese studies—sometimes after ignoring or even vilifying the People's Republic for a score of years—is added a sense of guilt: when they write countless papers showing that life in China's communes is the most prosperous, happiest possible, they hope that they will be more easily forgiven for choosing for themselves an "austere" American exile.

After the travelers comes the lower category of resident aliens. First you have to understand that there are two classes of them: the Maoists (professionals or "pensioners of the Revolution," who are comfortably set up in Peking in an arrangement paid for by the Chinese people) and the agnostics (diplomats and newsmen). The believers and unbelievers see little of each other: each community has its own ghetto, whether in Peking or in the country; even at Peitaiho, the famous seaside resort for bureaucrats and diplomats, the two groups coexist during the hottest weeks of summer without ever running into each other, since their camps are strictly segregated. (There used to be a third category, more varied and also more interesting, because it had more contact with Chinese life: the foreign students, professors, and specialists who worked in China on contract to the People's Republic. But these were sent back home, being undesirable witnesses, during the Cultural Revolution; they have now begun to return.)

In principle, resident Maoists who have spent long years in China should be better acquainted with Chinese realities than traveling Maoists. But in practice, this seems not to be the case. Sometimes they privately express a certain cool distance from the current propaganda slogans, but when they write, it is only to embellish the stale old clichés: one looks in vain for anything new, any fresh idea, any fact that has not been handed out twenty times already by New China News Agency or *Peking Review*. It is true that during the Cultural Revolution a few were brave—or ignorant—enough to express a personal opinion: they found themselves in jail, where some of them stayed for several years. This lesson was not lost on the rest, who follow the straight and narrow path with strict orthodoxy.

The community of unbelievers has grown considerably since Nixon made China fashionable again. They are mostly diplomats, with a sprinkling of foreign correspondents. These residents tend generally to be gloomy, ironic, fatalistic, bitter, or exasperated—depending on their temperament—in striking contrast to the excited enthusiasm of the passing visitors. It is easy to see why: visitors must try to fit a tremendous program into three or four weeks—monuments, hospitals, schools, factories, kindergartens, scattered over thousands of miles; the residents, on the other hand, must spin out over several years a life of small problems and large frustrations, of empty and monotonous routine. Passing travelers see a changing landscape, and they are less conscious that they are being carried everywhere in a cage; the residents, who must stay put in Peking, have plenty of time to count all the bars. I might add that they are paid well to live in Peking and would have no reason to play down the "hardships" of their post: these partly justify the generous allowances they are given.

Whereas the tourists pay a lot (more and more every year) to spend a few days in China, and of course what we pay a lot for and what makes us the envy of our friends cannot be silly or commonplace. . . .

The Peking authorities know only too well the foreign residents' state of mind and do their best to protect the tourists against their pernicious influence. Travelers who want to meet their ambassadors in Peking must endure the open disapproval of their guides, whose unwillingness to help once went as far as sabotage (although I believe this doesn't happen any longer).

However, one should not think that all the foreign residents have a poor opinion of Maoism from the moment of their arrival or before: on the contrary. In countries that have recently re-established diplomatic relations with China, to be posted to Peking is a coveted favor, and the diplomats in that city, however astute and intelligent, still feel some of the euphoria that surrounded their assignment and departure. This euphoria, and the Maophile hysteria that has swept the world, is difficult to explain in terms of political analysis. At the beginning of the People's Republic, when the regime was stable and dynamic and had the support of practically the whole population, the West ignored and isolated China, recognizing it only after the country had been shaken by the Cultural Revolution and its sequels: five years of upheaval, of blood and madness; the most gigantic frenzy China had known since the Taiping rebellion; a flood that swept away two-thirds of the governing elite; a military *coup d'état* considered as a means of government; purges and counterpurges that left two old men steering a rundown machine while in the murky corridors of power military gangs fought for control. The battle is still going on and is always on the verge of breaking out into the open; a deliberate destruction of intelligence and culture, of arts and letters, of the cultural heritage of the past—all this seems to have been nearly swept away by a magical Ping-Pong paddle. There have never been so many ambassadors coming to Peking as when there was no head of state to accept their credentials. For nearly four years, Chou En-lai, that good actor of classical opera, played suave and tirelessly glittering variations on *The Stratagem of the Empty Fortress*; as a new Chu-ke Liang,[6] he was able to bring off for a dazzled audience the mirage of a strong and powerful order, where in fact there is only incoherence and emptiness (receiving timely help, of course, from various guest actors such as Nixon).

Westerners know little about such tasteless doings, since no quality newspaper would have the heart to enlighten them.[7] What is more surprising, many diplomats posted to Peking recently were just as ignorant—though their job is to be well informed and the men who get such a good assignment are usually above average. Western governments that sent their very best personnel to Peking thought, perhaps, that Mao's court would be the focus for one of the most active diplomatic centers of the world. But, alas! the work that has to be done in Peking can be done by any old Blimp: raising the flag over the far-off suburban quarantine station that passes for the foreign quarter, and turning up for the official banquets, where everything—the food, the

6. Chu-ke Liang, a great statesman and strategist of the Three Kingdoms period (A.D. 220–80), managed by sheer bluff to save his empty fortress from enemy attack: he sat, relaxed, at the wide-open gate of the fortress and invited the enemy general to join him inside for a drink; wary of such confidence, the enemy general feared a trap and retreated from the fort, which was in fact utterly defenseless. The episode forms the subject of a very popular classical Peking opera. Chou himself was a talented amateur opera singer.

7. A French writer, well known in university and literary circles for his sturdy, independent judgment, who was writing regularly for the best-known French "left" weekly paper, was told by its editor: "My dear fellow, send us articles on any subject you want, but, please, not on China. Try to understand my position: I have quite a number of Maoist editors and I have to live with them." More than thirty years ago, Victor Serge had noticed the same thing about Stalin's Russia: "I have seen intellectuals of the left responsible for editing reputable reviews and journals refuse to publish the truth, even though it was absolutely certain, even though they did not contest it; but they found it painful, they preferred to ignore it, it was in contradiction with their moral and material interests (the two generally go together)." *Memoirs of a Revolutionary,* trans. Peter Sedgwick (Oxford, 1963) p. 376.

music, the speeches, and the participants—contributes to monotonous solemnity.

Needless to say, in a week or two the newcomers know every nook and cranny of the iceberg where they will have to survive for some two or three more years, living on their own resources of patience and humor, in a solitude made worse by knowledge that their governments are more or less incapable of imagining what life is like in the Holy City of Maoism. Diplomats are, by professional necessity, used to working and living intensely; here, they read the communiqués of the New China News Agency to fill in their reports or wait for the weekly mail from Hong Kong that will tell them what is going on under their very nose. Social activities are an important and normal part of diplomatic life; in Peking, the diplomats have only the rind of that fruit, for it is out of the question to have any kind of close personal relationship with any Chinese with a scientific, artistic, literary, university, or political background. They meet only a handful of bureaucrats, always the same ones, and always in the dreary rounds of official functions. In fact, the opportunities for meeting Chinese are so few that diplomats who speak Chinese worry about losing their knowledge of the language, and their fears are not groundless. Peking is probably the one city in the world where a non-Chinese has little chance of speaking Chinese; few other large cities lack a Chinese community where one can make friends with two or three people who speak Mandarin and see them regularly; that is more than can be said for Peking today.

Nearly all diplomats live and work in the same place. Following the old imperial tradition, the Maoist government has concentrated the embassies, chanceries, and diplomatic lodgings in two huge ghettos outside the capital. No foreigner can try to find a house in the center of Peking nowadays, and those who were lucky enough to have inherited a house in town cannot stay there for long: within a year or two they will have to move to the diplomatic ghetto.

Aesthetically, the diplomatic quarter is part army barracks, part railway station, part hospital. In these joyless quarters, you can hear all the world's languages spoken, but China is absent: its only representatives are the sentries posted at the gates and the hired help—the cooks, house servants, and drivers. Within these walls, it requires a large effort to remember that one is in Peking, in China, and not in some suburb of Newcastle or Stuttgart.

The recurring nightmare of the Maoist bureaucrats is that the foreigners might have fanned out into the countryside and even—this is the worst—managed to make some spontaneous and unsupervised contact with the people. In fact, this last fear is groundless: trained by five years of the Cultural Revolution, Chinese people will think twice before speaking to a foreigner. In some provincial cities, it happened to me that people—for one reason or another—refused even to give me directions. Who could blame them? Their caution is understandable: to own a Dickens novel or a Beethoven recording is enough to support the accusation that one has been in touch with cosmopolitan reactionaries (of what could a man who speaks with a living foreigner *not* be accused?). In my own case, in six months I had no conversation with any Chinese, except for bureaucrats or people who could justify their contact with me as being part of their jobs—as guides, railroad employees, waiters, and so on. Generally speaking, the resident foreigner who does not take the easy way out—relying upon the social amenities of the foreign colony—faces a most absolute solitude. After a few months of that life, one has been cut off for so long from human company that even the visit of an *agent provocateur* is a welcome diversion (the one I had to deal with was an attractive fellow, his profession notwithstanding).

With its nightmarish obsession that foreigners may eventually (though as I say quite hypothetically) achieve unmonitored contacts with the people, the Maoist government has revived a great many privileges, special status rights, and waivers for foreigners in order to keep them even more isolated. It is a shameful legacy of the old imperialist-colonialist epoch. The Chinese are not allowed, except on official business, into the luxurious hotels and clubs that are reserved for foreigners only. As soon as a foreigner appears in a restaurant, he is led away from the common room where the Chinese people are crowded, and for him alone a special lounge is opened, smelling of camphor; sitting there, the best meal in the world would be a kind of penance— or begin to feel like indulgence in a solitary vice. In railway stations, he has a special waiting room; on the train, he always travels first-class—alone, or with other foreigners, never with Chinese travelers. If you try to avoid this by saying that you have no money—no matter, you are issued a ticket on credit, and the bill is sent to your embassy, if necessary: never, never would you be allowed to travel second- or third-class with the Chinese crowd. In cities, you are made to go everywhere by car; any suggestion of traveling on foot or by bus is received by your guides with shocked disapproval. These petty bureaucratic heirs to the colonial dragomans bully their fellow citizens zealously on your behalf and do their best to worsen your feeling of isolation.

Obviously the Maoist dream would be to put all the foreigners on a small island where they could be watched all the time and heads could always be counted. The ideal would be a kind of national park where they could live, work, relax, eat, do their shopping, and mate by and among themselves, in conditions of such ease and comfort that they would no longer wish to escape from the paddocks. As in game preserves where the bears stay put due to the enticement of strategically placed barrels of apples, one should not be surprised if the Maoist government, in one of its pragmatic-revisionist phases, should install a jazz band or some go-go girls to keep the foreigners within the bounds of the International Club—that is, if the healthy pleasures of Ping-Pong and the marching bands of the People's Liberation Army fail to achieve the same results.

Still in all, we must recognize that the authorities are on

target: their reckoning meets certain constants in human nature too well not to be efficient. One can't go too far wrong when one bets on ignorance, foolishness, vanity, and stupidity. A good many foreigners not only get used to being cheered and applauded everywhere they go—there are claques at the entrances to and exits from every school, hospital, factory, even street—but they actually come to enjoy it. They like the colonial trappings. Enterprise and curiosity normally develop only under the pressure of necessity; these faculties atrophy among the foreigners, since they always have guides and interpreters who take care of everything. They get used to having their tickets taken care of—for trains, theaters, planes; they get used to being picked up, brought back, having their hotel chosen for them; their timetable is filled for them. After a few weeks of this, they drop even the simplest or most ordinary activity which might take them off their conveyer belt. The "organization" takes care of everything, answers all questions, deals with all problems, is never surprised with any request, is all-competent. The "organization" will arrange a real mass for you, with a Latin-speaking priest in a real church, or an all-night party in the Summer Palace with cooks, waiters, and gondoliers, so that you may entertain your friends in style; or it will find for you that special nutcracker or lemon-squeezer you could not find in the shops. Most foreigners have no desire to do without the help of the "organization," the less so because, while everything is simple and easy when they deal through it, any show of initiative or autonomy is fraught with difficulty, results in an appalling loss of time, and guarantees encounters with police obstruction and endless red tape. If you make a personal effort you will have problems, petty annoyances, delays, wear and tear—and you will end up with refusals, interdictions, and deadends. In the end you give up—if you are a traveler, because your time is limited; if a resident, out of sheer fatigue and because your instincts for independence have been worn away. After a few years of that life, some become like the caged canaries who are so accustomed to the comfort of their captivity that they could hardly survive in the wild. The "pensioners of the Revolution" are perhaps the worst cases: they are used to their Peking hideouts and are cut off from life, so if they go to Hong Kong, say, and for the first time in years do not have welcoming committees, guides, interpreters, cars all waiting for them, they are gripped by the same fear that afflicts the old monk who goes outside the cloister after a lifetime in sequestered quiet.

These strange living conditions are less shocking to those who have known China only under the present regime: they put it down to the exotic strangeness, which, according to a certain literature, has always been China's. But for anybody who had the privilege of living in the Chinese universe in earlier times, of enjoying its hospitality, of gauging the warmth, the depth, the humanity of its welcome, the walls that Maoist bureaucracy has built between him and those incomparable people create a sadness—nay, despair. It is hard to describe. In the old days (and still today in Chinese communities that are not under Maoist regime) any foreigner who spoke Chinese and adopted Chinese cultural values could participate wholly in Chinese life: he was accepted; his foreignness vanished, was forgotten; the natural flow of life, the friendly and unobtrusive pressure of the environment—everything worked to assimilate him. Now, however, his foreignness is underlined. Everything possible is done to remind him that he is an alien—a moat is dug around him. The authorities do everything to prevent him from enjoying the simple, warm welcome that Chinese people had always been ready to extend to him but can now reveal only stealthily, furtively. He lives in a perpetually false position. Around him, he hears the familiar language, feels at home with every face and gesture, thinks he will find his true home. But all along the way doors shut in his face, and he cannot participate at even the simplest level of popular life. Every attempt, however modest or timid, to get closer to the community of which he had once been a part, fails miserably in a welter of heartbreaking and ridiculous complications. He drags behind him his foreigner's status as a cat drags the tin can that ragamuffins have tied to its tail, and the authorities see to it that it is never removed, not for a moment. The more he tries to break the *cordon sanitaire* of privileges, the more he tries to join the crowd, the more dangerous his case becomes. Does he want to take a bus, like everybody else? In the bus, jammed as usual, his arrival causes a turmoil. The ticket taker orders somebody to give up his seat: They would order anybody to rise—an old man, a pregnant woman, a cripple— rather than have a foreigner strap-hang. In the restaurant, if he declines to be quarantined in the luxurious solitude of the private lounge, if he clings to the humble corner table he has found in the common room, they make him pay for his pretensions: the manager himself chases all the Chinese customers away from his table; the unlucky fellows (who had come well before him) will have to try to find room elsewhere or wait for other seats; now the blushing foreigner is sitting all alone, a hundred eyes upon him, at a table where an entire wedding party could have sat at ease. He has spoiled the evening for at least twelve people who had probably saved up for it and looked forward to it for a long time: a family celebrating because the father has returned on leave from the province where he works alone most of the year, a pair of lovers, a soldier and his old mother—people who can afford to have a party perhaps only once a year. The waiters bustle noisily around him in an excess of diligence, as if to say: "See! Why not do as we say and go to the private room for you and your kind? You've made everybody miserable with your silly ideas—including yourself! !"

And it is the same everywhere he goes. There will always be some officious lower-level bureaucrat representing the invisible, ever-present, omnipotent authorities and ready to create around the hapless foreigner a no man's land that nobody dares cross.

To isolate the foreigners is one thing; it is also necessary to pin them down. (This applies to foreign residents only: as I said

before, the travelers are neutralized by a frenzy of movement.)
But the residents have little to do—not that they are naturally
lazy, but the current Peking idea of diplomatic activity reduces
them to inactivity—and they might be tempted to use their
enforced idleness to visit the country. The government has been
compelled, of course, to curb this kind of inquisitiveness, and the
free circulation of foreigners is limited to Peking and its suburbs.
Once a year, in the autumn, foreigners are allowed to go and look
at the red, changing leaves in the Park of the Fragrant Hills,
some four miles northwest of the city. The only road open to
them on that occasion has soldiers and policemen posted every
five hundred yards, whose duty it is to prevent any communing
with nature.[8] North of Peking, thanks to an incredibly gracious
gesture on the part of the authorities, the Ming Tombs are open
all year round. In this sublime valley—where the thirteen imperial memorials raise their red walls and golden roofs under
the pines and junipers, in this sacred circle where the ageless
call of the plowman reverberates in the surrounding hills, while
the cry of the hawk echoes across the solitude of the azure sky
—here one can for a moment forget the ugliness and sadness of
the Maoist cancer that is gnawing away at the face of China, that
imposes everywhere the indiscretion of its slogans, the obscenity
of its loudspeakers, informing against the people, denouncing
and tracking down beauty, grace, and poetry wherever they may
be found. How is this possible? By what extraordinary over-
sight has this necropolis, so full of an unseen presence, been
spared by the proletarian revolutionary pickax? The visitor
should not delve too deeply into that question, but should come
secretly to drink at this pure spring of loveliness as long as it still
is there, in the midst of spiritual desert so industriously created
all around it by the propagandists of Maoist culture. Who can

8. The Park of the Fragrant Hills is now accessible all year round and
will probably remain so until the next *coup d'état*. It was closed after the
Lin Piao affair because the Peking garrison has most of its barracks in this
area.

guarantee that one of these days they will not convert this mystical place into a Monument to Sino-Albanian Friendship, a Permanent Exhibition of Imperialist Atrocities, a Coney Island of the Class Struggle?

But there is some hyperbole in the secret rapture I speak of, for the foreign visitor who strolls among the tombs (especially if he does it at night) can only enjoy his ecstasy under the watchful eye of three mobile sentries from the People's Liberation Army, who will follow him through the sacred valley on a motorbike with sidecar. If you pause to look at the moon on a cold, clear autumn night, those three poor devils, stamping their feet to keep warm, and longing for their heated barracks, will make you feel guilty, and the contemplative purity is spoiled. If only the incorruptible warriors would agree to share the wine you brought, but no, their orders are strict, and you're lucky if they take a cigarette. The only thing they really want is for you to go home so that they can go to bed. And go home you will, soon. Giving up, you have to accept the truth: in the People's Republic today, the whisper of the wind in the pines is a reactionary and subversive music, looking at the moon is a feudal leftover toward which one should adopt a clear and strong class position, a taste for being alone is an individualistic, petty-bourgeois—maybe worse, counterrevolutionary—tendency. Why should you ask these simple joys for yourself when they are now denied to all Chinese?

(On this totalitarian proscription of the enjoyment of nature, Orwell has some penetrating insights:

Is it wicked to take a pleasure in spring and other seasonal changes? To put it more precisely, is it politically reprehensible to point out that life is frequently worth living because of a blackbird's song, a yellow elm tree in October, or some other natural phenomenon which does not have what editors of left-wing newspapers call a class-angle? ... If a man cannot enjoy the return of spring, why should he be happy in a labour-saving Utopia? ... I think that by retaining one's childhood loves of such things as trees, fishes, butterflies, and toads, one makes a peaceful and decent future a little more probable and that by preaching the doctrine that nothing is to be admired except steel and concrete one merely makes it a little surer that human beings will have no outlet for their surplus energy except in hatred and leader-worship.[9]

During the Cultural Revolution, activists were seen busily forbidding the private ownership of songbirds and goldfish—two popular Chinese hobbies: even in the most miserable slums you will seldom see a yard without some lark in a reed cage and/or a couple of fish in a jar—in order to liberate the energy required for the worship of the Leader and the hatred of class enemies. Inversely, in 1972 the reappearance of bowls of goldfish in Sun Yat Sen Park in Peking was deemed a true harbinger of some "liberalization" in the regime, such as the rehabilitation of several political figures. This "liberalization" is of course very limited: the partial rehabilitation of goldfish has not been followed by an amnesty for songbirds.)

Apart from this run to the Ming Tombs—and beyond them, on the same road, you can go as far as the Great Wall, on which you can stroll for a 500-yard stretch, just enough to be able to follow Johnson's advice to Boswell[10]—nothing else is left but to wander round in Peking, a murdered town, a disfigured ghost of what was once one of the most beautiful cities in the world. Whatever the direction, as soon as you leave the center of the

9. "Some Thoughts on the Common Toad," in *Collected Essays, Journalism, and Letters of George Orwell* (London, 1968; New York, 1971), IV, 143–44.

10. "Johnson talked with an uncommon animation of travelling into distant countries; that the mind was enlarged by it, and that an acquisition of dignity of character was derived from it. He expressed a particular enthusiasm with respect to visiting the Wall of China. I catched it for a moment, and said I really believed I should go and see the Wall of China had I not children, of whom it was my duty to take care. 'Sir,' said he, 'by doing so, you would do what would be of importance in raising your children to eminence. There would be a lustre reflected upon them from your spirit and curiosity. They would be at all times regarded as the children of a man who had gone to view the Wall of China. I am serious, Sir.'" *The Life of Samuel Johnson* (Oxford, 1970), p. 929.

city, you encounter the big trilingual signs—in English, Russian, and Chinese, and guarded by sentries—which mark the end of the area in which you are free to wander. This is strictly controlled: any foreigner who goes beyond a sign, be it only by a few steps, is arrested; his identity is checked; he is questioned, checked, and rechecked; the whole procedure (including the final confession of the thoughtless stroller, written down and signed) may easily take three to four hours. Like a Pavlov dog conditioned by a few electrical shocks not to go near the fence, the foreigner will himself curb his wanderlust.

This narrowly confined existence and, even more, the lack of a normal human relationship with the Chinese environment, is hard on the nerves of even the most level-headed person. Quiet and courteous people astonish themselves by the uncontrollable tempers which may flare up in them over trifles. The Chinese who work in the foreign ghetto are not left untouched by this hysterical atmosphere. There is quite a large neurotic component among the personnel who cater to the foreigners, and this is not surprising when one thinks of the intense and contradictory psychological pressures that they have to endure in their work. They must work in a manner that satisfies not only the foreigners but their true and permanent employer, the party. Sometimes the party wants them to be efficient, polite, and unobtrusive, but at other times such behavior is treasonable. According to the political line, they must be pleasant or odious, cooperative or obstructionist in turn, but they can never follow their own inclination in dealing with their foreign employers. The perpetual violence done to their inborn feelings, the need to conceal what they feel and do the opposite, the duty to report to the authorities (they inform as informers, but they also confess), the sometimes subtle, sometimes brutal, wrenching distortion of all their human relationships—all this does not differ in kind from the common lot of the entire population, but it is brought to such a pitch for them that it can cause a real disruption of personality.

To escape this close and sickly atmosphere, it would be

tempting for the foreigner to take refuge in work or pleasure. Unfortunately neither can be found easily in Peking. The great state banquets that Chou En-lai has given with greater and greater frequency these last months do not really come under either heading, but since they take up a large part of the foreigner's time, maybe a word should now be said about them.

These banquets follow an unchanging ritual. They take place in the Great Hall of the People—a monstrous example of totalitarian architecture, a cross between an Egyptian temple and a Mussolini palace, whose uncouth mass defiles the noble perspective from T'ien-an men Gate to Ch'ien men Gate. The guests enter a large anteroom in double file; there they chat and drink before the arrival of Chou En-lai and his guest of honor. Maoist bureaucrats are ranged along the right-hand wall, foreign diplomats along the left-hand wall. No rule prohibits anyone's crossing the no man's land between the two groups to start a conversation, but the very incongruity of such an initiative strikes your would-be interlocutor dumb, and the would-be conversation falls flat at once. After a while, the guest of honor and his followers enter with Chou En-lai and his followers. A reception line forms, and everyone gets to shake hands with the guest of honor and Chou. Then everyone goes to the dining room. Each table seats twelve. How the places are chosen and where everyone sits is the result of some complex algebra that would have fascinated the Duc de Saint-Simon: it takes into account the rank of each guest as well as the degree of warmth in relations between China and his country. These delicate equations are not easy to solve, and one can easily understand that the civil servants in charge of etiquette do not want to repeat such mathematical efforts too often: this means that once you have been given a seat at one table, you will always have the same fellows with you, barring death or transfer, at all subsequent banquets. After a few such evenings, the conversational topics are exhausted (provided, of course, that a common language made it possible to converse in the first place, which is not always the case). During lulls, there is music: a band from the People's Liberation Army plays at regular intervals, like a well-oiled music box, from its vast repertory of about a dozen tunes. There are usually two Maoist bureaucrats per table: one, rather important, who can concentrate on the food, since he knows no foreign language; the other, less important, whose job it is to talk with "our foreign friends." So you talk about food and the weather in Peking; you move on to research, scientific comparisons of the various climatic conditions prevailing in the countries of the various guests, the seasons, the rains, and the winds. Once these meteorological questions have been examined, silence falls, until the band strikes up and plays for the sixth time that evening "The Chuang Minority Loves Chairman Mao with a Burning Love" or "The Production Brigade Celebrates the Arrival in the Hills of the Manure Collectors."

The cooking, by the way, may appear fabulous to American journalists raised on hamburger and chop suey, but on a Chinese scale, it rates only from "good" to "average." Actually, I rather like the mediocrity of the fare in the Great Hall of the People: I would be shocked if it were otherwise. I note it here only to state the plain unvarnished truth on a point where our new Marco Polos let their enthusiasm run amok.

At the end of the banquet come the speeches. As a rule they are very long. They may be also quite striking: to hear, for example, the Empress of Iran extol the virtues of the Thought of Mao Tse-tung and in return Chou En-lai lauding the wise government of the Shah,[11] or Li Hsien-nien welcome a delegation from the Greek government by singing the praises of the colonels' regime is certainly novel entertainment. But such humorous occasions are few; most of the time the waters of governmental eloquence flow smoothly and blandly, bearing their cargo of commonplaces down the canals of predictability, and you don't have to listen long to figure out what's around the next bend.

What kind of entertainment is available to the foreigner to

11. This was less than two years after the *People's Daily* had printed a telegram from Iranian revolutionaries on the occasion of China's National Day, describing the People's Republic as the major help of the Iranian people in their fight against the corrupt tyranny of the Shah. . . .

recuperate from those high-society duties that take up so much of his time? Once, Peking managed the paradox of being a northern city with a meridional liveliness; now the Maoist regime has razed its monuments and sterilized its genius (this murder is described in Chapter 2). Only the breathtaking courts and palaces of the Forbidden City have been kept whole: the stroller dare not wander elsewhere, because all around it Peking is a desert with nothing to entice him. The streets and markets have been shorn of their colors and spectacles; the noble city walls and gates have been pulled down; all the pailous, which gave rhythm and graceful fancy to the streets, have disappeared. The "Cultural" Revolution closed down the museums; the few temples that it left standing have become barracks, factories, dormitories, or garbage depots. The jugglers, booksellers, story-tellers, puppeteers, the thousands of craftsmen, the inns, the little shops and pubs, the antique dealers and calligraphy shops (except for two catering only to foreigners), in short, all that gave Peking its lovely, diverse, and wonderful face, all that made it into an incredibly *civilized* city, all that made the ordinary Pekingese—with their truculence, their verve, their quick and subtle minds, their art of living—a natural aristocracy within the nation, all this has gone, disappeared forever.

Once upon a time in Peking, culture was not the privilege of the few; it was not something to be put under a glass case in a museum; it was a component of everyday life. You met it on the streets, you breathed it in at every corner; it gave color and taste to the common speech, it expressed itself in the unending panorama of festivals and traditional shows that were so enthu-siastically followed by everyone—illiterates and aesthetes, rich and poor, bourgeois and proletarians, all of whom came to cheer their favorite artists, the best in the country. The Cultural Revo-lution put a stop to all that. Nowadays the curious foreign resident will want to rush to all the concerts, ballets, operas which can be seen, now and then, in the two or three theaters that are still extant; but he should take care not to quench his thirst too rapidly; he may see in one week the entire repertory that is available to him over the two to three years of his stay. In the case of the Peking Opera, in particular, whose incredibly rich repertory was reduced under the supervision of Madame Mao to six Revolutionary Model plays—a monstrous breed, by *Sicilian Vespers* Bolshoi-style out of academically stilted, hideously cloth-capped Chinese opera—the foreigner will soon realize that the problem is not how to get to see it but how to avoid doing so. For several years now, in all of China, *nothing* has been produced except these six measly plays; on top of that they have been made into films—the only feature-length movies to come out of Chinese studios for eight years[12] and they are broadcast over the radio seven days a week, twelve months a year—one hears them, thanks to the ever-present loudspeaker, in restaurants, railway stations, trains, planes, and even in the fields.

As far as films are concerned, apart from these cinematic versions of Madame Mao's six Revolutionary Model operas, there are only some newsreels and technical documentary films: the best one is on how to apply dialectical materialism and the Thought of Mao Tse-tung to the growing of peanuts in Shantung. Movie fans can also "enjoy" some North Korean and Albanian productions.

In the end, the only thing left more or less untainted by ideology and for this reason popular among Chinese and foreigners alike—is to go and gorge oneself (the low quality of the fare does not warrant a more refined word) at a restaurant.[13] Few of these are left in Peking. The cheap ones have the spartan

12. Since this was written, the Chinese movie industry has timidly resumed some measure of activity.

13. During the high point of the Cultural Revolution, attempts were made to have "revolutionary meals"—spartan meals of boiled bark, unhusked rice, or other inedible fare—which were consumed liturgically in remembrance of the famines and hardships of prerevolutionary society. Could it be that the memory of more recent famines and hardships prevented these rites from becoming popular? Anyhow, the idea was quickly abandoned.

look of an army canteen, with customers standing in long lines, or if it is one of the posh places where bureaucrats like to entertain foreign guests, the place will be decorated like a small-town dentist's waiting room. If you are invited by a bureaucrat with clout, whom the restaurant wants to treat well for some reason, the food may be delicious; otherwise, it will be rather poor. Obviously the customer is not very important: if he is not satisfied, let him go; twenty people are waiting for his seat. There is no competition: the other restaurants will not treat him better. Restaurants are open at fixed times, like post offices, and close very early; long before closing time the waiters stop customers from coming in and discourage the ones inside from ordering more food. Who can blame them? Why should the poor devils work overtime for nothing?

When the newly arrived foreigner has thus explored all the possible pleasures for the mind and body—it does not take long —the day will soon come when he will cry uncle and do as his colleagues do: spend his evenings in the French Embassy seeing old Fernandel movies, or in the British Embassy seeing old Peter Sellers movies, and wait for an American Embassy to come so that he can see old Dean Martin–Jerry Lewis movies.

These pages give the situation as I knew it in Peking in 1972. If the present détente lasts, I am sure that changes will occur: museums will reopen; some ancient temple or other will be restored for the benefit of foreigners; bookshops will sell books again. With the passage of time the shocks of the Cultural Revolution will fade and be forgotten, and the man in the street will again display, in his chance dealings with foreigners, his customary courtesy and friendliness. Instead of having only six Revolutionary Model operas, theaters will have twelve, then twenty. The signs announcing where it is "Out of Bounds to Foreign Visitors" will be put two miles farther away, then four, then six. All these changes will make life in Peking more interesting and more pleasant, but I think it would be a mistake to believe that under the cosmetic improvements anything basic has changed. All the changes of direction in the party line, not only since the liberation in 1949, but since Yenan or even since the Kiang-si soviet, have been only *tactical* changes. The vital dynamics of the Chinese Communist regime comes from the constant shifting from "left" to "right," and the continual changes of the tiller's direction do not in the least affect the ship or her final destination. Among various descriptions of Communist China made at different times, one may note differences, yet if these descriptions have been made conscientiously and perceptively, they will show more than ephemeral journalistic truths, for modifications will be in *quantity*, never in quality—variations in amplitude, not changes in basic orientation. Only observers who lack a sense of historical perspective can entertain the illusion that at such and such a time the regime turned a new leaf or started in a new direction. In fact its choices are severely limited by its very nature: in a totalitarian system where authority is held by a military-bureaucratic class, and where power expresses itself through periodic military coups, it is inevitable that times of stress will be followed by times of relative relaxation; it would be absurd to take one or the other of those cyclical phases for a new development.

2 | Follow the Guide

*Let's face it: most of the time, foreigners know us
better than we know ourselves. To take a very
elementary example, the Peking Guide prepared by
the Chinese is much less reliable than the one made
by the Japanese.*[1]

—Lu Hsün

The Border

One enters the People's Republic from Hong Kong. The Lohu
frontier post, where travelers spend a few hours before board-
ing the train to Canton, is in many ways an exemplary summary
of the official China, the only one foreigners are allowed to see.
I forget who it was who compared Lohu to a convent, but the
image is very apt, the likeness striking: long white corridors,
spotlessly clean; high windows; green plants in pots; quiet
shadowy parlors; edifying portraits; gray muslin slipcovers on
the furniture; a whiff of camphor and wax; pious boredom;
orthodox literature in several languages freely available to
visitors; a kind of solicitude on the part of the personnel who
serve you, knowing well that thereby they acquire eternal
merits with Chairman Mao—it's all there.

Indeed, ecclesiastical metaphors are virtually irresistible when
describing the People's Republic. And, too, Maoism has a
peculiar fascination for some clerical-minded souls. Those who
harbor a certain nostalgia for totalitarianism and unconsciously
regret the passing away of the Inquisition and the Pope's Zouaves

1. *Lu Hsün ch'üan-chi* (Peking, 1963), III, 62.

will find in Maoist China the incarnation of a medieval dream, where institutionalized Truth has again a strong secular arm to impose dogma, stifle heresy, and uproot immorality.

Canton

In contrast with the starchy formality of Peking, Canton has a southern kind of casualness that is rather fetching; compared to the bustling modernity of Hong Kong, it seems decayed, run-down. It reminded me of the drowsy seediness of Macao, yet if the seediness is certainly genuine, the sleepiness may be only apparent, for Canton has a front-rank place in the annals of revolutionary China. One may apply to its province, Kwangtung, the old proverb about Szechwan: "The first province to rebel, the last to be pacified."

Indeed, thanks to its outlying position, the province has never been tightly controlled by the central Chinese government and was more openly exposed to outside influences. Unorthodox lines of thought and subversive movements could easily develop, putting down deep roots in that far-flung corner of the empire before the Court could learn of them and take repressive measures. It was also an important outpost in China's contacts with foreigners: the main port for trade with Southeast Asia, a landing place for foreign ships, and, from the sixteenth century onward, the point of entry for foreign missionaries. After the mid-sixteenth century, the Portuguese settlement in Macao, right on Canton's doorstep, was a subversive presence that gave witness to the existence of a whole world alien to China, of which the rest of the country was still unaware.

The Cantonese have always shown a touchy spirit of regionalism, and this was in turn exacerbated by the patronizing condescension of "northerners," who never failed to point out that this poorer and less refined province had weaker historical and cultural traditions. Their condescension only reinforced Canton's will to manage its own affairs and oppose interference from the central government. This bent toward autonomy, combined with the distance from the center of traditional culture and the proximity of foreign influence, naturally favored intellectual ferment and new ideas. A propensity to question the reigning orthodoxy, coupled with vigorous regionalist enthusiasm, explains at least in part why the revolutionary current always ran strong in Kwangtung.

What is remarkable is that these factors, which in the past helped to make the region a hotbed of rebellion, are still active and they give Kwangtung province a very special aspect and a distinct flavor. The presence of party cadres from other provinces is a cause of frequent friction, and "Cantonese chauvinism" has often been denounced in Maoist China. The battles of the Cultural Revolution were especially long, hard, and bloody here, and Kwangtung remains a troubled region.

The proximity of Hong Kong and Macao to Canton is a breach in the almost total isolation of China; many people in Kwangtung have relatives on the other side of the border, and they keep in touch with them. Elsewhere in China, the outside world might as well be on another planet. Even in Tientsin or Shanghai, nothing remains but incongruous colonial buildings and neo-Gothic cathedrals—ghosts, the vestiges of a world that has long since been submerged. But in Canton, the outside world is *there*, not only twice a year, when thousands of foreigners from all over the globe visit the Trade Fair, but all year round, when the tens of thousands of Chinese visitors from Hong Kong and Macao bring, with the news from the outside, a heady whiff of foreign air.

Because of this, for Chinese to go to Canton is to get a secondhand tang of Abroad; in this sense, now as in the old days, the southern city gives Chinese travelers something different—something not quite respectable, vaguely tainted, the fascination of exoticism. And for the foreigner living in Peking, Canton is a welcome change, far from the formal rigidity of the capital. Strolling around is much more pleasant, since it does not attract notice, and in the more relaxed atmosphere the foreigner can almost behave normally; going to a public place —a restaurant or theater—does not cause a commotion, people won't leap out of their seats for him on a bus, he can stand in line like everybody else at a movie, and so forth.

In Canton, I was surprised to see the sidewalks along the Pearl River embankments crowded with people doing *nothing*— lots of young men squatting, smoking, talking, and playing cards. In the People's Republic, with its permanent mobilization of the masses, this behavior is most surprising, subversive even. At the time I observed this, a fallback and a demobilization could be seen in nearly all the cities of China, but never so shamelessly as in Canton. The Cultural Revolution had been hard on Chinese nerves—the years of unremitting tension, battle, uncertainty, and violence—and the authorities evidently realized it was necessary to give the masses some breathing space; for two years, no new mass movement was started and everyone made the most of it, relaxing and recovering their balance.[2]

In comparison with Peking, Canton appears destitute, from what one can see in shop windows (which are almost bare) and in the rather coarse food offered in ordinary restaurants. The sybaritic habits of the Cantonese—preserved in Hong Kong even among the poorest classes—are now only a memory. I am thinking, for example, of the sacred custom, once observed at all levels of society, of spending a good part of the morning eating *tim-sun* (*tien-hsin*) in the teahouses (*ch'a-lou*): the teahouses have disappeared, and in the small restaurants that formerly offered a choice between four kinds of tea, you now get no tea at all, but only hot water, as among peasants. (This leveling down, which brings urban life to the level of the impoverished countryside, is not unique to Canton but is happening all over China.) In a

2. The lull ended in 1973 with the launching of various new campaigns—Fan ch'ao-liu, P'i Lin p'i K'ung, *et al.*—but that is another story.

small eating place in the suburbs, I was struck to see a ragged old woman gleaning crumbs of food from under the tables and carefully putting them one by one into her sack. In some quarters you see little workshops where even children are carding hemp, as in the most destitute alleys of Hong Kong or Macao. In the evening, to save electricity, public as well as private lighting is at a minimum, and the streets look like those of a besieged city: under the arcades that in the southern fashion serve as sidewalks, passers-by appear like wraiths in the balmy night; far off, the darkness is broken by a naked bulb casting its feeble ray over the quiet intimacy of some domestic scene: through the curtainless window, the passer-by might see the standard furnishings, the gray mosquito net on its wooden frame, a few makeshift shelves, a Thermos bottle, a peeling shadowy wall where glows, ever-present, benign, the sun face of Chairman Mao.

As everywhere else, the Cultural Revolution in Canton is an invisible but gigantic presence, overshadowing everything; its scars are barely hidden by a hasty whitewash. Of the many temples which once distinguished Canton, only one can now be visited, the Temple of the Six Banyans (Liu jung szu). It is open to foreigners only: Chinese are not admitted. The monks who lived here until the Cultural Revolution have disappeared without a trace; the temple lost all its rich sculptured decoration in the lootings of the Cultural Revolution and has retained only a great bronze statue—Sung period, and very beautiful—of the sixth patriarch, Hui-neng. A visit is made under the supervision of young guides—girls, really—who are very nice but prodigiously ignorant of the basic data of Chinese culture and history; one cannot hold this against them, since it is not their fault that the Cultural Revolution virtually deprived them of a secondary education. What is more surprising is their complete ignorance of the revolutionary history of modern China; for instance, they mixed up the uprising of the Canton Commune in 1927 with the incident of 1839, when Lin Tse-hsü burned British opium!

The Temple of the Six Banyans has been impeccably restored and maintained. Tourists—who will not ask what happened to the other ancient temples of Canton, the Hua-lin Temple, the ancestors' temple of the Ch'en clan, the Kuang-hsiao temple, and so forth and so on—will conclude that "contrary to the rumors circulating abroad, *all* the temples and ancient monuments in China are open and in excellent condition." The fact that in each city one or two Potemkin monuments are specially kept up to satisfy their curiosity fits in so well with their opinion that they do not feel the need to inquire further.

In the Old Citadel (Wu ts'eng lou, or Five-Storey Tower— also called Chen-hai lou, or Tower Overlooking the Sea) there is an exhibition of "archaeological objects dug up during the Cultural Revolution." Similar exhibits have been organized in all the provincial capitals, and the best pieces from all over China have been pulled into Peking—a spectacular grouping that is going to tour the world. In the new foreign-policy line archaeology is a tool not to be despised: to lend credibility to its diplomatic initiatives, the People's Republic is trying to change the bad image that the iconoclasm and violence of the Cultural Revolution gave it in the West. Archaeological exhibits of pieces "discovered during the Cultural Revolution" play a dual role: they show that far from destroying the cultural heritage, the Cultural Revolution enriched it; they prove that Maoism and humanism can live together. And a regime that respects the cultural treasures of antiquity must be worth talking to—it must be steady, reasonable, and serious. This archaeological maneuver, though rather obvious, has succeeded completely; on this question, lucid and competent witnesses to the real truth are few, and fewer still are those who would have the bad taste to speak out.

But there is at least one person who was not convinced by the exhibition held in the Citadel: one art historian I know, a specialist in Cantonese painting, went to Canton three times hoping to see various paintings that had been in the Provincial

Museum prior to the Cultural Revolution. The poor fellow's hopes dwindled from one trip to the next; not only was he unable to see the paintings or even to get a catalogue of the museum collection but he could not learn what had happened to the paintings or to the museum itself; not only was he unable to talk to any curator but he did not even succeed in learning the name of a single one, or an address to which he could have sent a letter to another specialist in his field. During his inquiries, he met with the immense good will of the young so-called curators, but it was good will mixed with dismay; these "curators" were youngsters promoted after the Cultural Revolution whose experiences was limited to dusting the showcases, and on his behalf, they spent whole afternoons on the telephone (phoning in Canton is always a lengthy and nerve-racking experience; shouts get through only sporadically), but their efforts brought no result. Obviously, those who could have enlightened our art-lover were still adjusting their *Weltanschauung* in a more revolutionary-proletarian direction by healthy farm work in the countryside.[3]

But enough of decadent aesthetic curiosities. On the subject of museums, let us speak instead of those dedicated to modern revolutionary history—the Canton Commune Museum, the Lu Hsün Museum (Lu Hsün taught at the Sun Yat-sen University in Canton in 1927), the Chinese Trade-Union Congress Museum. This won't take long: all three are closed and will reopen only when the historians of the regime have finished rewriting history to make it conform to the latest dogma.[4] Theirs is not an easy task: not only must it be done all over again after each *coup d'état*, but in some instances—as recently, for example—when the power struggle lasted for some time without one unified team

3. Eventually, in 1973, the dogged art historian managed to meet briefly one of the real curators—a charming fellow—but the paintings still could not be seen. It is not possible to know where they are or if they still exist.

4. The Lu Hsün Museum was reopened in 1973. It is notable mostly for its omissions and falsifications.

and one political line triumphing, they are in a dangerously un-- certain position. This is true not only for historiographers and curators but for all propaganda operations and cultural activities. The *People's Daily* seldom has ideological editorials; the book-shops are empty of books; the Arts and Letters faculties cannot start their teaching and research programs again; the studios have not produced a single feature film since 1966; the theaters are restricted to Madame Mao's half-dozen Revolutionary Model operas—all this happens not only because many intellectuals, writers, professors, and artists are still busy carting manure and raising pigs but also and mostly because the minority who are still on the job have received no clear-cut instructions. With no criteria to establish the orthodoxy, but only vague and contra-dictory instructions, they dare not take any initiative that might be considered a crime tomorrow.

Still, the ideologists and "soul engineers" must do some-thing, put some sort of show on in the cultural desert: this is where the Mao cult comes in. Various reporters have said that this was toned down after the Cultural Revolution, and especially after the downfall of Lin Piao, but this does not appear to be totally true, as any traveler can find out by himself. Mao images are everywhere, in all possible materials and formats, from the façades of official buildings to the inside of hovels; in photo-graphs, paintings, embroideries; in plaster, on medals, as posters. Mao's Thoughts, Mao's poems are there in gigantic letters on all walls; Mao's calligraphy adorns historical monuments, hotel rooms, street corners, waiting rooms, public gardens, post offices, zoos, railway cars, schools, hydroelectric dams, screens, fans, the frontispieces of diaries, and the entrances to army barracks. Quotations from Mao spice radio programs, are given at the start of movie shows, plays, concerts, music-hall revues; they are on the front pages of all newspapers every day. No periodical, be its subject archaeology, pedagogy, or linguistics, is published with-out having its front page exclusively devoted to some *Thoughts* of Chairman Mao, printed in boldface; since the Cultural

Revolution even *books* (on philosophy or electronics or any-thing) have that invariable, ritual, propitiatory front page.

Yet it is not entirely false to say that this cult has lost its original stridency. Some practices that were in vogue during the Cultural Revolution have been discouraged: speed contests in reciting the "Quotations" (some champions could give them not only in the right order, but also *backward*) and Quotation Calisthenics (where movements followed not a tune, but quota-tions from Chairman Mao: bend the arm on this phrase, flex the legs on that one, and so on) are out of favor now. In a concert some years ago, the whole program would have cele-brated the Chairman (hymns to him, his poems set to music, and so on), and now, sometimes, two or three out of ten pieces will be unrelated to him.

In the end, what has changed in the Maoist cult is perhaps less its intensity and breadth than its character and aim. It was a conquering religion, a fighting weapon; it has become an alibi, a ruse, a formal occupation whose wholly negative virtue is to cover a void, fill up the silence, people a desert. Since the museums exist, something must be shown; bookshops exist, so something must be on their shelves; professors must teach some-thing to their students, and journalists must fill their columns for their readers. But in the present uncertainty—with *coups d'état* that sometimes succeed but also sometimes fail, mysterious attempted assassinations planned by leadership groups against each other, well-known and seemingly unassailable figures dis-appearing and others unexpectedly reappearing—the safest pro-cedure is to put Mao, and only Mao, everywhere. At worst, it may become monotonous; but this is a paltry danger compared to the perils of taking a more subtle line.

A good example of this cautiousness was given in Canton by the Museum of the Institute for Cadres of the Peasant Move-ment—which with Shaoshan and Yenan was one of the only three museums of contemporary revolutionary history open in all China. Shaoshan is the birthplace of the Great Helmsman;

Yenan corresponds to the period when his personal power was consolidated; it was therefore natural that these two museums were dedicated essentially to him. To adapt their contents to the changing needs of orthodoxy, it was necessary only to have an eraser and scissors, so that on various group photographs the figures of some "closest comrades in arms" could be obliterated when their historical role, or even their very existence, had been retrospectively reduced to that of non-persons. As for the Museum of the Institute for Cadres of the Peasant Movement, more serious distortions of history and chronology were required to transform it into a museum dedicated to Mao. Mao taught only the last class of the institute, in May–October 1926; the guides thus—with a straight face—tell visitors that the institute was *founded* in 1926, so that the institute's life starts with the coming of Mao. P'eng P'ai, who headed the institute as early as 1924 and was the first organizer of the peasant movement in China, is mentioned only once in the last room of the museum, with one photograph and three lines of commentary. (His name is not even pronounced correctly by the guide. The "P'ai" ideogram is rather uncommon, but it looks very much like another very common one, pronounced differently.) This shows how much this remarkable revolutionary and martyr has been deliberately forgotten (he was executed by the Kuomintang in 1929). From a Maoist point of view P'eng P'ai is an unimpeachable figure, but the fact that he was active *before* Mao in a field where Mao became the specialist is a breach of the revolutionary monopoly of the Great Teacher: all praise, all glory can be given only to him, no independent merit can be tolerated.

It is always dangerous, even futile, to generalize from isolated incidents. A shopkeeper and some passers-by running after a teen-ager shouting "Stop thief!" would not merit mention if it did not illustrate what a waiter at my hotel had told me some days before in one of the few interesting talks I had during my stay in Canton. We got to talking—I forget how—about juvenile delinquency. This was still a serious problem in .Canton, he told me, though it was not so bad as it had been two or three years before. The delinquents are usually urban young people who have been sent to the countryside, cannot fit into rural life or endure perpetual exile, and return to the city clandestinely. They have no means of livelihood except stealing; with no jobs and no fixed abodes, they sometimes form roaming gangs. When people catch a thief, said the waiter, they usually give him a good beating—often at the request of the thief himself, who would rather have this expeditious punishment than be handed over to the police. (It should be noted that the same practice prevails in Hong Kong: the Chinese on both sides of the border apparently share the same lack of trust in law enforcement.) If the thief is not a vagrant, his case will be referred to his place of employment. Only more serious matters—armed robbery, organized crime, or murder—are brought to court, and are punishable, according to the seriousness of the crime, either by death (by a firing squad), a prison sentence, or corrective labor. I made a show of disbelief: how could theft still exist in China today? The waiter laughed and told me I would hardly experience it myself: Chinese who have any contact with foreigners have strict instructions, and the worst thing that might happen to them would be to have a traveler in their charge complain to the Ministry of Foreign Affairs about bad service or, much worse, a theft. This is why hotel personnel go to such great lengths to return anything the foreigners may have left behind, lest they believe that something which they lost or forgot had been stolen.

Thus do many foreigners come to believe that theft has disappeared in the People's Republic. In fact, though the regime has succeeded in building up a remarkably law-abiding society, it would be naïve to think that it is entirely free from the vices of a consumer society. The instinct for possession (by legal or illegal means) still exists, but can only be expressed in minor ways. Some objects, such as Swiss watches (one of the few imported consumer goods in China) or cameras (Chinese-made), fascinate the Chinese, especially the young people, and their envied owners derive considerable prestige from the possession of such goods. Bicycles in China are like cars in the West: both a vehicle and a status symbol. In rural areas, many girls ask boy friends to guarantee them the "three things that go round" (*san chuan*: a watch, a bicycle, and a sewing machine) before agreeing to marry them. In the cities, from heavy utility bicycles made in Shenyang to the light Shanghai bicycles, luxury and prestige machines named Swallows, the wide range of models can help you place their owners nearly as exactly as you can European carowners, Mini or Jaguar. As for the foreigners who say there is no more theft in the People's Republic, I am afraid it shows that they have never been to a bicycle parking lot: most of these, which one has to pay to use, have watchmen; bicycles have chains and the watchman always reminds you about locking them up.

In all fairness it must be said that most bicycle thefts are committed by youngsters out for a joyride, and, in general, Chinese society maintains its very high standard of discipline—even after the Cultural Revolution. To find such a standard in the past, one has to go back more than twenty-two centuries to the brief Ch'in dynasty (221–209 B.C.), when, according to the chroniclers, "people could leave their luggage on the wayside without fear that anybody would touch it"—but the Ch'in regime was also the one in ancient times that managed to come closest to being a totalitarian system in the modern meaning of the word.

The Cultural Revolution and its years of violence and anarchy endangered that discipline for a time by undermining the prestige of traditional authorities—the party, the cadres, and the police. In the end, the army was entrusted with re-establishing order, and it now keeps the situation under tight control. Under the shadow of the guns, the old order can slowly be rebuilt. For instance, in Canton I saw wall posters telling the people about road, street, and river traffic. These are normally police matters; here, the ordinance was issued by the army (from the military command for Canton), telling the people to obey the police, who were charged with effecting these orders—the implication being that the police had no authority except when cautioned and assisted by the army. In the city itself, the armed forces are clearly in evidence; sentries are posted in front of official buildings and hotels for foreigners; some buildings have become temporary barracks; in the streets and parks, the large numbers of soldiers on leave suggest the existence of major city garrisons. Officers are the new aristocracy; you see them on planes and in the best hotels; their sleek cars speed down the boulevards, and they are practically the only Chinese who travel first-class on trains.

The army has the situation well in hand and has succeeded in restoring order in the streets, but it is not so easy to see to what degree spirits have quieted down. Youth is—at least potentially—the biggest problem. During the Cultural Revolution young people had the chance to be on their own, to look for adventure, to taste political action, to have a direct influence on the life of the country. The taste of such experiences is not easily forgotten. In contrast, their present position seems all the more unendurable. Under army guidance, back under the authority of the same mandarins whom they managed to overthrow briefly in 1967–68, they are deported for life to distant and unfriendly regions, far from their families. Yet paradoxically, of all the Chinese population these young people are spiritually the most free. They are completely unfettered by the taboos or fetishes of the regime because they have nothing of their own; having lost everything, they have nothing to protect or save; they do not believe in anything anymore; their cynicism is total. A group of students from the Chinese University in Hong Kong, on tour in the People's Republic, was approached in a Canton alleyway by some young vagrants who started to speak out in such daring and incendiary terms about the Maoist regime that the students went back to their hotel in a panic, fearing that they would be accused of fostering a counterrevolutionary plot. Before the Cultural Revolution, such an encounter would have been unthinkable: not that the regime had no opponents, but they would never have dared to voice their complaints so openly to outsiders.

It is probable that the Cultural Revolution has left other, even deeper scars on Chinese minds and feelings. It represented, after all, the climax of twenty years of periodic, sometimes violent purges, twenty years of systematic training in aggression, of legitimizing violence and hatred. The daily witnessing of looting, revenge, cruelties, humiliations inflicted by children on their elders under the pretext of "class struggle"; the obligation to be present at, if not to take an active part in, the public denunciation of neighbors, friends, fellow workers, and parents—all this must have put its mark on the society as a whole. It would be interesting to know the statistical curve of suicides and mental illness; such information, if it exists, is of course not available to us. But from my own limited, myopic, subjective view as observer and traveler, I could not help being struck by the electric tension in the atmosphere, a tension for which none of my previous experiences of Chinese life had prepared me. For instance, in my six-month trip in China I saw more quarrels, even brawls, than in five years in Hong Kong—which is not a markedly relaxed or gracious city. I do not mean to suggest that social life in the People's Republic is based on violence: on the contrary, and especially when compared to other societies, Chinese society is remarkably peaceful and balanced. But if we compare it to *itself*, I cannot but wonder if the history of the last twenty years has not borne fruit, twenty years of systematic incitation to "class hatred" and the denunciation of basic human impulses, such as compassion for suffering, whoever is the victim (this is now condemned as the expression of a bourgeois humanism that denies the class struggle), has not brought about the general and *willed* lowering of the traditional virtues that gave harmony to

Chinese life. On this point, the Maoist regime has only repeated Soviet experiences, and the witness of Nadezhda Mandelstam to the psychological and moral impact of Stalinism on Russia could perhaps well apply to Maoist China:

There were once many kind people, and even unkind ones pretended to be good because that was the thing to do. Such pretence was the source of the hyprocrisy and dishonesty so much exposed in the realist literature at the end of the last century. The unexpected result of this kind of critical writing was that kind people disappeared. Kindness is not, after all, an inborn quality but it has to be cultivated, and this only happens when it is in demand. For our generation, kindness was an old-fashioned, vanished quality, and its exponents were as extinct as the mammoth. Everything we have seen in our times —the dispossession of the kulaks, class warfare, the constant "unmasking" of people, the search for an ulterior motive behind every action—all this has taught us to be anything you like except kind.[5]

Strolling in the streets of Shamien, the former European quarter of Canton, I saw a huge banner on the front of an old church, now transformed into a meeting hall. It announced a meeting of parents of young people sent into the countryside. The despair of the youngsters banished for life, to faraway villages where they are often unwelcome, is shared by their parents: they suffer not only from the final separation but from the terrible thought that their children's future is, in their eyes, forever ruined. (Twenty years of socialism have not succeeded in crushing the age-old contempt of mandarin society for manual work; and it must be added that the condition of peasants remains so low in China that city dwellers still look down upon a countryside posting as exile or disgrace; to send people to the country remains a disposition of the penal system.) Sending so many urban young people to rural areas created many problems, which

5. *Hope Against Hope: A Memoir*, trans. Max Hayward (New York and London, 1970), p. 134.

the authorities try to solve by a two-pronged attack: giving the young some ideological framework, and, more indirectly, working with the parents to persuade their offspring to try to adapt to their new life and forget the notion of returning to city life. To what extent do parents accept this role? What happens when they try to carry out those instructions? What the official press tells us is very theoretical: *Red Flag* has published several stories about model parents (one of them, for instance, said that it was better to send the children Marxist encouragements and tonic doses of Marxist literature than candies and chocolates that would sap their will; as for the author, he had spent his savings to buy and send to his offspring no less than *ninety* books by Marx, Engels, Mao, and Stalin), but in the end this kind of article does not tell us much except that the parents' morale itself is a problem. I would have been a thousand times more interested to go to the meeting in the Shamien church and hear the parents speak in their own words: needless to say, it is out of the question for a foreigner to attend such a gathering on the spur of the moment.

An Aside on Means of Transport

Air travel in China is full of unexpected charms, but if one is in a hurry, better take the train. The charm of air travel—apart from the apple or the banana (sometimes both) that one gets during the flight—is that one never knows when one will depart or when one will arrive, or even where one will land. The element of surprise, nay adventure, gives back to air travel some of its former romance. On provincial lines, the aircraft are little twin-engine planes that fly slowly at four to six thousand feet, and in clear weather (the weather will always be clear: if it were not, the plane would not fly[6]) one has the most gorgeous imaginable

6. Planes are expensive, and the Chinese reckon (wisely) that they should not be jeopardized just to keep to a timetable; if there is wind or rain, the planes are grounded.

lessons in Chinese geography. Sometimes the planes have seats —taken, it would seem, from old buses—on one side only, and the other side is filled with crates, boxes, and parcels. These little planes are even more irregular than the big ones, and more fun.

The trains, prosaically, run on time. Sybaritic meals offered in the buffet car contrast with the austerity of the airline fare. (Have the railways fallen back, like other sectors, into the hands of the revisionists, while the airways are still the preserve of the extreme left?) The first-class sleeping car is always three-quarters empty, and the only travelers the foreigner will meet are highly military officers. Mealtimes are arranged so that he will never be in the buffet car with ordinary Chinese travelers. But to break the isolation, the foreign traveler can talk to train personnel— the porters, waiters, and cooks. These are mostly agreeable and sociable types, and thanks to the peculiar nature of their professional obligations, they lack the inhibitions that paralyze the rest of the population in dealing with foreigners. They can always find a good reason to come and have a chat with you in your compartment: travelers are few in first-class, and they have plenty of time. I never traveled without Hong Kong Chinese-language newspapers, of which the citizens of the People's Republic, for obvious reasons, are extremely fond.[7] I never figured out exactly what fascinated them most—heretical revelations about recent developments in the power struggle in Peking, or prurient details about the private lives of Hong Kong starlets; but in any case, on each trip the word would go around, and before long my compartment would be a reading room; the conductor, the guard, the policeman on duty, the porter, and the cook would each in turn knock on my door; after securing the lock to discourage any undesired visitor, they would sit down comfortably and become absorbed in back numbers of *Ming pao*.

Traveling always on the same lines—Peking-Canton, Peking-

7. For the same reasons inhabitants of Taiwan have the same ravenous curiosity for publications from Peking.

Shanghai—it happened that I met the same attendants several times, and I was able to establish fairly coherent and friendly relationships with them. We had long talks on all kinds of subjects—purposeless, sloganless, filled with friendly curiosity. We had time. To chat for hours about everything and nothing with these straightforward and warm-hearted people was for me a source of the deepest happiness, and it wasn't only because I had been cut off for so long from the most basic social exchanges. In contrast to officials—big or small bureaucrats, fanatics or success-hounds, arrogant or shabby, proud parvenus or pathetic prostitutes—whom I had to meet daily and exclusively, those workers appeared to me, in their simple human truth, as the rightful heirs of a civilization that the new mandarins had not yet succeeded in entirely destroying. Their natural ease, their wisdom, their mixture of courtesy and craftiness, their richly expressive language—all this put these naïve and subtle people in complete contrast with the unidimensional cardboard robots who rule them; more, they offered me the revelation (or illusion) of a Chinese humanity that had kept itself intact, as if protected by its very simplicity. Orwell had an intuition of this essential and secret hope, with people lacking intellectual formation (or deformation?) remaining its trustees amidst the universal nightmare: I am thinking of this passage from *1984*:

In some ways, Julia was far more acute than Winston, and far less susceptible to Party propaganda.... But she only questioned the teachings of the Party when they in some way touched upon her own life. Often she was ready to accept the official mythology, simply because the difference between truth and falsehood did not seem important to her. She believed, for instance, having learnt it at school, that the Party had invented airplanes.... And when Winston told her that airplanes had been in existence before he was born, and long before the Revolution, the fact struck her as totally uninteresting.... In the ramifications of Party doctrine she had not the faintest interest. Whenever he began to talk of the principles of Ingsoc, doublethink, the mutability of the past and the denial of objective reality, and to use

Newspeak words, she became bored and confused and said that she never paid any attention to that kind of thing. One knew that it was rubbish, so why let oneself be worried by it? She knew when to cheer and when to boo, and that was all one needed. If he persisted in talking of such subjects, she had a disconcerting habit of falling asleep. She was one of those people who can go to sleep at any hour and in any position. Talking to her, he realized how easy it was to present an appearance of orthodoxy while having no grasp whatever of what orthodoxy meant. In a way, the world-view of the Party imposed itself most successfully on people incapable of understanding it. They could be made to accept the most flagrant violations of reality, because they never fully grasped the enormity of what was demanded of them, and were not sufficiently interested in public events to notice what was happening. By lack of understanding they remained sane. They simply swallowed everything, and what they swallowed did them no harm, because it left no residue behind, just as a grain of corn will pass undigested through the body of a bird.[8]

This reminds me of the interview given in Hong Kong in the early 1960s by a peasant who had escaped from China. The interviewer was asking him what he knew about other countries. When asked, "What do you know about Yugoslavia?" the peasant, painstaking and placid, answered, "It is a pseudosocialist country run by revisionist hyenas in the pay of American capitalism."

Somewhat later, the interviewer asked: "If you could choose, where would you like to live?"

"Well, in Yugoslavia, for example."

"Why?"

"It seems that in pseudosocialist countries run by revisionist hyenas in the pay of American capitalism, oil and cotton cloth are not rationed."

8. George Orwell, *1984* (London, 1948; New York, 1949), pp. 154, 155, 157. Rereading this book, written before the People's Republic was founded, one is aghast at its uncanny prophetic quality. Without ever dreaming of Mao's China, Orwell succeeded in describing it, *down to concrete details of daily life*, with more truth and accuracy than most researchers who come back from Peking to tell us the "real truth."

Peking

It is not easy to foresee how future centuries will judge the Maoist rule, but one thing is certain: despite all it has done, the name of the regime will also be linked with the outrage it inflicted on a cultural legacy of all mankind: the destruction of the city of Peking.

For what they wanted to do to their own capital city, the rulers of the People's Republic would have been better inspired to have a hideous modern city such as Tientsin, for instance; they could have bulldozed whole neighborhoods, laid out grids of those endless straight boulevards they seem to be so fond of; created vast esplanades and exalting deserts of tarmac for their mass manifestations in the best Stalino-Fascist style; in a word, they could have slaked their thirst for destruction without causing irreparable damage to the monumental legacy of Chinese civilization. Moreover, the architectural ugliness of a city like Tientsin, which reaches almost surrealist dimensions, could have inspired the architects of the new regime as it challenged them in the category of delirious kitsch and petty-bourgeois pretentiousness; the competition would have been keen between the imperialist-colonialist and the Maoist city planners; even better, the various monuments given to China by the Soviet Union which now disgrace Peking would have found in Tientsin a background more in harmony with their aesthetic. But alas, from a Maoist point of view Tientsin would not do: it had no imperial tradition.

In Peking stands one monument that more than any other is a dramatic symbol of the Maoist rape of the ancient capital: the Monument to the Heroes of the People. This obelisk, more than a hundred feet high, the base of which is adorned by margarine bas-reliefs, would by itself be of no particular note if it were not for the privileged place it has, exactly in the center of the vista from Ch'ien men Gate to T'ien-an men Gate. A good sneeze, however resonant, is not remarked upon in the bustle of a busy railway station, but things are somewhat different if the same explosion occurs in a concert hall at just the most exquisite and magical point of a musical phrase. In the same way, this insignificant granitic phallus receives all its enormous significance from the blasphemous stupidity of its location. In erecting this monument in the center of the sublime axis that reaches from Ch'ien men to T'ien-an men, the designer's idea was, of course, to use to advantage the ancient imperial planning of that space, to take over to the monument's advantage that mystical current, which, carried along rhythmically from city gate to city gate, goes from the outside world to the Forbidden City, the ideal center of the Universe. The planner failed to realize that by inserting his revolutionary-proletarian obscenity in the middle of that sacred way he was neatly destroying precisely the perspective he wanted to capture for it.

The brutal silliness of the Monument to the Heroes of the People, which disrupts and annihilates the energy-field of the old imperial space by trying to appropriate it, epitomizes, alas, the manner in which the Maoist regime has used Peking: it has chosen the old capital in order to give its power a foundation of prestige; in taking over this city, it has destroyed it.

The destruction of Peking started in the 1950s, when all the pailous that spanned the main thoroughfares of the old city were eliminated. These graceful arches broke the monotony of the streets and gave them a kind of rhythm that was at the same time noble and elegant, but they were guilty of two crimes: they hindered traffic and worse, in the heart of the Red capital, they were feudal and reactionary remnants (most of them had been built to commemorate chaste widows or upright mandarin officials). At that time, an expert in ancient Chinese architecture, Liang Ssu-ch'eng (son of Liang Ch'i-ch'ao, the famous publicist who did more than anyone to introduce modern ideas in China at the beginning of the century), defended the pailou and fought bravely against the destruction committed in the name of Russian urbanistic principles. He paid for it: not only was his struggle in vain (*not one* of these charming constructions remains in all of

Peking), but he became the target of various attacks, which stopped only when he had recanted publicly, praised the merits of Soviet architectural planning, confessed his errors, and (for good measure) denounced the memory of his father.

After pulling down the pailous, whole blocks were razed to assuage the hunger of socialist town planners for immense avenues, boulevards, and squares; these are intended for the parades, mass meetings, pageants, and rallies, mobilizing hundreds of thousands of participants, that are as essential to the good working of a people's republic as the old circus games were to the Roman Empire. During the off-season for political grand opera—and this is so in all socialist metropolises, from Moscow to Peking—the paltry car traffic, contrasting with the giant size of these roads, gives them a ghostly appearance. The vast boulevards call to mind the false airports which cargo-cult devotees in New Guinea hack out of the jungle in the hope that this will persuade their gods to send planes full of treasure: one is sometimes tempted to believe that the building of the *Autobahns*, now used only by a few dismal cyclists or donkey carts, might similarly be part of a magic ritual, as if miles of macadam might generate the sudden appearance of hordes of hooting, stinking, triumphant cars—simultaneously the nightmare of the consumer society and dream of the socialist one.

In the obliteration of Peking, the next step was to demolish the city walls. Here it must be noted that Peking was not an ordinary city born of the meeting of various economic, demographic, and geographical factors. It was also the projection in stone of a spiritual vision: its walls were, therefore, not so much a medieval defense apparatus as a depiction of a cosmic geometry, a graphic of the universal order.

Before coming back to Peking in 1972, I had known already that I would not see the walls again: the government of the People's Republic had razed them all. This Herculean labor, begun in 1950, was completed in 1962. But, I thought, if the walls have gone, at least the essential things are still there: the glorious series of monumental gates that still define and organize the city's ideal space. Even if the physical appearance has changed, at least the gates are there, perpetuating on Chinese soil, as an ideographic character painted on silk or carved on a stele, the sign of Peking.

The panic that seized me when I could not find the gates is not easy to describe. Everyone who has known them must naïvely believe, as I did, that they were immortal, and they will understand my state of mind that day in May 1972, as I rushed breathlessly from Ch'ung-wen men (Hata men is the popular appellation of this gate, from the name of a Mongol prince, Hata, who had his palace nearby) all the way to Hsi-chih men, finding only, in place of each gate, the dull flatness of an abnormally wide and empty boulevard. For a while, I tried to tell myself that I had gotten lost, that since the streets had changed I had lost my sense of direction, that at the next crossroads I could not miss the massive and protecting shape of a gate, rediscovered at last. This could only be an absurd nightmare: sooner or later I was bound to find the road back to reality —the gate to Peking. I must be having hallucinations. —Any hypothesis seemed more acceptable than the truth. Finally, at Hsi-chih men, dead-beat after rushing around madly for a whole afternoon, I could not deny the evidence: this obscene stump among the rubble, which the workmen were beating down with their picks, this was all that remained of Peking's last gate. . . . As I learned later, its destruction had been postponed because the wreckers had found, during their work, the foundations of a gate of the Yuan era (A.D. 1234–1368). Archaeologists and photographers were summoned; the *K'ao-ku* (*Archaeology*) review published articles by the first and pictures by the second, to show the world how much care was taken with China's cultural heritage under the Maoist regime; when this formality was accomplished, the destruction of the entire monument continued until completed—Yuan remains included. In order to make people believe that it was both revolutionary and cultural, the Cultural

Revolution thus practiced (simultaneously or successively) iconoclasm and archaeology. Dead stones loom large in specialized periodicals for the export market, while living stones in the city are murdered.

But why all the demolition? In the particular case of Hsichih men, for instance, the only result of reducing it to a field of rubble is to clear the perspective of the Exhibition Palace, that poisonous gift of Soviet friendship, a masterpiece of Stalinoid architecture, whose neo-Babylonian tower in lard, now visible from all sides, succeeds in changing West Peking into a suburb of some dismal Irkutsk or Khabarovsk. Elsewhere, the disappearance of the gates has permitted the widening and straightening of the streets; muleteers and bicyclists do not have to waste two or three minutes going around those majestic sentries; now they can dash in a straight line across a desert. In Europe one is, alas, used to seeing the beauty of historic cities destroyed to make room for cars. In Peking, it is more original; the city has been destroyed not under the pressure of existing traffic, but in prevision of traffic yet to come. This, at least, is what one must conclude if one accepts the most common official explanation. But official doctrine on the matter is not unanimous; some bureaucrats defend the destruction of the gates by the need to clear the way for future traffic; others say that it was done to obtain building materials—but this is not very convincing, since the army of demolishers could just as well have opened new quarries in the hills around Peking. When cornered on the subject, authorities are vague and strangely laconic. It is rather remarkable that nobody seems to know the true reasons for a job that took so much effort and so many people and lasted for so many years.

In the end, chronology can give us the clue to the riddle. It appears that the destruction of the gates started in 1967 or 1968: in other words, the operation took place under the master slogan of the Cultural Revolution, "Destroy the old to establish the new." Today, however, various tactical considerations have led the authorities either to deny the depredations of the Cultural

Revolution or to lay them to the account of various saboteurs: Liu Shao-ch'i's disciples, Lin Piao's followers, rightists, leftists, rightists disguised as extreme leftists, and so on. When one is confronted with a case such as that of the gates of Peking, whose destruction was the work of specialists, well planned and well organized, employing a large work force over many years until long after the end of the Cultural Revolution, one becomes skeptical of the official theory that maintains that all acts of vandalism committed during the Cultural Revolution were the work of irresponsible extremists at the base, acting against the directives of the central power.

One should not be led astray by this "archaeological nostalgia" which seems to appear now and again in my impressions of the People's Republic. If the destruction of the entire legacy of China's traditional culture was the price to pay to insure the success of the revolution, I would forgive all the iconoclasms, I would support them with enthusiasm! What makes the Maoist vandalism so odious and so pathetic is not that it is irreparably mutilating an ancient civilization but rather that by doing so it gives itself an alibi for *not grappling with the true revolutionary tasks*. The extent of their depredations gives Maoists the cheap illusion that they have done a great deal; they persuade themselves that they can rid themselves of the past by attacking its material manifestations; but in fact they remain its slaves, bound the more tightly because they refuse to realize the effect of the old traditions within their revolution. The destruction of the gates of Peking is, properly speaking, a *sacrilege*; and what makes it dramatic is not that the authorities had them pulled down but that they remain unable to understand *why* they pulled them down.

A passage in the autobiography of Kuo Mo-jo throws a strange light on this subject. In the last years of the empire, Kuo, still a child, goes for the first time from his village birthplace to the next town, Chia-ting (in Szechuan), and he describes the arrival:

... At last, on the left bank, appeared the red walls that surrounded Chia-ting; the high cornices of the ramparts, rising in a sweeping movement, the imposing arch of the great gate and its gaping black hole like an abyss, was, for all of us, children of the countryside, a prodigiously unusual sight. The grown-ups on the boat said to us: "Those who cross the city walls for the first time must first bow three times to the great gate." We knew it was a joke; nevertheless, on approaching the gate doubts seized us, and we could not rid ourselves of the notion that some kind of ceremonial would have been fitting. In fact, I am not sure that the adults did not themselves have the same sense of religious awe when confronted with the severe majestic splendor of that gate; otherwise, how could they have thought of telling us about that rite? Powerful is the work of man! The walls they build end by having a sacred prestige. ... The least provincial town has its temple to the god of walls: psychologically how does this differ from our childish response to the great gate of Chia-ting? Those superb walls are typical of the Szechuan landscape, and one seldom encounters them in other provinces —except in Peking, of course, where the walls are truly majestic.[9]

A countersuperstition is not less a superstition: under the old regime town walls were venerated; under the new one they are under attack. The fury of the iconoclasts is a negative measurement of the permanence of the sacred powers that ruled feudal society. The tragedy is that the sacred powers dwell not in those innocent stones, whose beauty is sacrificed in vain, but in the minds of the wreckers. Seen in this light, the Maoist enterprise appears hopeless; the regime may well change China into a cultural desert without succeeding in exorcising the ghosts of the past: these ghosts will continue their paralyzing tyranny so long as the regime is unable to identify them within itself. But will it ever be capable of such clear vision? Certain foreign Sinologists, guilty of having noted traces of the traditional way of thinking in the Maoist systems, are the focus in Peking of surprising hatred out of all proportion to their limited audience or influence.

9. Kuo Mo-jo, *Autobiographie: mes années d'enfance* (Paris, 1970), pp. 75–76.

This shows, I'm afraid, how little the Maoist authorities are ready to re-examine critically the old clichés in which they have locked the concepts of "old" and "new," "feudalism" and "progress," "reaction" and "revolution." By refusing to examine the nature and identity of its revolution in depth, the People's Republic condemns itself to marking time, to struggling in the dark, producing such periodic sterile explosions as the Cultural Revolution. It can have little hope of liberating itself from the slavery of the past as long as it hunts it among old stones, instead of denouncing its active reincarnation in the ideology and political practices of the new mandarins.

For those who knew it in the past, Peking now appears to be a murdered town. The body is still there, the soul has gone. The *life* of Peking, which created never-ending theater in its streets and squares, the noisy and enjoyable life of the city has gone, leaving only the physical presence of a mute and monochromatic crowd, oppressed by a silence broken only by the tinkle of bicycle bells.

But for foreign tourists, this dead city continues to offer a number of monuments that amply warrant the visit. The Forbidden City has miraculously been preserved (is it because Mao Tse-tung likes now and again to play at being emperor from the balcony of T'ien-an men?). Whatever the reason, this vast gathering of courts and palaces remains one of the most sublime architectural creations in the world. In the history of architecture, most monuments that try to express imperial majesty abandon the human scale and cannot reach their objective without reducing their occupants to ants. Here, on the contrary, greatness always keeps an easy measure, a natural scale; it is conveyed not by a disproportion between the monument and the onlooker but by an infallibly harmonious space. The just nobility of these courts and roofs, endlessly reaffirmed under the changing light of different days and seasons, gives the onlooker that *physical* feeling of happiness which only music can sometimes convey. As a body loses weight in water, the visitor feels a lightening of his being to swim thus in such perfection—in curious contradiction to the explanatory notices that the authorities have put at the entrances to each court and building, describing the Chinese imperial regime in terms which would best evoke the dark and cruel horror of some Assyrian tyranny, and which would hardly account for this quality of equilibrium that seems to have inspired the whole city.

The Temple of Heaven belongs to the same aesthetic and spiritual world. Here again, greatness is reached through means that are wholly foreign to gigantism. It represents a perfect harmony, the result of the organization of a homogeneous and unique space where the buildings, the empty spaces, the perspectives, the old trees, and the blue of the sky are all active elements. I do not know to what miracle this pure perfection owes its survival—under a regime for which, elsewhere, beauty in all forms appears to be the sure mark of feudal vice or bourgeois corruption. Up to now, the Maoists have been content with building (in the middle of the avenue linking the Huang-ch'iung yü, the Imperial Heavenly Vault, to the Ch'i-nien tien, the Hall of Prayer for Good Harvest) a huge crimson cement screen on which you can read the text of the inevitable Mao poem (to tell the truth, it is the least bad one: 'Snow") in the poor and pretentious calligraphy of the author. In 1972 truck convoys were bringing dirt to a spot just west of this sacred way: I was told there was a plan to build an artificial hill there. The plan was evidently to make some sort of proletarian Tiger Balm Garden in the heart of the Temple of Heaven, for the healthy relaxation of the working masses. . . .

I shall say little of the Summer Palace, carefully restored after the lootings of the Cultural Revolution. (But the tomb of Yeh-lü Ch'u-ts'ai has disappeared: the new guides there, promoted after the Cultural Revolution, not only did not know that the tomb had been there until 1966, but knew nothing about this famous historical figure. Yeh-lü Ch'u-ts'ai (1190–1244), a Khitan aristocrat who served as minister to Genghis Khan, exerted a civilizing and moderating influence upon the savage Mongol conquerors.) That was not the first time the Summer Palace was ransacked, and the buildings are of a decadent *chinoiserie* architecture in the purest style of the 1900 International Exhibition. Still, the surroundings are lovely.

The other Peking monuments have suffered various fates. One can always reread the *Nagel Guide* on this subject, for it remains a remarkable piece of work, but since the Cultural Revolution its usefulness has become rather academic. It should not be read for practical purposes, but rather for historical information, as one reads the accounts by eighteenth- and nineteenth-century missionaries, or the descriptions by Madrolle or Segalen: to visit in one's imagination the monuments which have disappeared or have become inaccessible.

The eighteenth-century Temple of the Lamas (Yung-ho kung, or Palace of Eternal Harmony) was being restored in late 1972; it was to be open to foreigners (visitors by appointment). The fifteenth-century Temple of the Five Pagodas (Wu-t'a ssu), built in imitation of an Indian model, was used for Study Groups on the Thought of Mao Tse-tung for young people, and entry was forbidden. The Temple of Confucius, founded in the fourteenth century, was closed down and closely guarded, with barbed wire and electrified wires running on the tops of the walls; it was evidently inhabited by important military persons. The Temple of the White Dagoba (Pai-t'a ssu), an eleventh-century Buddhist temple rebuilt in the fifteenth century, was a warehouse and refuse dump with a padlocked entrance, and all one could see over the wall was ruin and desolation. The seventh-century Fa-yuan (Source of the Law) Monastery (restored in the fifteenth, seventeenth, and eighteenth centuries) and the Buddhist Association were closed; the main gate and walls bore traces of various outrages, and the whole seemed dead and dilapidated. The Great Mosque was similarly closed and abandoned; the buildings of the Islamic Society were empty, with no sign of life except for some soldiers strolling in the garden. The T'ien-ning Pagoda—one of the oldest monuments in Peking, an early thirteenth-century construction (the Buddhist monastery to which it belonged has disappeared completely)—is inaccessible: it is in the backyard of a factory, and you can only see it from afar. The Pa-li-chuang Pagoda, the only remains of a Buddhist monastery built at the end of the sixteenth century, is in less dreary surroundings— you can get near to it and even go around it—but it is in bad condition, with its stucco high reliefs exposed to weather and to the catapults of passing boys. The famous Taoist Temple of Po-yun kuan, established under the T'ang (618–905) and until the Cultural Revolution the only Taoist temple in Peking still in use, has become an army barracks; the tourist should not go too near if he wants to avoid trouble. The T'ai-shan Temple (Tung-yüeh miao, or Eastern Peak temple, a Taoist temple dedicated to the worship of the god of one of China's sacred mountains) has been converted into offices; entry is forbidden. The House-Museum of the famous modern painter Hsü Pei-hung, a beautiful example of Pekingese traditional domestic architecture, with an interesting collection of the painter's works, was razed, along with the entire surrounding block, when a subway was dug there (so it is said). The Wan-shou Monastery, established in the sixteenth century and rebuilt in the eighteenth, has become sleeping quarters for workmen. And so forth. And I might add that in 1972 all the museums—the Historical Museum, Museum of the Revolution, the Lu Hsün House-Museum (Lu Hsün lived in Peking from 1912 to 1926)—were closed, the historiographers not yet having finished rewriting history in the light of the latest purges.

The Pei-hai and Ching-shan parks were closed "for maintenance work," according to signs at the entrances, but the silhouettes of sentries who could be seen patrolling at the crest of those two natural observatories that dominate the city suggested another explanation. It should not be forgotten that the last military *coup d'état* in China (or countercoup?—since the Cultural Revolution, the question of who holds "legal" power in China is purely academic) took place in 1971. The Chung-nan-hai district—which shelters Mao Tse-tung and most of his staff, as well as the Central Committee, the State Council, and various national executive organs—was still in a state of semi-siege; not only were the two parks forbidden to the public and under military control but the neighborhood streets were stuffed with barracks; on the bridge between the Chung-nan-hai and the Pei-hai, whence one can see a bit of lawn near the holy of holies, every twenty yards one could see a notice reminding passers-by that it was *forbidden to stop while crossing the bridge*; at each end sentries made sure that this order was respected. At night, in the same quarter, it was not unusual to meet patrolling groups of soldiers with fixed bayonets. This situation was of course temporary; we were assured that things were on their way to "normalization." Except that when normalization is completed it may well appear that it was only temporary, before the next Cultural Revolution. In the end, the problem remains: which, the *coup d'état* or the period of "normalization," is the really normal condition for the Chinese government?

Tientsin

In the diesel train that links Peking to Tientsin, there are no compartments where the foreign traveler can be isolated. The conductor puts you in the first seat facing the front and clears the seat next to you and the ones opposite. The train I took, one cold autumn morning, was full; many passengers had to stand in the aisle. I was surprised when a young woman defied the conductor's instructions and quietly sat down opposite me. I quickly learned the secret of her audacity: she was an *Overseas* Chinese. Overseas Chinese, even if they have lived on the mainland for years, keep a special status and enjoy several material privileges—and if they want to leave China they can sometimes get an exit visa. But more than those various advantages, what perhaps really sets them apart is their more individualistic attitude, a sum of reflexes of a people used to freedom, which the citizens of the People's Republic seem to have forgotten. We chatted about one thing or another till we came to Tientsin. Normally, the traveler in Maoist China must observe a ponderous and didactic program, in which the Chinese bombard him with numbers, statistics, Thoughts of the Chairman, official pronouncements made by various "responsible persons" and other spokesmen, which the zealous visitor is supposed to write down in little notebooks. By contrast, any human contact, however short, however commonplace, stands in sharp relief. I want to note down here the cold-pinched face and sad smile of that young woman on the Tientsin train, not that this image has any particular meaning: I note it because it has *no* particular meaning, which is what made it so precious and so rare in a world that was so meticulously organized, rigorously planned, and heavily pedagogic.

Tientsin has the funereal and grotesque poetry of a décor by Kafka. Soldiers of the People's Liberation Army quartered in a neo-Gothic cathedral. The proud façade of imperialist banks —colossal imitations of fancy Parthenons—with patched tatters of laundry fluttering between the columns. Once luxurious palaces belonging to captains of industry and barons of finance, false Roman villas, imitations of medieval castles—and then, suddenly, a whole street borrowed from a quiet European middle-class suburbia, with plaster gnomes in derelict gardens. A nightmare Disneyland, with old Belgian tramways shaking along the boulevards; everything tawdry, peeling, decrepit, ramshackle. Once pretentious mansions have become warehouses, or have been subdivided into flats and subflats for a whole population of tenants who have organized themselves with an abundance of planks and cardboard. Tientsin should be visited by night— the streets are all but blacked out, although here and there a lamp glows in the darkness—and the whole city, with its walled-up windows, its blind and leprous façades, seems to be a sleepwalker's dream. The paradox of this ghost city is that it is one of the major cities of the world, with more than three million inhabitants. To the passing visitor, the very existence of these millions of lives seems to have been sucked away by the vampire shadows of the past.

The only human confidence I received in Tientsin was given me by a wall: I found a small stenciled notice from a private citizen glued near a bus stop. The man who had signed it, a technician from Tientsin working in a factory in Sian, more than six hundred miles from his family, was trying to learn if there were not in Tientsin a technician from Sian with qualifications similar to his and willing to exchange posts; he wanted the exchange urgently because "the fact of being permanently away from his wife and small children worked on his mind in a way that prevented the full development of his revolutionary enthusiasm for the edification of socialism."

The hotel for foreigners in Tientsin is worth the journey. This monstrous and gloomy construction, a relic of the imperialist era, is usually empty; an army of idle servants yawns and naps along the corridors. In the high-ceilinged rooms, shadowy even in the middle of the day, the guest has the feeling of a vague presence—as if the previous occupant had hanged himself there. In the gloom, as in a cave, can be heard the crystalline music of a leaking toilet, tinkling that monotonous melody of socialist plumbing which can be heard in all the hotels from Prague to Vladivostok, from Canton to Novosibirsk.

Peitaiho

Peitaiho is a seaside resort for bureaucrats and diplomats, some seven hours from Peking by train, not far from the place where the Great Wall meets the sea. It has a certain charm, but this cannot always be felt right away.

The essence of this subtle magic lies in the fact that after a few days one is assailed by doubts about the very existence of the place. If any holiday resort to fulfill its aim of making evasion possible must suggest a kind of "elsewhere," Peitaiho represents an absolute evasion, because it is a true "nowhere." Imagine turn-of-the-century villas from Folkestone or Ostend, transposed in colonial terms, with wide verandas, servants' quarters, and corrugated-iron roofs, and set down in a space dotted with pines and sentry boxes of the People's Liberation Army, on a low cliff overlooking the blue horizons of the Po-hai: this will give you in a nutshell an idea of this ineffable place, neither Chinese nor Western, this incredible bastard of a clandestine mating between colonialist imperialism and the dictatorship of the proletariat. Peitaiho in its eeriness raises the notion of a seaside resort to the quasi-metaphysical plane: it is less a holiday resort than the Platonic idea of a holiday resort.

During the holiday season, all the foreign diplomats of Peking and their families may be found parked on the beach, which is the size of a handkerchief. On the land side, you find every fifty yards a sentry of the People's Liberation Army, marking off a perimeter that is perhaps two miles long and a mile wide: a magic and unreal holiday zone carefully cut off from China—which from Peitaiho seems to be on another planet. On the sea side, an underwater net marks the area allotted to swimmers—ostensibly this is to protect them from sharks, but since at that latitude sharks do not exist or are no bigger than a large herring, I cannot help thinking that the net has, not a practical, but a mystical function; the counterpart of the line of sentries on the land side, it makes that small diplomatic world completely watertight, sealed off against any contamination from reality that might emerge in contacts with peasants from the countryside or fish from the Po-hai.

But the Peitaiho atmosphere is insidious. I have observed that some vacationers who stay too long almost fall back, gently, into childhood. One dozes at the sound of the surf; the moon washes over a blue-and-silver world; the wind sighing in the pines brings back old memories from a forgotten youth. In the touching old bungalows the floors moan, the musty drawers give out heady Proustian odors. Secretaries from the Scandinavian embassies, varied but interchangeable, make up a permanent and poetic contingent of *jeunes filles en fleurs*. The local pastry shop, a branch of Kiesling and Bader, a venerable Austrian firm founded in Tientsin in the last days of the reign of Kuang-hsü, sells not *madeleines*, but strudels and little pink marzipan pigs which melt in the mouth with such a powerful taste of vanished childhood that even the most hardened diplomats in that weird exile can be found with moist eyes. Higher cadres of the People's Liberation Army who have villas nearby are no less appreciative of the Viennese pastries of Kiesling and Bader (even soldiers are human beings!), and from time to time one can see their black limousines parked in front of the shop, while drivers and orderlies pile up cakes and confectionery cartons in the trunk.

Loyang

China has two faces: the immemorial one of the Yellow River and the Wei, cradle of Chinese civilization, site of prehistoric cultures and of the great dynasties of antiquity, driving force of the country until the end of the northern Sung dynasty; the other is that of the lower Yangtze River, where beginning in the twelfth century a string of dynamic and prestigious cities developed, the modern locus of Chinese history while the Yellow River China fell into a kind of torpor. It was not until the present regime that an effort was made to shake these old provinces from their lethargy and misery.

Loyang is one of the richest historical sites to be found in all of China; founded about 1200 B.C., it was the capital of ten dynasties before losing its rank in the tenth century A.D. In the twelfth century it was stormed and sacked by the Jurchen invaders, and never recovered from the disaster. What remains of Loyang today is a group of archaeological sites and a picturesque, rather squalid old town, vegetating quietly on a small area of the vanished capital, phantom of the past. After 1949 a new industrial city was created some distance away, and foreign visitors are taken to model factories there. While the new city is less picturesque than the old one, it is nearly as run-down; block after block of sordid apartment dwellings are uncared for, as cheery as barracks.

The Lung-men cave-temples nearby, one of the landmarks of world sculpture, were miraculously spared during the Cultural Revolution. A friend who visited them in 1967, during the most anarchic period, told me that he had found them open; nobody was watching over them, and anybody could go in. The fact that they are some distance from the city may well account for their survival without mishap during this troubled period. On the other hand, I could not get permission to visit the famous Temple of the White Horse (Pai-ma ssu) or the Temple of Kuan Yü (Kuan Ti Miao); and these prohibitions make me fear the worst about their state of preservation. The first is one of the most venerable Buddhist shrines in China: the present structure, dating back essentially to the Ming (1368–1628), was erected on the site of the earliest Buddhist temple built in China, under the western Han, in the first century B.C.; the pagoda dates partly from the tenth and partly from the twelfth century. The second is a sixteenth-century Taoist temple dedicated to the Three Kingdoms hero Kuan Yü, later canonized as the god of war; after 1958 the temple housed a municipal museum.

In 1972 the local population of Loyang did not seem used to seeing a foreigner walk freely in their streets. A tourist who managed to part from his guide and driver would be followed by a crowd that in a few moments might number a thousand people, which meant that one Western visitor walking alone could bring traffic to a standstill for whole streets—although zealous activists would spring up out of nowhere, organizing the confusion and directing the show. Twenty paces ahead of the visitor, they would shoo away anybody who might offend his sight or slight China's national prestige: people in rags and naked children were told curtly to get lost. But soon responsible types arrived: two or three breathless policemen on bicycles, alerted by telephone. By now it is too late, the human flood cannot be dammed, the policemen give up and let themselves be carried along in the wake of the poor "foreign devil."

Spy fever was still as prevalent in Loyang as in other provincial towns. This psychosis is maintained by huge wall posters placed at random throughout the city. ("Increase our Vigilance and Protect Our Fatherland!"), with the result that nobody dares even give directions to a foreigner. "I don't know, I am not from here," said several passers-by. "I am sorry, I do not go out very often, I do not know the streets," said a shopkeeper behind his counter. Finally I had to ask my police escort for the topographic information I needed.

Though Loyang is not much more miserable than cities like Chengchow or Anyang, it gave me a feeling of unspeakable sorrow—due, I think, to the wide gap between the magical poetry of its name and the commonplace misery of its present reality. As I walked past monotonous workers' flats, under the heartbreaking beauty of a May sky, I was haunted by the famous verses of Wei Chuang, weeping over the ruin of Loyang at the fall of the T'ang dynasty (A.D. 907), and they obsessively reverberated in my head, so relevant still, after a thousand years:

> Spring is bright and splendid in the city of Loyang;
> But the flower of its youth grows old under other skies. . . .

Sian

Sian too was the capital of successive dynasties almost as far back as Loyang, but it had preserved its antique nobility much better. While Loyang has been only a kind of backwater village for eight centuries, Sian—though now covering only a sixth of its size when it was capital of the T'ang empire under the name of Ch'ang-an (A.D. 618–907), and one of the largest cosmopolitan cities in the world—has kept intact the majestic order of its imperial plan, its walls, and its gates. It seems to have been left aside by the turmoils of recent history, and it keeps some of the charm and beauty that the Maoist regime has succeeded in erasing in Peking.

It is wonderful to see how the inhabitants of Sian are aware of their city's glorious past and proud to show its monuments. The official tour is limited to the Pagoda of the Great Goose (Ta yen t'a: attached to a Buddhist monastery from the seventh century, the pagoda itself is from the seventh and eighth centuries) and the provincial museum of Shensi (located in the former Temple of Confucius and including the famous Forest of Steles), but one afternoon I managed to get rid of my keeper and visited by myself the fifteenth-century Temple of the City Gods (Ch'eng-huang miao) and the Great Mosque (Ch'ing-chen ssu), founded in 742 and rebuilt in the fourteenth century. Maoist bureaucrats are not eager to let foreigners discover the pitiful state to which these monuments were reduced by the Cultural Revolution, but what is surprising (and would have been unthinkable in Peking) is that people from the neighborhood very kindly unlocked the doors to let me visit both of them. The Temple of the City Gods has lost all its statues, the great gate with five carved wooden arches which marked the principal entrance has disappeared, the sanctuary itself is now a warehouse. The dilapidated buildings are a sorry sight. As I gazed silently on this desolation, one of my volunteer guides who had let me in said, as much for himself as for me: "Oh well, the Red Guards destroyed everything here!"

At the Great Mosque, which had been furtively opened for me by an old Muslim with a white skullcap, I did not have time to meditate very long on the scars left by the Cultural Revolution, for the guide who was officially in charge of me in Sian had discovered my truancy, traced me, and finally managed to catch up, panting and in a great state—my disappearance had obviously made a lot of trouble for him. He explained that the Cultural Revolution was only just over and the revolutionary temperature of the "masses" was still feverishly high; people were not used to meeting foreigners on the streets, and a misunderstanding could happen so quickly. . . . He was a nice fellow, and we had got along well. He was of course responsible for supervising all my activities, and by escaping him, I had exposed him to the reprimands of his superiors, who would probably accuse him of negligence. My escapade shocked him: in a way, I had betrayed his confidence. I felt full of remorse, but it was too late: after this adventure, I did not see him again until he showed up on the railway platform to say good-by when I left. When I asked where he had been, he said in a rather embarrassed way that he had not been well. The carelessness or imprudence of foreigners in China seems to cause a lot of sickness among the personnel who must take care of them—especially when these are young and inexperienced. In the end, it is that feeling of being a perpetual source of problems for your escort—who is so friendly and full of good will—which may be the most powerful brake on the foreign traveler's longings for more freedom of movement. Except when the guides are dogmatic and disagreeable, one abandons any plan that may bring trouble to the people whose responsibility it is to care for you. Their job is hard enough as it is under the best of circumstances.

I did not try to launch other independent expeditions in Sian, but I doubt if they would have brought me unexpected revelations; one guide whom I had asked several times if I could visit the Five Western Terraces (Hsi-wu t'ai, a Sung monastery that used to contain some fine Ming sculpture and that was, I knew, not far from the hotel) and who had given me dilatory answers, ended by saying, with unusual frankness: "It's not worth it: there is nothing to see, the Red Guards burned everything." More research on the fate of the other famous monuments in or near Sian—the Buddhist Temple of the Reclining Dragon (Wo lung ssu), built under the Sui (581–618); the biggest Taoist temple in Sian, the Temple of the Eight Immortals (Pa Hsien an), founded under the Sung and still in use before the Cultural Revolution; and others[10]—was fast becoming mere prurient curiosity. "But if these things interest you so much, why not go and visit the provincial art workshop? If you like, we could easily organize a visit for you." So there I went: a small factory with about a hundred workmen sculpting billiard balls, polishing seashells, and gluing fake ostrich feathers on plastic objects, making out of a bewildering variety of sickening materials huge quantities of trinkets depicting "Chairman Mao surrounded by peasants, soldiers and workers," "Souvenirs of Yenan," and "Greetings from Shaoshan." You would have to be Huysmans to describe adequately the production of that place—in all its cloying hideousness, its breathtaking saccharine, its viscous, suave vulgarity. Meanwhile, what philosopher will explain why the natural bend of proletarian art is to petty-bourgeois academicism?

About ten miles from Sian, at the foot of the first ridges of the Ch'in-ling mountains, one finds Hsiao-hsin ts'un, one of the model villages that are supposed to represent, for the foreign visitor, the peasant realities of all China. This village is exemplary because of the hydraulic works that have allowed it to control the flow of a nearby torrent. Technical commentaries are given out by an old peasant who explains how the conception of the whole work rests basically on a living and creative application of a Thought of Mao Tse-tung and—here he takes a deep breath, knits his brow, and proceeds cautiously into the memorized gibberish—di-a-lec-ti-cal ma-ter-i-al-ism. Any suggestion that there could have been any advice or intervention from engineers and technicians in this remarkable and complex work is rejected

10. The early eighteenth-century Pagoda of the Small Goose (Hsiao yen t'a) is still standing, but it is in bad shape. I saw it from a distance: one could not get near it. During an excursion to Hua-ch'ing (where tourists are brought to see the site of the famous "Sian Incident" of 1936), I asked if it were possible to visit the Temple of Yü the Great and the Temple of Lao-tzu, since both had interesting sculptures and the first was until the Cultural Revolution inhabited by Taoist hermits, but I was told curtly that it was impossible, the first one having been "remodeled" and the second one being "closed."

with horror: it is the Thought of Mao Tse-tung which has liberated the hidden genius of the toiling masses, making unnecessary any intervention on the part of those specialists so dear to Liu Shao-ch'i & Co.—specialists who, meanwhile, have learned that the best way for them to help build up socialism is to break stones and cart manure.

What was noteworthy was that the political personnel of the village was totally unaffected by the Cultural Revolution: the team in charge has not changed at least since the beginning of the 1960s, when the hydraulic works were started. This confirms what we already know: the Cultural Revolution was essentially an urban movement, and its main effect in the rural areas was, for a while, to relax external controls and to favor a temporary return to village autarky—a double evolution that brought only benefits to the peasants.

Tachai

In the Maoist religion, which teaches that the spirit dominates matter and that revolutionary will by itself can move mountains, Tachai is a holy place and is for the faithful a kind of Lourdes or Fatima. China is covered with inscriptions that repeat: "Let us learn from Tachai!" Since eight hundred million Chinese must model themselves on the six hundred inhabitants of Tachai, the task of these last seems to have been reduced to bearing their own holiness, as a monstrance, under the gaze of the myriads of pilgrims who trundle daily to the miraculous village. Since part of the herculean labors said to have been done by the peasants with their bare hands was in fact done by the army, and since the other Chinese villages can hardly hope for such help, one realizes that the model offers to its imitators a rather discouraging perfection.

In fact, Tachai is a fantastically snobbish place (snob: in the sense that word may describe a well-known English-Maoist novelist, chattering at a diplomatic cocktail party in Peking about pig-breeding methods, the comparative values of human manure and chemical fertilizers, manure-spreading techniques, and so forth, *as if those questions interested her, as if she had any real experience of them*). I had the chance to visit Tachai with a cosmopolitan group of foreigners, piloted through China by officials from the Ministry of Foreign Affairs. The village head-man, whose photograph is nearly as common in China as Mao's, was there for once (he spends most of his time traveling around the country, taking part in conferences and other bureaucratic activities) and he gave us a banquet. For this occasion he came with his head wrapped in a carefully knotted towel, which in the fields under a glaring sun would be useful for wiping the sweat away but at an official gathering or other social occasion becomes something like the feathered headdress of an Apache chief selling souvenirs to tourists. This operetta peasant dress was balanced by the proletarian-postcard disguise of some of the Foreign Affairs officials: one of them, who as a rule wears im-peccably cut Sun Yat-sen jackets,[11] came down the first morning in old clothes, artistically patched and rumpled, which he had kept in his suitcase for the visit to the Holy Places. The lodging house at Tachai had subtle rustic touches: international capitalists and other tourists who "do" China are like Marie Antoinette playing at being a shepherdess; the meals are no less delicious or less abundant than in the Peking, Canton, or Shanghai palaces for foreigners, but here they are touched with a well-studied primitivism, a shrewd naïvety. In the usual vast array of dishes, some dissonant notes are skillfully struck—a dozen hard-boiled eggs on a tin plate here, a bowl of gruel there—and added to the usual choice of wines, beers, soft drinks, and alcohol is a fearful local spirit. The gourmet brave enough to taste it is suddenly drenched in sweat, giving him the virile and exalting sense that he is somehow communing with the hard task of building socialism.

11. Chung-shan chuang, which a silly vogue in the West persists in calling a "Mao jacket"—as if the present regime had invented it.

Linhsien and the Red Flag Canal

Linhsien, with the famous Red Flag (Hung-ch'i) Canal, an enterprise worthy of the Pharaohs, is the second Holy Place of Maoism. To irrigate the Linhsien district, a river was rerouted through a tunnel beneath a mountain and then along a new bed built on the side of steep cliffs. Here again, the guides insist on the fact that this colossal work was done by the local populace with their bare hands, without the help of engineers or machines. If engineers had been consulted, they would probably have objected that, instead of mobilizing thousands of people for ten years "to dig by hand 1,500 kilometers of canal, level hills, pierce 134 tunnels, build 150 aqueducts, displace by hand 16.4 million cubic meters of earth and rocks—enough to build a road 1 meter high, 6 meters wide, and 4,000 kilometers long," it would have been more rational and more economic to use that energy for some productive use, and to use the proceeds to buy a pump that could bring water directly over to the other side of the mountains. But by making such a suggestion, the engineers would have shown that, like true "experts," they knew nothing of the real nature of the problem. The function of the Red Flag Canal is only accidentally economic, agricultural, or hydraulic; its real significance is religious, and it is probably for that reason that it will be passed on to posterity. Monuments like the Great Wall or the Pyramids capture the imagination of millions, though the first was of dubious military effectiveness and the second never seemed (from an economic point of view) a rational practice for burial. Maybe psychologists and anthropologists will be able to explain why slave societies feel the need to pursue such gigantic endeavors. Meanwhile, I note that visitors from the Third World—especially Africans—are usually overcome by the lesson of Linhsien, and this is something we should think about. That this epic work makes little sense for the technician or the economist doesn't cut much ice with people who from their own national experience know the illusory value of credits and experts. Maybe they think that only the ancient secrets of the

Pharaohs and of Ch'in Shih-huang, as applied anew in the heroic mobilization of the antlike Linhsien people, can rescue the Third World from the morass into which, each day, it sinks deeper.

Chengchow and Anyang

Visitors who go to Linhsien usually break their journey at Chengchow, the provincial capital of Honan. I have spoken already of the weighty, luxurious fortress-hotels where, far from the city centers, foreigners are deposited: the Chengchow hotel is the most Babylonian of all (a close runner-up is the hotel in Ch'angsha, where people stay when they visit the Birthplace of the Great Leader). The Chengchow hotel was designed by Russians for Russians; its vulgar gigantism and monstrous daintiness, which seem to have been devised for half-breed customers (by Cyclops out of shopgirls), are a fascinating projection of Stalin's genius. Stalin, for all too obvious reasons, is very much honored in Mao's China: his portrait hangs in most public buildings next to Lenin's, Engels', and Marx's; his complete works fill whole shelves in bookshops. But nowhere is his presence so evident as in the Chengchow palace. In the nightmare of its endless corridors, the weight of its triple velvet curtains, the perpetual gloom of its vast lounges filled with gray-covered furniture, I could feel almost physically the permanent presence of the man whom Osip Mandelstam (paying for it with his life) called "the hillman in the Kremlin, the wide-chested Ossete":

> His thick fingers are fat like worms
> And his words fall like hundred-pound weights.
> He laughs in his enormous cockroach mustache
> And his boots glisten, catching the eye. . . .[12]

On the other hand, Anyang is barely equipped to greet foreign guests, and this gives it much of its charm. Here is where the history of China starts, in a corn field next to the city, where

12. Nadezhda Mandelstam, *Hope against Hope*, Appendix I. The poem does not appear in the English edition, but only in the *French* edition: Nadejda Mandelstam, *Contre tout espoir* (Paris, 1972).

seventy years ago were found the oldest exemplars of Chinese writing on the site of a Shang capital (1765–1162 B.C.). Every year, this hallowed piece of ground yields some archaeological harvest, sometimes under the hoe of local farmers, sometimes in the sieves of the Permanent Mission of the Academia Sinica.

The center of the modern city is "modern" only in comparison with the three-thousand-year-old remains that sleep in the surrounding soil. It is made up of a maze of low houses and courts planted with willows and junipers, and it has been nicknamed—quite rightly—Little Peking. From the Wen-feng t'a, a curious pagoda dating from the time of the Five Dynasties (A.D. 907–960), one can have a general view of this poetic small world, with its gray roofs creeping under green trees, keeping up the memory of a Peking that has nearly completely disappeared in Peking itself.

In the main street of Anyang, I met an old-style funeral convoy: a lacquered coffin, whose curves recalled pagoda roofs and the bows of junks, followed the standard-bearers and the classical band, its high-pitched noises marked by the rhythm of rasping cymbals. The parents of the dead followed in traditional mourning dress: a white band on the forehead and a hemp chasuble on the shoulders. Did they not know that China had just gone through a Great Proletarian Cultural Revolution? This fleeting vision, in a city where few foreigners came, brought suddenly to the mind the suspicion that the China we are forbidden to see—nine-tenths of the cities and 99.9 per cent of the countryside—may well be somewhat different from the China we are allowed to visit.

Ch'angsha and Shaoshan

Ch'angsha is a compulsory stop for all pilgrims on their way to Shaoshan, the holy place of the Maoist Nativity. The Ch'angsha Hotel, therefore, has been built along especially grandiose lines so as to accommodate the cosmopolitan battalions of the faithful coming from all over the world. It is also a high spot of gastronomy: the great traditions of the Hunan cuisine are maintained remarkably well—at least for foreigners and high cadres.

In Ch'angsha, after spending two days visiting everything my guide wanted me to see, I felt, after my last factory, a certain fatigue. The idea of going back in a limousine to the closed world of the hotel was no more attractive than the idea of visiting a shoe factory or a workshop where they made marbles. (I would have been interested by Hunan University, but it appears that it had not yet recovered from the Cultural Revolution: seven years after the events, a visit was still not possible.) All I really wanted to do was stroll in the streets—without aim or purpose. I wanted to taste the mildness of twilight after a pretty summer day, in the leisurely jostle of a southern crowd, and then to come home in an ordinary, ramshackle town bus—in other words, I wanted to spend an hour or two like a normal human being. My guide was first nonplussed by this strange ambition; neither he nor the driver seemed ready for the free afternoon I was offering them. First, he tried to convince me of the strange problems I would face trying to move about with only my legs and the buses at my disposal, but then, since he was tactful (which made all my dealings with him a pleasure), he changed his approach, wished me good afternoon with a wide smile, and was gone. I disappeared into a maze of streets—with all the naturalness one can muster when surrounded by a hundred or a hundred and fifty onlookers, amazed, amused, or curious. After a while, I reached the bridge that crosses the Hsiang, and finally found some peace and quiet at the tip of the big island in midstream. I stayed there for an hour, enjoying the sunset and the sight of the delicate Hsiang junks.

The next day, while visiting the Mao Tse-tung Museum in Shaoshan, I saw displayed an old photograph of a view that seemed vaguely familiar.

"Now, what is this Shuilu chou?" I asked.

"Don't you recognize it?" replied the guide, abstracted. "It is the island where you went yesterday!"

It is not easy to lose oneself in the People's China.

Shaoshan, the birthplace of Chairman Mao, is about fifty miles from Ch'angsha and is visited by about three million pilgrims every year. A railway line has been built from Ch'angsha to transport them there, but one can also reach the village by a good macadam road (in contrast to the dirt roads common in the Chinese countryside) devised for the special needs of the pilgrims. Every two hundred and fifty yards or so, this Sacred Way is marked by a large red board on which one finds in golden letters some quotation from the Chairman. Shaoshan lies in a bright and prosperous valley; the red Hunan soil is rich and fertile, as is attested by the prosperous appearance of the farms (and the well-known gastronomy of the province). The influx of visitors does not give the village animation and bustle—far from it. All is orderliness and hushed devotion. The pilgrims move in ranks, by sections, red banners flying. They line up patiently to visit the House where He was born (a large farmhouse which must rouse the envy of many a visitor) and the Museum. This Museum has been twinned. There are two identical sections, completely and entirely alike in all respects. All the objects to be seen have been made in two sets, so that more visitors can be accommodated at the same time. I cannot imagine what strange reticence prevented the organizing committee from applying the same ingenious solution to the House where He was born also, or why it has not been done half a dozen times over: this would allow at least a million more tourists a year to satisfy their curiosity. No superstitions and childish fetishism about the "authentic thing" here, especially in the museums of revolutionary history, of which the contents are duplicated, multiplied, modified, falsified, eliminated, fabricated, and renewed at will.[13]

13. The best example of this museographic industry belongs to the great movement to emulate Lei Feng. Lei Feng was a conscript who died at the age of twenty in a banal accident. Only after his death was it discovered what a humble and admirable pupil of Mao Tse-tung he had been during his short and hidden life. His ideal had been "to be a small cog in the machine" working for the party and Chairman Mao. The biography of Lei Feng had some strange variants before the definitive version

The passage of the Great Man, discreetly noted by small signs, has transfigured Shaoshan. For instance, the duck pond is not an ordinary duck pond but "the duck pond where Chairman Mao used to swim when he was a boy"; the meadow that appears to the ordinary visitor to be a common pasture is "the pasture to which Chairman Mao led the cows." And so on. On the other hand, the Chairman's subjects get only scanty information on his biography—whereas foreigners can at least read the autobiographical confidences he gave Edgar Snow long ago.[14] To this American journalist, Mao had described his father as a decidedly unpleasant character, a prosperous farmer who ended as a landowner and speculator in grain; they had some violent quarrels, and it was then that Mao, still a child, discovered the brutal realities of oppression and class struggle. These old family quarrels seem forgotten nowadays. In the Museum, a large photograph of Mao's father is made acceptable with the sober caption, "Member of the Working Classes." Communist historiography follows quite closely the canons, conventions, and patterns of traditional historiography: positive heroes always have humble working-class origins, the baddies are invariably of doubtful origin and suckled vice with the milk of their wet nurses. In this way, Lin Piao, for example, who is one of the few leaders who could claim to have experienced childhood poverty, has gratuitously been given a wealthy capitalist background. As for Chou En-lai, whose mandarin-patrician origins are well

---

was prepared by the writers of the Propaganda Department in 1964. "Lei Feng Exhibitions" were organized in the large cities, simultaneously showing many "original" copies of the hero's diary. These exhibitions also showed remarkable photographic documents, such as "Lei Feng helping an old woman to cross the street," "Lei Feng secretly [sic] doing his comrades' washing," and "Lei Feng giving his lunch to a comrade who forgot his lunch box," and so forth. Only cynical and impious spirits will wonder at the providential presence of a photographer during the various incidents in the life of that humble, hitherto unknown soldier.

14. An integral Chinese translation of Red Star over China was made in Shanghai in 1939 by Shih Chien-k'ang under the title Ch'ang cheng. Reprinted in 1949, this translation was taken out of circulation some years later.

known, there has been a courteous convention that he was born
without a navel. . . .

Hofei

I spent a day and a night in Hofei, the provincial capital of
Anhwei, thanks to one of those unforeseen incidents that make
the Chinese airlines so charming. One morning I left Shanghai
for Peking in a small plane. The other passengers were military
officers—loud-mouth types who discussed the merits of various
hotels in Peking with the self-satisfied air of true businessmen—
plus some civilians with much lower profiles. Two hours later,
we landed in Hofei, where we were stuck in the airport, flattened
by an African heat (this was in August) bristling with cicadas.
Our little twin-engine plane, guarded by a sentry with a fixed
bayonet (was it a precaution against local hijackers, or against
saboteurs of the Lin Piao gang?), began to look quite majestic,
a *rara avis* destined for the capital, for the local traffic was made
up of single-engine biplanes that seemed to have come from
some Museum of Air Pioneers.

We spent the time quite pleasantly lolling about on the
benches in the waiting room, and a delicious lunch was served at
noon. There was a rain cloud near Tsinan, evidently, and we were
waiting for it to dissipate before proceeding on our journey.
Around five o'clock, probably because the cloud had not burst,
we were told that the plane would not leave until the next day.
I was delighted with the notion of this unexpected sojourn in
Anhwei. It happens that I have dear and intimate links with that
province, and I had given up the hope of visiting it—I could not
find an official pretext to do so—and now I had the chance, given
to me by meteorological accident! The authorities in charge decided that I would stay in the Hofei Guest House, a luxurious
place recently built on a hill outside the city, with a very nice
garden and a lotus-covered pond. This superb guest house was
used exclusively by passing civil and military personnel, as was

clear from the registration form I had to fill in. In Chinese only, it asked such questions as: Nature of your mission? Employed by what department? Functionary of what class? (As is well known, there are thirty echelons in the Maoist bureaucratic hierarchy, and each has its well-defined privileges: in the mandarinal guest houses, it is important for the staff to know to which class each guest belongs; probably this determines the size of the room and the number of courses at dinner.) The military must have been in the majority, judging by the number of cars with army markings in the courtyard.

Though Hofei is the provincial capital and must have about a million inhabitants, it appears that it never receives foreign tourists; it has no model factories and no Maoist relics—nothing worth organizing a guided visit. To get from the airport to the guest house, you cross the city itself; as far as I could judge, it appeared rather commonplace and poor. The general decrepitude of Chinese cities after twenty years of Maoism is not redeemed here by any antique buildings. I asked the guide, an open and pleasant man, a native of the place, if there were any interesting monuments to be seen. With disarming candor he laughed and said, "What do you think! After the Cultural Revolution? We had the Red Guards here!"

"Was there anything interesting before that?"

"Well, two or three old temples, but nothing remains, everything was pulled down."

But Hofei did have—like Peking, Canton, Soochow, Loyang, Sian, and most of the other cities I visited—an exhibit of archaeological objects "found in the province during the Cultural Revolution." This, at least, I gathered from a wall poster. But when I asked to visit it, there was a lot of uneasiness and, in the end, for various reasons and very courteously, my request was not granted. These exhibits were hemmed in with precautions and strange restrictions—not everyone can go, not open at all times— as if the cultural objects on display were some kind of dynamite that the authorities were using for a very precisely defined tactical purpose, and very carefully, lest they explode in their hands.

After leaving my luggage at the guest house, I wanted to have a look around, but as soon as I left the grounds, my guide caught up with me on a bicycle. It was not "opportune" for me to walk about, he explained. This could bring "problems" for the people and for me. His reasons were unconvincing, but his tone was anxious, and he was obviously operating under strict and precise instructions. I turned back. He was happy to see me so cooperative and added, "But since you really want to see the city, perhaps I can try to take you for a car ride this evening." Fortified with this happy plan, I returned to my suite—a drawing room with the dimensions of a ballroom, a terrace, and a bedroom just as large. There, in solitude, I had a six-course meal, with plenty to drink, while a platoon of servants was busy shining my shoes, brushing my coat, ironing my handkerchiefs. After dinner I was visited by someone who must have been rather important, to judge by my guide's attitude, and I knew at once that our car ride was not to be. True enough. After welcoming me to Hofei, the VIP told me courteously but in no uncertain terms that it would be best to limit my movements to my suite and that a car would pick me up the next day and take me to the airport.

Why was I not allowed to visit the city? It is not easy to say. We all know that savage incidents occurred in Hofei during the Cultural Revolution; but time has passed and the scars would not have been noticeable to a passing and superficial observer —I doubt that my welcoming committee had anything to fear on that score. The most likely explanation, I think, is that like all bureaucrats they were seized with classic administrative panic at the idea of making any decision without an official stamped paper to back it up. Foreign residents traveling in the provinces must always carry a pass that lists in detail the places they are allowed to visit, and at what date; when they go to each city, this document is stamped by security officials—and is stamped again on departure. I had left Peking two days before for a short visit to Soochow and Shanghai, and I had already five more stamps on my pass: one at the departure from Peking, one for arrival at Soochow, one for departure from Soochow, and one each for arrival to and departure from Shanghai. The Hofei stopover was due to bad weather and had not been planned; therefore, I had no permission to visit it. In that case, the most innocent stroll was an unthinkable bureaucratic heresy, a sin against Security. Any accident or incident—not probable, of course, but not impossible ("You never know" is one of the bureaucrats' golden rules)—during such a visit, which was technically illegal, would have brought trouble to the local authorities who would have been deemed guilty of acting on their own. Such being the case, to give me a grand meal in solitary splendor appeared to them the wisest solution.

Shanghai

The Peking-Shanghai Express leaves Peking early in the morning and gets to Shanghai in the morning of the following day. I have never tired of this trip and I recommend it to all travelers because they can then see for themselves how natural physical conditions render an extraordinary diversified universe, despite the monochrome varnish that has been painted over it during two decades of Maoism.

During the first part of the trip, one traverses the great agricultural plain of northern China; late in the afternoon, after crossing the Yellow River, the countryside changes: it becomes hilly and takes on a distinct character. First you have isolated stony hillocks rising here and there out of the flat plain, then the hills multiply and grow larger and are strung together in ranges. The highest point on the line is reached at T'aian Station, where one can see T'ai-shan, the most prestigious of the Five Sacred Mountains. Confucius climbed to the top, over five thousand feet high, and claimed that "seen from the heights, the world is small." It is on the T'ai-shan that the most solemn sort of the imperial sacrifice to Heaven and Earth was celebrated: in the entire history of China, only five sovereigns were sure enough of their virtue to dare celebrate that rite.

In the harsh Shantung countryside I rediscovered for the first time the graves scattered in the fields, marked by a stele, an old tree, or a copse, that are such a feature of the Chinese landscape. Instead of our death-ghettoes, our corpse quarters, here the whole earth is a vast and welcoming cemetery: the dead nourish the earth that had nourished them, and their tombs, like a protecting presence, witness the work of their offspring from generation to generation. The new regime—both for technical and economic reasons (regrouping the fields, leveling the countless tumuli that prevented continuous plowing) and for political and ideological reasons (the fight against "superstition," the desire to break the old clan ties, woven around the tombs of common ancestors, that bridged the class differences between "poor farmers" and "rich farmers")—started long ago to expropriate the dead, and has generally succeeded, despite desperate peasant resistance. Shantung was about the only place that I could still find some remnants of this celebration of the mystical union between life and death, between man and earth, which once could be seen all over China.

It is also in Shantung that I saw the enormous amount of work being done to build up the roadbed so as to double the rail line—and this took me back seventeen years. In 1955 I had been struck with the sight, all over China, of such gigantic enterprises done entirely by hand, without the aid of any mechanical equipment. There had been something deeply moving in seeing a whole nation grapple thus with its destiny barehanded, and one sensed a life-force that could not fail to win. But here we were *seventeen years later*, and long files of coolies were still balancing baskets of dirt on their shoulders. In 1955 that work had been lightened by the hope of better days that were soon to follow; how much of that faith remains? How much of it *can* remain for these hard-pressed men, with no donkeys to pull their carts or plows, working themselves like beasts of burden, twenty years after being liberated by socialism?

The next day at dawn the traveler discovers an entirely different world. The austere world of northern China has been left far behind; he has crossed the Yangtze in the middle of the night, and now he wakes up in the mellow softness of the Chiangnan ("South of the River"). In this rich, water-saturated plain, the brilliant green of the rice fields is crisscrossed by canals on which sails pass slowly by. Northern China is the color of dust and earth; here is the freshness of the "land of fish and rice," China's Cockaigne. Dotted over the countryside are neat white farmhouses, freshly whitewashed, with black slate roofs. From Nanking to Hangchow, one finds a string of old towns built on trade and arts, commercial centers and places of leisure. The cultural and economic development of the region was already well advanced in the Six Dynasties period, but received its main impetus under the southern Sung, and since the twelfth century it is here more than anywhere else that the Chinese bourgeoisie directed trade and commerce, while cultivating aesthetic leisure as well. This world, where the art of living had been brought to an extraordinary degree of perfection, has disappeared, but its memory still lingers in the atmosphere of cities like Soochow and Hangchow. On the other hand, since the beginning of this century, Shanghai has been the economic and cultural heart of China, and it expresses the creative genius of its region in raucous modernism. What is striking is that after twenty years of Maoist leveling, each city has remained faithful to its old image: Soochow and Hangchow still keep some of their charm and elegance, and even practice their arts of living to some degree; but Shanghai keeps up the strenuous rhythm of a great commercial metropolis, and remains proud of the skyscrapers dating from its imperialist-colonial past.

Shanghai is a paradox: to the Maoist regime it is suspect, the city in China most marked by foreign influence and open to the outside world; but it also led the vanguard of the Cultural Revolution. In the "rightist" restoration that marked the early

1970s, it was the last "leftist" bastion, and it may well become again the base from which extremists try to recapture power in Peking.

Shanghai may have changed radically since 1949, but its atmosphere and populace still have something unique and different about them—quite potent, too, for someone used to the stiff formality that Peking has acquired since becoming Mao's capital. This is partly due to the size of the conurbation (ten million inhabitants!). In such a crowd, anonymity is possible, individuals have a chance for solitude, personal activities, a degree of privacy. In addition the revolutionary tradition of the city that was the vanguard of the political, social and cultural struggles of modern China is still alive. The two social elements which, mixed, can bring on explosions—an urban proletariat and an intellectual elite—are larger here than anywhere else. It is not surprising that the regime has tried—and still tries—to use Shanghai's revolutionary potential; this was where the first shot of the Cultural Revolution was fired—the famous article written by Yao Wen-yuan under Mao's direction, which the Great Leader, restricted in power at the time, could not get published in any newspaper in Peking and in the end had to have appear in the Shanghai paper *Wen-hui pao*. And, again, when Peking is back in its conservative rut and serves forth the latest Maoist slogans in such a way as to defuse their explosive power, Shanghai restores the dynamite in a new review, *Hsüeh-hsi yü p'i-p'an* (*Study and Criticism*), which is stiff competition for the traditional *Hung ch'i* (*Red Flag*) of Peking. Between Peking and Shanghai, acrimonious dialogue or mutual boycott can be felt today, in the propaganda papers and among the political personnel; they crystallize the contradictions and antagonisms that have torn Chinese leadership apart since the beginning of the Cultural Revolution and have prevented the emergence of a homogeneous leadership and stable power.[15]

15. The downfall of the "Gang of Four" (Madame Mao, Wang Hung-wen, Chang Ch'un-ch'iao, and Yao Wen-yuan) in late 1976 marked the end of Shanghai as a citadel of radical Maoism.

The revolutionary character of Shanghai is a two-edged sword in the hands of Maoist power, when this power tends to deny its own revolutionary vocation. At the beginning of the Cultural Revolution Mao recruited his first partisans here in 1965–66; but here he also made his bitterest enemies, when he crushed the proletarian strikes that could have given him his revolutionary vanguard and when he betrayed the hopes of those activist youth who had enthusiastically answered his first call.

As for now, in any case—a remnant of bourgeois individualism? a cynical lack of commitment on the part of people whose hopes were betrayed? or just typical defiance?—one is happy to see pairs of lovers everywhere, completely indifferent to their surroundings, and a striking lack of those proletarian uniforms (virtuous patches and right-thinking cloth caps) which are *de rigueur* in Peking, and by the general fact that Shanghai girls refuse to shroud their grace in dreary potato sacks as their sisters do in Peking.

Such manifestations of independence, not all that important but at least visible, combine with the quick lilting rhythm of the Shanghai dialect and the agile minds of the people to make Shanghai's atmosphere tonic and stimulating (in complete contrast to the Peking stiffness and slowness) and to give the city a specific and irreducible quality of which the inhabitants are very proud. The rest of the country views it with a mixture of fear and suspicion, and Shanghai brings nightmares to Peking bureaucrats. China looks at Shanghai rather the way provincial and puritan America looks at New York: as an urban monster that drains the intelligence, dynamism, and daring of the whole nation, a fascinating and disquieting Babylon in which the country cannot recognize itself.

Economically, Shanghai is a heavy burden on China's resources, with its ten million customers who must be fed every day. Twenty years ago, the regime decided to decongest this dangerous and restless concentration of humanity, mainly by deporting young people to the countryside and especially to outlying provinces such as Sinkiang. This movement, started in the late 1950s and gaining impetus at the end of the Cultural Revolution, resulted in a decrease of eight hundred thousand people in the municipality.

The First Congress of the Chinese Communist Party took place in Shanghai in July 1921. In retrospect, this has assumed an enormous historical significance, but it appears that at the time the participants did not imagine what prodigious development would follow their modest clandestine meeting: those who described the First Congress—Ch'en Kung-po, Pao Hui-seng, Chang Kuo-t'ao—seem to have only a hazy recollection of what happened, and apart from the political motives that everyone may have in rewriting history in his own way, it is puzzling to find that the witnesses do not agree on such simple basic facts as the number and the names of participants, the time and the place where they met; the best historians share this vagueness and uncertainty.[16]

The authorities have organized a museum with pedagogical aims at 76 (formerly 106) Hsing-yeh Street, which is presented as the site of the First Congress. It was the house where one of the delegates, Li Han-chün, lived in 1921; the Po-wen Girls' School, often mentioned in connection with the First Congress, is in the neighborhood but appears not to have been a meeting place, only to have housed some delegates. For practical reasons, the organizers of the museum seem to have chosen arbitrarily from among the various contradictory accounts of the event. On the ground floor, one is shown a room furnished austerely with a table and twelve chairs; on the table, there is a teapot and twelve cups; on the wall, a portrait of Mao as a young man, and

16. See Wang Chien-min *Chung-kuo kung-ch'an tang shih kao* (*Draft History of the Chinese Communist Party* [Taipei, 1965]) or Jacques Guillermaz, *A History of the Chinese Communist Party: I, 1921–1949* (London & New York, 1972).

the guide explains that the First Congress met here, with twelve participants, on July 1, 1921. Actually the date is far from certain; according to the memory of witnesses, the meeting took place upstairs; and twelve is certainly the wrong number. After a moment of silent meditation, the visitors go to the house next door, where one can find conference rooms and convent-style parlors. There, foreigners are offered cups of tea and a short talk on the First Congress, the quality of the discourse being in direct relation to their own level of information. For example, when questioned, the guide will admit rather easily that two foreigners took part in the Congress[17]—though this appears to be denied by the twelve chairs and the twelve cups, unless one supposes that the foreigners did not drink and sat on the floor, but since those fellows later "sank into Trotskyism," perhaps they do not warrant more attention. But, alas, the same appears to be true of about half the delegates: Ch'en Kung-po and Chou Fo-hai left the party some years later, joined the Kuomintang, and finally collaborated with the Japanese. Chang Kuo-t'ao, who was one of the most influential party leaders, defected after losing to Mao in the power struggle. Liu Jen-ching became a Trotskyist and later (during the war) joined the Kuomintang. Li Ta early ceased to play an active role in the party, though he was never a turncoat; after the Liberation, he became president of Wuhan University, but in 1966 he was violently attacked by Red Guards and died of the treatment received at their hands—after having appealed to Mao in vain. Li Han-chün left the party—or was excluded—early, and was executed in 1927 by Kuomintang soldiers; his martyrdom rehabilitated him. Ho Shu-heng, Ch'en T'an-ch'iu, Wang Chin-mei, and Teng En-ming all gave their lives for the party. When one has accounted for the traitors and martyrs—almost equal in number

17. These were Maring (Henrik Sneevliet), who died in 1942, shot by the Nazis in Amsterdam; and Nikolsky. Nikolsky was a representative of the Profintern, the Trade Unions International, but I heard him called "Niknosky" in Shanghai. Most historians mention Maring and *Voitinsky*, but it seems that in July 1921 Voitinsky was not in Shanghai.

—there remain only two famous living members: Mao Tse-tung and Tung Pi-wu.[18]

What the Congress did is usually passed over discreetly, since the main decision adopted by the delegates was in fact to confirm the authority of Ch'en Tu-hsiu, who was later expelled from the party and became the leader of the Trotskyist opposition.

I asked the curator of the museum, who was taking me around, what basic books he could recommend, in Chinese, on the history of the Chinese Communist Party. This question seemed to take him unawares.

"Well, er, that is to say, I mean, since the Cultural Revolution, nothing has been published on the subject."

"And before the Cultural Revolution?"

"Before that? Oh, yes, well, before that . . . in fact, there was nothing then either."

He was telling the truth.[19] *A directive of Lu Ting-yi in the 1960s explicitly forbade the writing of the history of the party.* This is a good example of Chinese pragmatism: rather than have to write and rewrite the history of the party, according to purges and successive crises (as the Russians do), better not write it at all.

Should I describe my visit to the famous diesel factory, where for some years now the welcoming committee for foreign visitors has performed a very convincing act? A worker describes with great gusto and verve his experiences during the Cultural Revolution. Since his tale has already appeared in twenty different reports, to write it down here once again would tire the reader; and in any case, I do not want to compete unfairly with K. S. Karol.

18. Tung Pi-wu died in 1975 and Mao in 1976.
19. Except for the short work (forbidden today) by Hu Ch'iao-mu, *Chung-kuo kung-ch'an-tang ti san shih nien* (*Thirty Years of the Chinese Communist Party* [Peking, 1951]).

As in Peking, the Lu Hsün Museum in Shanghai (where Lu Hsün spent the last ten years of his life) was still closed: official historiographers are rewriting his biography to make it conform to the last mutation in orthodox thought, and this is no mean task. As a melancholy compensation, I was allowed to visit the house where he died. The inscription at the entrance was calligraphed by Kuo Mo-jo. Now Mo-jo, a man of versatile abilities (poet, playwright, archaeologist, historian, philologist, politician), is a pillar of China's cultural establishment who has been showered with countless official titles and honors. But his ruthless opportunism and shameless sycophancy have earned him the universal contempt of all Chinese intellectuals. In the 1930s Lu Hsün described him as a "talented scoundrel." Why not have ordered the inscription from Chang Shih-chao and go the whole hog? Lu Hsün tirelessly denounced *him* with wit and with rage. His writing, Lu Hsün said, was the "acme of obscenity."[20]

Not only has the Maoist regime eliminated the closest disciples of this great writer and heaped honors on his foes but, to add insult to injury, it has now turned a writer who was ex-

20. Chang Shih-chao was such a reactionary that even the Kuomintang did not want to employ him, and after discrediting himself in the service of warlords (he was Minister of Education under the warlord Tuan Ch'i-jui and took that opportunity to kick Lu Hsün out of his job in that ministry), he was mercifully forgotten until the People's Republic, after the Cultural Revolution, decided to make this repulsive mummy (he was then ninety) a herald of "revolutionary culture." One of his essays written in classical language was published in a luxury edition, at a time when all living literature was gagged. When he died in 1973, the regime paid national homage to his memory. I asked the curator of Lu Hsün's house how in China today one could conciliate the homage paid to Lu Hsün and to someone like Chang Shih-chao. He answered that the latter, "despite the regrettable mistakes he made in the old days, completely rallied to Mao *after* the Liberation." It is the unchanging law of this kind of power: that it employs spineless opportunists while survivors of the revolution are eliminated one by one, since only the first will be unconditionally obedient. In the same manner, in the old days, despots gave preference to eunuchs over their ministers of state.

tremely touchy about his independence into a caricature of a
model pupil, studying with application the Thoughts of Mao
Tse-tung, whom in fact he neither met nor read. Lu Hsün's house
in Shanghai is a cold and empty shell with a few pieces of furniture: a table, a chair, a bed. One is shown a cabinet "that con-
tains Lu Hsün's books," but the cabinet is locked and the books
are invisible[21]; after visiting the house, one goes to the writer's
tomb, transferred to Hung-k'ou Park; it is crushed by a heavy
mausoleum, with an inscription calligraphed by Mao Tse-tung,
and in front of it stands a monstrous bronze effigy of the writer.
His brother Chou Tso-jen, a considerable writer in his own right,
commented on it in a letter written from Peking to a writer in
Hong Kong: "I have just seen a photograph of the statue they
put up in front of Lu Hsün's tomb in Shanghai: really, this is the
supreme mockery! How could this personage sitting as on a
throne be the effigy of someone who hated all solemn attitudes?
Ch'en Hsi-ying & Co.,[22] if they had wanted to mock him, could
not have dreamed of a better way to do it!"

In the famous Foochow Street, the secondhand bookshops
were still closed in 1972 and 1973. In Nanking Street, the To-yun
hsuan shop (which specialized in paintings and artistic reproductions) sold only propaganda posters and portraits of Chairman
Mao in the part of the store accessible to the public. However,
for foreigners, a back room was unlocked: there, one could see
paintings in the traditional style and reproductions of old paintings. These prophylactic measures to isolate the Chinese from
their own culture are applied throughout China. A better example still could be found in the Shanghai Museum in 1973: a won-

---

21. A year later the curator had found the key and he opened the
cabinet for me when I came for a second visit. One could find on the
shelves some Japanese works on Chinese calligraphy, some Japanese translations of Western works, and some Chinese books on the classical novel.

22. Ch'en Hsi-ying (Ch'en Yuan) was a writer with whom Lu Hsün
had violent polemics.

derful exhibition of ancient calligraphy had been organized, but the public was not allowed to view it. One had to be a foreigner or get a special permit, delivered on application forwarded by one's "unit": to go by the notes and commentaries written on the register, few connoisseurs managed to become authorized visitors.

Strolling in the streets of Shanghai. In T'uan-ch'eng, the old "Chinese city," the hovels are still miserable. The temple of the protecting deities of the city (Ch'eng-huang miao) has been half-razed, half-transformed into a small factory. But the streets around it still shelter a very busy market.

In the crushing heat of summer, Shanghai gives the impression of a human sea that has burst through the dams. Toward evening, the crowds fill the streets seeking fresh air, and the almost total absence of cars leaves the boulevards to them. Slow-moving masses drift to the banks of the Huang-p'u River, and at that blessed hour an antique grace fills the river with a swarm of red and brown sails, as the junks go down on the ebb tide to Wusong and the muddy immensity of the Yangtze.

Soochow and Hangchow

A famous saying links Soochow and Hangchow: "Above is Paradise, here below are Soochow and Hangchow." These sister cities, with the same traditions, the same natural, economic, and cultural backgrounds (the Chiang-nan, the "South of the River"), the same arts of living, and the same language (the gracious Wu dialect, used in south Kiangsu and north Chekiang), show opposite and complementary qualities: Soochow is an exquisite town in commonplace surroundings, Hangchow a commonplace town in exquisite surroundings.

During the last eight hundred years, the prosperous Chiang-nan has enjoyed a concentration of the best intellectual activity in China, as well as the best of its artistic and literary production. The capital was moved to Peking for good in the early fifteenth century, but even that did not dim the prestige of these southern cities, whose wealth and elegance remained unrivaled down to the mid-nineteenth century. Even now the Chiang-nan remains exceptionally prosperous, and this explains partly why the atmosphere is so relaxed and pleasant. During the Cultural Revolution, physical violence was uncommon in Soochow and Hangchow, and one feels that their courteous and urbane peoples were spared the psychological traumas that scarred so many other Chinese cities. Here, for instance, people are much less formal and fearsome in their dealings with foreigners, and notably less inhibited by "revolutionary" conformism in their daily life. Beauty is not automatically suspect: people dare to decorate parks and gardens with calligraphed poetry that is not Mao's; especially in Soochow, the girls, who since antiquity have had the reputation of being the most beautiful in China, seem to keep up the tradition, and show in their hair styles and clothing a touch of art. How refreshing it is after the virtuous ugliness of Peking fashion! Last but not least, the army is absent from the landscape. The traditional *dolce vita* of the Chiang-nan is still there, at least by comparison with other Chinese regions.

Soochow is a small city by Chinese standards (six hundred thousand inhabitants): one crosses it easily from north to south in an hour. Some industry (chemicals) were started here after the Liberation: mercifully, they have been put outside the city walls, beyond the southern suburbs, along the Imperial Canal (dug in the fifth century to link Peking and Hangchow, and still in full use); despite the silly boast of guides who say that factory chimneys have replaced towers and pagodas, they have not marred the old skyline.

Soochow is surrounded by moats: the Imperial Canal meets the moat at the northwestern corner of the walls and leaves it at the southeastern corner, heading toward Hangchow, thus ringing the city with a wonderful watery girdle, with junks, barges, and other boats. The city itself is crisscrossed by narrow canals, spanned by high-arching bridges; the backs of the houses front on the canals, with stone staircases leading to landing places. One sees washerwomen at work, and from time to time a boatman sculling a junk.

Soochow's paradox: the city, traditionally given over to pleasure and luxury, with no industries except artisan ones (embroidery, silkweaving, paper-, ink-, and brush-making) and not much commerce except the antiques and art trade—in other words, its past is "feudal" and bourgeois—seems least able to adapt itself to the new order and is relatively little influenced by the present regime, but it also happens to be the neatest, best-kept, cleanest, and well-cared for city I was allowed to see in China. The houses are freshly whitewashed and in good repair; there are few slums; the streets, shaded by plane trees and very clean, positively invite you to stroll around. The people are easy to meet and very pleasant (although in the suburbs the appearance of a Western visitor is an event and causes a crowd to gather at once—rather embarrassing).

The buildings themselves do not appear to have suffered during the Cultural Revolution. The activists probably lost heart when they saw how much work had to be done: to do a proper job, the whole town would have to be razed. Still, as everywhere else, only a few monuments can be visited. Also as everywhere else, there was in 1972 an exhibit of cultural objects "discovered during the Cultural Revolution," and again entrance to it was strictly limited and by appointment only. In the Temple of the Western Garden (Hsi-yuan ssu), the garden was open to the public but the temple was open to foreigners by appointment only: always this fear of the authorities that the Chinese people may be contaminated by any contact with their past. Tiger Hill (Hu-ch'iu) is again a popular spot for walks, and many people go there; personally, I am not very fond of its pseudo-antiques all jumbled together: Shen Fu's opinion seems perfectly valid after nearly two centuries: "I think the sites of Tiger Hill too contrived; everywhere, the hand of the architect has pushed Nature out. Even more recent works, such as the Temple to the Memory of Pai Chü-yi or the Bridge of the Pagoda's Shadows, are but elegant curiosities."[23]

I had wanted very much to go to T'ien-p'ing Hill, which must be one of the finest sites near Soochow: the tomb of the eminent statesman and scholar of the Sung dynasty Fan Chungyen (989–1052) was there, in the former Kao-yi Garden, and that charming fellow Shen Fu loved the place—he made several excursions there, related at length in his *Six Chapters of a Floating Life*—and this for me was reason enough to make the pilgrimage. Unfortunately, T'ien-p'ing is some distance from the town, and being a foreigner I could not go there alone; the local guides, for unexplained reasons (it could well have been laziness), showed a total resistance to the idea. "There is nothing to see there," they told me (fueling my burning desire to go, for I knew that by their standards the more smokestacks the more noteworthy the site), and added: "In any case, the tomb of Fan Chung-yen no longer exists." To allay my disappointment, they had the kindness to let me visit the Cold Mountain Monastery (Han-shan ssu), which usually was not open.[24] The monastery is near a canal a stone's throw from the Maple Bridge: near the spot where Chang Chi spent a melancholy night, more than a thousand years ago:

23. Shen Fu's opinion of the Garden of the Forest of the Lions remains so vivid that we may think this site (different in this from many famous gardens) has changed little in the last two centuries: "Some people say that the Forest of the Lions is the work of Ni Tsan, but for my part I see nothing very remarkable in it; one sees some very nice rocks and many old trees; but if one thinks of it as a composition, the whole looks rather like a heap of cinders covered with moss and tunneled like an anthill, and the breath which gives life to hills and forests is, alas, wholly lacking." Shen Fu, *Six récits au fil inconstant des jours* (Brussels, 1966), p. 181. (Lin Yutang translated this into English under the title *Six Chapters of a Floating Life*, in *T'ien Hsia Monthly*, Hong Kong, 1935; later it was reprinted in *The Wisdom of China*, a Modern Library volume [New York, 1942].)
24. So-called in memory of the monk-poet Han-shan (Cold Mountain), who lived there during the first half of the seventh century.

The moon sets, the crows croak in an icy sky.
At Maple Bridge fishermen's lamps watched over my restless sleep
When the bell from the Cold Mountain Monastery at the entrance
of Soochow
Woke me up at midnight in my boat.

Hangchow was terribly devastated in the nineteenth century when it was sacked by the T'ai-p'ing (1861). Few monuments survived that destruction; many that did have disappeared now, victims of the Maoist regime and the iconoclasm of the Red Guards. The tenth-century Buddhist sculptures in the three caves of Yen-hsia san-tung ("the most beautiful to be seen in Hangchow," according to the Nagel Guide) were destroyed by hammers during the Cultural Revolution. The Temple of the Great Buddha is only a memory; the Temple of Yüeh Fei, a heroic general (1103–1141) who was executed by the felonious minister Ch'in Kui, was closed in 1972, and I could not find out what had happened to its famous statues.[25] The Fang-sheng Monastery (Monastery where Living Beings Are Given Their Liberty; its real name was Ch'ing-lien ssu) has been razed; in place of the old convent buildings, full of poetic charm, which I had seen fifteen years earlier, they have built, in the style of a modernistic public convenience, a gallery for photographs and propaganda posters. The monuments that still stand (Huang lung tung, or Yellow Dragon Spring, a Taoist temple; Hu p'ao, a ninth-century Buddhist monastery but entirely rebuilt in modern times, and others) have by and large lost their sculpture. Some of the destruction seems to have been ordained by the most random obscurantism: the tomb of Su Hsiao-hsiao (Dainty Su), the fifth-century courtesan, which for fifteen hundred years was the site of a poetic and sentimental pilgrimage, so famous that

25. I have since learned that the temple was entirely ransacked during the Cultural Revolution, after which someone wrote on the wall: "Was it Ch'in Kui who did this?" I am grateful to Professor Ivan London for this information, which he learned from a former Red Guard.

it had become a stop in visits to the Western Lake, has disappeared completely and no trace of it is left. Perhaps the ghost of that witty and beautiful woman troubled the sleep of some "revolutionaries." Let us hope, for Madame Mao's sake, that her followers will not one day peruse her life with the same touchy puritanism: they would certainly find enough lovers to damn her ten times over, but—different in this from Dainty Su—how many poets would plead for her?[26]

The Ling-yin Temple in Hangchow was the cause of a ferocious debate between moderates and radicals during the Cultural Revolution, the latter wanting to destroy it because it

---

26. Except of course if you consider Kuo Mo-jo a poet. One remembers the "poem" he dedicated to Chiang Ch'ing (Madame Mao) during the Cultural Revolution:

> . . . With all our heart and with all our minds, we shall act following the directives of Chairman Mao.
> Devoting our whole life to the service of workers, peasants and soldiers, changing the subjective world and the objective world.
> Down with American imperialism! Down with Soviet revisionism! Down with all reactionaries! . . .
> Dear comrade Chiang Ch'ing, you are a good example we want to follow.
> You have mastered the living study and the living application of the invincible Thought of Mao Tse-tung;
> Fearless, you advance in the vanguard on the front of letters and of art. . . .
> The luminous Thoughts of Mao Tse-tung will always be our spiritual nourishment. . . .
> O Chairman Mao, you are the red, supremely red Red Sun which shines in our hearts,
> We wish you a long life, a long life, a life without end!

1976 Post-Scriptum: In fact, the old rat (he is now eighty-five) was still agile enough to jump off Chiang Ch'ing's ship when it began to sink. Kuo, who had been the first to praise her when her star was rising, wrote another poem just after her downfall, to denounce her and to glorify his new master, Hua Kuo-feng:

> Our hearts are jumping with enthusiasm at the crushing of the "Gang of Four,"
> At the destruction of this white-skeleton witch who thought she was Empress Wu Tse-t'ien.
> Those who attempted to assassinate the Red Sun deserve ten thousand deaths!
> Our new leader is a hero without equal!
> How magnificent his achievements!
> Let us all support Chairman Hua!

had a religious significance, the former wanting to keep it for historical reasons. The problem was submitted to the Hangchow municipality: they did not dare decide the case and thought it wiser to refer it to the highest echelon, the State Council. In the end, Chou En-lai himself gave the order to preserve the temple, as well as the rock sculptures on the Fei-lai Cliff opposite. Its responsibility thus discharged, to prevent vandal incursions, the municipality built a wall at the entrance to the gorge that climbs toward Ling-yin. The community of monks who lived there was scattered, the monks reduced to a lay state and sent to work in the fields. Recently, however, some old monks, invalid and useless, have been allowed to come back to die in the shadow of their old monastery. They live in a small outbuilding on the hillside behind the temple.

During the most ferocious phase of the Cultural Revolution, some extremists even suggested tearing down the Tower of the Six Harmonies (Liu-ho t'a), which has been standing guard on the bank of the Ch'ien-t'ang for a thousand years: it was accused of being a legacy from the "feudal" past. Fortunately it is such a sturdy building that an army of "specialists" would have been necessary to demolish it, and it is dear to the hearts of Hangchow citizens—for them, it is the symbol of the city. In the end, the project was abandoned.

Hangchow was once a center of intense intellectual and artistic activity, but its cultural life was brought to a total stop by the Cultural Revolution, and has not really gotten going again. Its Fine Arts Institute, one of the most famous in China, had to leave town and settle "for good" with all its teachers and students in a small city (Fen-shui) deep in Chekiang province, to insure closer contacts between the artists and the toiling masses. I do not know if the work of its painters and calligraphers has been improved by that migration, and we cannot gauge to what extent the cultural life of inaccessible Fen-shui has been stimulated by their arrival. Meanwhile, one thing is certain: the flight of the institute impoverished cultural life in Hangchow and, thus, the whole country. The name of the institute is still there on its old buildings, which now stand empty. Given the way things go in China, and the lessons from the past (the current revolution in education is not a new experiment: all the reforms brought about by the Cultural Revolution were tried first in 1958–59 during the Great Leap Forward and were rescinded two or three years later, when experience had shown them to be unrealistic), I am sure that one day the Fine Arts Institute will discreetly slink back to its old haunts and start up again in Hangchow (if it is not happening as I write). But meanwhile, what a waste of time, what a waste of human and material resources—all because of a utopian whim of the Great Teacher!

I would have liked to see P'an T'ien-shou again; alas, I was told that the great painter had died in 1970 (he was eighty-one). During the Cultural Revolution, he had been attacked by Chiang Ch'ing, who said that his eagles (which he painted in the deadpan and sarcastic style of Pa-ta shan-jen) had a defeatist expression.

A visit to the Hsi-ling yin-she (Hsi-ling Society for Seal-Carving) is disappointing. Some of the most remarkable modern seal engravers used to work here, but nothing remains except a pavilion where idlers come to drink tea, play chess, and gaze at the soft horizons of the Western Lake. The setting is charming, but no trace can be found of the great artists who are linked with Hsi-ling.

In the center of the city, a large studio for the mounting of paintings and calligraphy is very active, and in its windows one can see a choice sampling of the work of local calligraphers— there is always a crowd of onlookers and connoisseurs discussing their respective merits. One must live for a while in the bleak cultural desert called Peking to enjoy these scenes to the full.

I had come to Hangchow essentially in the hope of visiting the museum dedicated to the memory of Huang Pin-hung (1864–1955): I am quite sure that world opinion will end by recognizing him as one of the greatest painters of this century. Alas, the museum (set in the Ch'i-hsia ling residence, where the artist spent the last years of his life) was closed by the Cultural Revolution and has not reopened since. Still, most of the works it sheltered have been put in safekeeping in the Chekiang Provincial Museum. Of course, that museum has also been closed for seven years—the main effect of the Cultural Revolution has been to dry up and seal all the springs of culture, in all fields—but my local guide, seeing how disappointed I was, managed to persuade a young curator to let me have a look at a dozen of Huang Pin-hung's paintings. For some mysterious reason, this could not be done in the museum itself, and I was not allowed to go near it; an appointment was made to meet in an arts shop in the center of town. I went there at the appointed hour and was led to a small room at the back. The young curator was waiting for me, with the twelve promised masterpieces rolled up in a bundle of brown paper. We spent two or three hours unrolling and looking at them; silently, some employees and shop attendants slipped into the little room to take part in the feast. One by one Huang Pin-hung's landscapes, triumphant "abstractions following nature," offered up their savage joy; their splendor abolished the dingy walls, even the compulsory and trivial Maoist chromos. As if conscious of taking part in some clandestine ritual, our small gathering was silent. At most, someone would whisper a technical remark, a connoisseur's note about the date or some detail. Afterward the group scattered as discreetly as it had gathered, and the curator retied the paintings into their brown-paper bundle. I thanked him and the guide for all the trouble they had gone to for me, but I wanted to thank them for much more: I wanted to thank them for being, simply, what they were. As always, in China, individual thoughtfulness and subtlety victoriously counterbalance the stupidity and obscurantism of the system.

In the Hangchow region grows one of the finest varieties of green tea, the Lung-ching, or Dragon's Well variety (named for the place of its origin, some ten miles from the site). A visit to a Tea Production Brigade is the indispensable complement of a visit to Hangchow, but it is a very pleasant one, for these Production Brigades[27] are in fact traditional clan villages, prosperous and picturesque, well situated on the hillsides or in the valleys.

The one I visited specialized in growing tea but also in welcoming foreign researchers. It has already been described so intensively and extensively by so many sociologists, journalists, economists, writers, politicians, and other roving polygraphs that it would not be easy to find a patch without their footprints. But since it is from this particular place that the newspaper image of rural China is largely built up for foreign consumption, it may be interesting to stop here for a moment. The average monthly family income here is 133 to 66 ¥, while in the rest of the country the monthly peasant-family income is about 30 ¥ (which gives an individual income of 15 to 20 ¥), and in poor provinces, it must fall well below that. (Workers' families earn about 100 ¥ monthly, which gives an individual monthly income of 40 to 50 ¥.) For instance, in 1972 I read in the *People's Daily*, in an article about health cooperatives, that in a Shensi cooperative the *yearly* contribution of 2 ¥ a person could not be completely paid because of the members' economic situation—which gives a telling indication of the level of poverty in the less favored areas.

In this charming village, the class struggle does not seem to have been very harsh: during the land reform, out of two hundred and fifty households only three were classified as "landowners" and five put in the "wealthy-peasant" category. During the Cultural Revolution, the village bowed to the wind and re-

27. The terms Production Brigade and People's Commune date back to the Great Leap Forward era of 1958–60. Since the party is infallible, even the names and slogans attached to its worst mistakes are never taken out of circulation: they are simply emptied of their contents and given another meaning. In this way, "Brigade" has become practically synonymous with "village," while "Commune" is an administrative unit, a kind of subdistrict covering several villages.

named its small leadership team "revolutionary committee" without changing its membership much. As in other villages, the Cultural Revolution was apparently a family affair, with no outside intervention. Its activities were limited—there were meetings "to denounce the agricultural policy of Liu Shao-ch'i" and so forth (the same policy that is now actively fostered under another name![28]).

When I asked how many young intellectuals sent down to the countryside lived in this village, I was told that there were only three. On our way back to Hangchow, my guide explained, without any prompting, that the authorities would never make

28. Since the fall of Ch'en Po-ta in August–September 1970 and of Lin Piao in September 1971, the partisans of "Liu Shao-ch'i's agricultural policy" have had a free hand in making their ideas prevail. That policy, which had been "exposed" in numerous articles in the *People's Daily*, is comprised principally of the following points: (1) to denounce "the apparently-extreme-leftist-but-in-fact-rightist" error that gave "primacy to politics" over the "concrete demands of production"; (2) to denounce all the principles underlying the Maoist ideology of the Great Leap Forward—warning against local improvisation and against decentralized and unplanned industrial initiatives started spontaneously by villages (because this kind of enterprise disperses energy and wastes materials, labor, and equipment, and priority given to agricultural production over industrial or paraindustrial activities (mining and so on) at the village level; (3) to re-establish material incentives, keeping and protecting individually owned plots, allowing and encouraging the private raising of fowls, pigs, and so forth, remuneration on the basis not of political merit but of work done.

All this did not occur without some verbal somersaults. Liu Shao-ch'i's "material stimulants" are still officially banned, but they must be distinguished from "reasonable incentives," which should be encouraged. The suppression of those incentives is now considered as a sabotage due to Lin Piao, who tried to disorganize the socialist mode of production. Any attempt to replace material incentives by pure political motivation, and to take shortcuts in the evolution from socialism to communism, is condemned as the expression of an "apparently-extreme-leftist-but-in-fact-rightist" error, the same error that is at the root of all Lin Piao's crimes.

Without jargon and cleansed of its rhetoric, the new agricultural policy is a very faithful expression of the charter of agricultural economy as formulated by "revisionists" in 1961–62.

1976 Post Scriptum: These trends are even more pronounced now that, with Mao dead, Maoism mummified, and its last exponents purged, the old "revisionist" policies inherited from Liu Shao-ch'i can at last be developed without hindrance.

the mistake of sending a bunch of urban youths to such a prosperous place: the Tea Production Brigade, which was large and well paid, would be most reluctant to welcome a major group of newcomers who could only lower its living standards.

3 | A Short Hagiographic Interlude

The Maoist authorities in China have had some disappointments with the individuals they gave as examples to emulate. One remembers Shih Ch'uan-hsiang, the model sewerman, who was later exposed as a disciple of Liu Shao-ch'i and was pulled down from his pedestal. They have learned the hard way what the church has known for a long time: before canonizing someone, wait until he is dead—and sometimes, to be quite sure, choose someone who never existed.

The most recent of these Maoist saints who are periodically proposed for the veneration of the masses is called Ch'en Tai-shan, and he died (so it is said) in December 1971, still quite young. The *People's Daily* recently published his photograph and related his life.

After the military saints of the Lin Piao era—Ou-yang Hai and others—come now the civilian saints. In 1968 Ch'en Tai-shan finished his middle school in Ch'angch'un at the far-from-early age of twenty-one and was sent to work in a factory, apprenticed in a car shop. He accepted his posting with enthusiasm and quickly became a model worker. As in all golden legends, or revolutionary operas, at the moment when the action seems in danger of falling into the mush, the Evil One arrives—with temptations—to rekindle interest. In Ch'en Tai-shan's factory, there are shady fellows bent on corrupting the young workers, and in particular they do their best to bring to ruin a promising young militant. Their conversations are suspect: they talk about *gastronomy* and *fashions!* Their insidious corrupt purposes are expressed in hundreds of little ways: to those who like to smoke, they offer luxury cigarettes from a pack of "Peonies" ("Mu-tan"),[1] to those who have a sweet tooth they offer chocolate, and they lend "dubious books."[2] These maneuvers go on until the day when Ch'en lays open their evil ways in a striking wall inscription entitled "What Is Concealed by Candy and Cigarettes." The young party stalwart is saved by this initiative just as he is about to sink into the mire, and he is brought back to the path of virtue in the nick of time.

Ch'en does thousands of other virtuous acts—so many that it would be tiring to report them here. One detail must suffice: he spends his pocket money buying Mao's complete works and reads them *all*, all four volumes (manifest sign of heroism, that). But his heroism should come as no surprise, for he has good antecedents: his father, a rickshaw "boy," always beaten up by capitalists, was covered with welts and scars; his mother, who had worked in a factory since the age of fourteen, had lost an eye in a work accident. And so forth.

His health undermined by a mysterious disease and a never-ending fever (phtisis?), Ch'en does not take the prescribed medical leave of absence; when a fire starts in the factory he does wonders and is terribly burned. (I'll skip the details: truly, vice and sadism are the two resources of hagiography, all over the world.) He lies in agony for forty days suffering horribly, given strength only by his desire to get back to the production line. Finally he dies, uttering edifying last words. Everyone weeps. Among his belongings is found a diary, full of lofty thoughts: "A match, even if it later goes out, if it has lighted others can start a fire ten times, a hundred times, a thousand times, millions of times bigger than itself. I want to be the match that lights the fire of socialism." After the man-as-small-cog-in-the-machine (Lei Feng), here we have the man-as-match. We must admire

1. And people will say there's no advertising in the Chinese press!
2. Unfortunately, no titles are given.

the literal though somewhat macabre imagination of the Peking hagiographers who make their man-match end his career as a human torch, for the edification of the faithful.

In his remarkable essay on Chinese literature for children, J. P. Diény has noted very perceptively, "China treats children as adults and adults as children."[3]

3. *Le Monde est à vous* (Paris, 1971), p. 8.

4 | A Short Philosophical Interlude

In the desert of Chinese bookshops in 1972,[1] the few new books drew attention at once and promptly became best sellers. Among those, I'd like to say a word about the *Vade-mecum of the Pig Breeder* (*Tsen-mo-yang yang chu*) and *A Short History of European Philosophy* (*Ou-chou che-hsüeh shih chien-lüeh*). The second of these works was mentioned in *Le Monde* by a correspondent who, protected by his blessed ignorance of Chinese, saw in the very fact that such a book could be published on that subject irrefutable proof of the rebirth of intellectual activity in the People's Republic of China. And it is true that the book can give us a telling illustration of Chinese intellectual life after the Cultural Revolution; for this reason we should look at it closely.

The book, written in partnership by three authors, covers Western philosophy from Heraclitus to Sartre. Marx is not included in this very broad syllabus; his philosophy, being "an unprecedented revolution in the history of thought," can be dealt with only in specific and separate studies. In any case, in this short treatise he would find himself in bad company. In a foreword, the authors explain the reason for their enterprise: "When reading Marxist-Leninist books, and especially in the study of the classics of Marxism, we constantly encounter concepts that refer to the history of European philosophy," a problem that also crops up when one must "denounce idealism, apriorism, and the bourgeois theory of human nature as they were developed by

1. A year later I found the situation unchanged. But today (1976), since the fall of Madame Mao, a modest measure of liberalization is at long last taking place in this field.

crooks of the Liu Shao-ch'i type." Therefore, "to answer the concrete needs of the class struggle and of the struggle between the two lines within our Party, it is necessary to study systematically some history of philosophy, including the history of European philosophy."

Thus, we are dealing with a practical work, a fighting book. ("Philosophy exists only as a function of the class struggle," say the authors on line 1 of page 1.)

Before the Cultural Revolution it was quite usual to see this sort of profession of faith at the start of what turned out to be excellent studies in the human sciences; after opening his ideological umbrella, the author could deal with his subject without bothering about possible dogmatic interferences. But this is not the case here: the introduction of the class struggle into the history of European philosophy turns that history into a shooting gallery where no one is spared. Here are some examples:

Nietzsche pursued and developed the esoteric voluntarism of Schopenhauer. He announces fascism. He publicly defended enterprises of cruel oppression and aggression launched by the reactionary-bourgeois class. Nietzsche's philosophy reflects the period when the reactionary-bourgeois class, having developed to the point where it could shed its democratic trappings, openly adopted a policy of violent dictatorship: it developed in the last part of the nineteenth century, at the time when capitalism was changing into imperialism. . . . In short, the philosophy of Nietzsche is a philosophy of robbers, at the disposal of the reactionary-bourgeois class to oppose openly and shamelessly the people and democracy. In fact, this philosophy preaches a return to barbarism; it expresses the bestial nature of the bourgeois-reactionary class. And, moreover, Nietzsche was completely mad. In Nietzsche's philosophy, there is a perfect marriage of the abject and shameless thought of the reactionary-bourgeois class with the madness of the philosopher himself. . . .

Bergson is a French reactionary philosopher of the late nineteenth and early twentieth century. . . . He has illustrated clearly the particular way in which, in the imperialist era, the bourgeois-reactionary class opposes science. . . . Bergson's philosophy is the expression of a blind spasm of the reactionary-bourgeois class, which in the imperialist era is in its death-throes. In his late works, Bergson was still more openly a defender of fascism. He thinks that the invasion of another country is simply a "vital impulse," that it is the necessary expression of the life of societies, and that it is therefore a "natural" and "normal" phenomenon. Which shows very clearly that Bergson's philosophy is an imperialist and fascist theory. . . .

Existentialism is a reactionary and bourgeois philosophical school, very common now in the capitalist world. . . . During and after the Second World War, the French writers Marcel and Sartre spread existentialism through their literary works, and in this way existentialism became the fashion in France for some time. . . . Imperialism is capitalism rotting in its death-struggle. In the imperialist era, the monopolistic-bourgeois class, sensing itself condemned to death, for one thing struggles in its death-throes by starting expansionist adventures and by trying to anesthetize the people's revolutionary will to fight, and, for another, is prey to anxiety, pessimism, and despair, and feels itself to be without strength. Existentialism is an expression of the corrupt decadence and despairing pessimism of the monopolistic-bourgeois class in the imperialist period; it is the dead philosophy of capitalist imperialism, it is the philosophy that the monopolistic-bourgeois class uses to paralyze the revolutionary will of the people to fight. . . . The existentialists, even if some are apparently atheists, in fact link their philosophy to religion. . . . In concrete political problems, most existentialists have adopted openly reactionary positions. They defend the policy of the monopolistic-bourgeois class of the U.S.A., helping it to spread the reactionary thought of universalist ideal.

I shall not offer too many quotations, for their monotony may be tiring. Dare I confess that, in content as in style, this second book appears to me clearly inferior to the other best seller I mentioned, the *Vade-mecum of the Pig Breeder*? Though less ambitious in its aims, this last seems to be the work of a competent man, remarkably free from prejudice. Let us not cast the stone too quickly at the poor philosophers on duty: in the People's Republic of China, not everyone has the luck to be a swineherd.

5 | Bureaucrats

As the day is divided into ten periods, so men are apportioned into ten classes, in such a way that the inferiors serve the superiors, while the latter serve the gods. In that manner, the king gives orders to dukes, the dukes to high officers, high officers to gentlemen, gentlemen to lictors, lictors to intendants, intendants to majordomos, majordomos to servants, servants to footmen, footmen to grooms. There are also stableboys to look after the horses, and herdsmen to care for the cattle, so that all functions are filled.

—*Tso Chuan (7th year of Duke Chao)*[1]

In the sixth century B.C., at the time the *Tso Chuan* refers to, China's social hierarchy had only ten degrees. We have progressed since then: the Maoist bureaucracy today has thirty hierarchical classes, each with specific privileges and prerogatives.[2] Its scrupulous care, nay obsession, for protocol is a permanent cause of wonderment for Western diplomats in Peking, just as the lack of formality in the embassies of some new nations (where quite often a Third Secretary will call the Ambassador by

1. An ancient commentary, composed somewhere around the third century B.C., on the Confucian classic the *Spring and Autumn Annals,* a chronicle of events in the state of Lu from 722 to 481 B.C.

2. It is noteworthy that the Cultural Revolution brought no change in this thirty-class division. This has been confirmed to me several times by different civil servants to whom I put the question in 1972 and 1973, in Peking and in the provinces. The system, adopted in 1956, is described in *Yi-chiu-wu-liu nien chung-yang ts'ai-cheng fa-kuei hui-pien* (Peking, 1957), pp. 226–47. See also on this subject F. Teiwes, "Before and after the Cultural Revolution," a report to the Symposium on Contemporary China, Australian National University, Canberra, November 1973.

his Christian name) has the Chinese mandarins flabbergasted. In all their contacts with foreigners, the Maoist civil servants insist on being given the exact titles, functions, and positions of each person, so as to be able to gauge precisely the length of red carpet each should have: any uncertainty about this makes them uneasy to the point of anxiety. In fact, they only want to apply to others the precise and rigid classifications that rule their own official life and give it such splendid orderliness. Nothing, no futile detail is left to chance: the place of an official photograph in the newspaper, its size, the presence (or absence) of important persons in it, the order in which the names of leaders are given—all have meaning, all are organized more formally than any Byzantine ritual.

To avoid mixing sheep and goats is another obsession, and no sacrifice is too great to keep the classes, castes, and hierarchies strictly separate. For instance, in Peking's diplomatic ghetto, it would have been very easy to organize one big cafeteria for *everybody*, but not only are the Chinese kept apart from the foreigners (of course!) but for the Chinese there are two different cafeterias, one for the intellectual aristocracy of employees and interpreters, one for the lower classes (drivers, sweepers, and other domestics).

The original purpose of the so-called May seventh schools[3] was to allow bureaucrats to be periodically in touch with workers and peasants. In practice, nothing of the kind occurs: one cadre, when I asked him whether he lived with the farmers during the periods when he worked in the fields, was quite shocked by my question. One should know that since the May seventh schools have been institutionalized,[4] they have become bureaucratic

3. Thus named after a directive issued on 7 May 1966 by Chairman Mao (actually it was a letter addressed to Lin Piao, but since Lin's downfall, this historical context is conveniently forgotten), underlining the necessity for the cadres to participate in manual labor together with workers and peasants.

4. During the Cultural Revolution, the May seventh school had a punitive-corrective character: disgraced bureaucrats were sent there. Later on,

islands in their rural environments. Their inmates plant cabbages and feed pigs, granted, but they do it *with other bureaucrats*, on the school grounds. Do they get any chance to learn about the life of the peasants? Of course! Once or twice a week some farmer comes and gives them a talk, and tells them how Chairman Mao and the party have changed his existence out of all recognition.

In old China, the mandarins were called, in a very telling phrase, "Those-who-eat-meat." Various gastronomical privileges still distinguish officials of a certain level from mere mortals: for them (especially in the provinces) any pretext will do (the visit of a foreign delegation, a visiting ambassador, anything) to organize private galas, and the extravagance of these can be quite extraordinary. (For anyone who has enjoyed attending these intimate banquets, the vaunted *haute cuisine* of the state dinners so often given by Chou En-lai in the Great Hall of the People to honor Nixon, Farah Dibah, or the like is by comparison something like the army-canteen level.) But if a new phrase must be found to qualify modern mandarins, "Those-who-ride-in-cars" would probably be the most appropriate. In China, there are no cars but mandarinal cars: all mandarins travel in cars and only mandarins travel in cars. (Old people, people gravely ill and on their way to the hospital, if they are unlucky enough to be just ordinary people, must do with a wheelbarrow or cart pushed by parents or friendly neighbors.)

Since all cars are official cars, the simple fact of sitting in the back seat of a limousine is equivalent to a *laissez-passer*. If you have to do business in a government building and you come on foot, you are sure to be stopped by a sentry, or a doorkeeper, or an usher with whom you will have to discuss your visit at length before being allowed to pass through the first gate. If you come by car, on the other hand, the various watch-

---

however, a routine was set, and they became a kind of institution providing all bureaucrats in turn with regular opportunities to have short study sessions in the country.

dogs will swing the iron grille of the gate wide open as soon as they espy you from afar and you can zip through without even having to slow down. In professional bureaucratic life, not to use a car sometimes seems as indecent as dressing only in underwear. A young European diplomat in Peking, new in the job, a decent fellow if somewhat naïve, thought it fitting in this proletarian-revolutionary capital to replace his car by a bicycle— as much as possible anyway. One day he had an important meeting at the Foreign Affairs Ministry; the interpreter-dragoman of the embassy caught him just as he was getting on his bike. "But Cultural Attaché, Sir! What are you doing! You're not going to go to the Ministry on a bicycle, are you?" Our young friend had to admit sheepishly that such was his intention. The interpreter, on his own initiative, called for the embassy car, and under his stare our progressive attaché had to climb meekly in. Thanks to the intervention of a Chinese employee, a shocking outrage to the Peking bureaucratic order was thus avoided.

To ride in a car marks you as an official, but the model, color, and size will vary according to your importance. At the bottom levels, one finds Russian, Czech, and Chinese medium-size cars, cream-colored or gray; at the top, one has long black Hung-ch'i limousines, with tulle curtains that conceal the passengers from the crowds. Peking is thick with these capacious hearses; their blinded windows have an aura of august mystery, suggesting at the same time the Coach of the Holy Sacrament and the limousines that Arab sheiks shuttle their harems around in. One of the favorite pastimes of Peking people—they do not have many—is to crowd around the entrance of the Peking Hotel or near the Great Hall of the People on gala nights to see the long processions of official cars go past with drawn curtains. Those people, one feels, have no envy or bitterness—they have the experience of three thousand years of despotism—but only the normal curiosity of gapers who try to glimpse, however fleetingly, the faraway magical world where their mysterious rulers live.

The Cultural Revolution has hypocritically masked some of the most obvious forms of class divisions, without changing their substance. In trains, for instance, first, second, and third classes have disappeared *in name*, but you have now "sitting hard" (*ying tso*), "sleeping hard" (*ying wo*), and "sleeping soft" (*juan wo*), which are exactly the same classes as before and with the fares, as before, ranging from single to triple prices. External insignia have nearly completely disappeared in the army; they have been replaced by a loose jacket with four pockets for officers, two pockets for privates. In this way, a colonel traveling first-class on the railway is now merely a four-pocket military man "sleeping soft"—with a two-pocket man respectfully carrying his suitcase. In cities one can still distinguish between four-pocket men in jeeps, four-pocket men in black limousines with curtains, and four-pocket men who have black limousines with curtains and a jeep in front.

In addition to the visible signs of their hierarchical dignity (to which they cling tenaciously: their absence is immediately interpreted as a sign of disgrace), the mandarins also have material advantages meticulously doled out according to their level. Salary differentials are quite steep in all sectors (a young university lecturer begins at 50 ¥ a month, a full professor gets 340 ¥; in a factory, the salary range may be from 35 to 210 ¥), but they are most marked for government officials, whose monthly salaries range from 20 ¥ at the bottom to 728 ¥ at the top. But for those who rise in the hierarchy, the salary is of course only a minor consideration compared to all the other advantages deriving from more influence and power: the possibility of going abroad, of sending one's children to university, of finding comfortable jobs for relatives, of getting goods in times of scarcity, and so on, in short, all that the colloquial language sums up in the phrase "going through the back door" (*tsou hou-men*). From time to time those practices are severely repressed—the Cultural Revolution was one of those times—but bureaucratic nature quickly prevails and the situation normalizes.

It must be said that examples come from on high: Chairman Mao's nepotism can be seen by all. What would Chiang Ch'ing be today, with her starlet demimondaine talents, if she had not become the wife of the Great Leader?[5] The case of Wang Hai-jung, Mao's niece, is equally remarkable: after getting her diploma at the Institute of Foreign Languages in 1965, this inexperienced young woman entered the Ministry of Foreign Affairs (which, curiously enough, shares with the Institute of Foreign Languages a kind of aristocratic prestige) and became Chief of Protocol almost at once; barely thirty, she was propelled into the position of Assistant Minister! What about Mao Yuan-hsin, the Chairman's nephew, who, not yet thirty, became vice-chairman of the Revolutionary Committee for Liaoning province in 1968, and shortly after was promoted Secretary of the Party Committee for that province.[6] One can go on: there is Hsiao Li (Li na), Chiang Ch'ing's daughter, who at an early age filled an important post on the staff of the *Liberation Army Daily;* and many others who owe their brilliant careers to family influence. But why continue? Everyone knows it, and the practice shocks no one: Mao was only following an ancient tradition in government practice that has become solid as a law of nature.

The meteoric rise of certain young people should not make one think that the regime trusts youth. On the contrary: promotion in principle goes by seniority. Given the number of echelons and the slowness of promotion, the regime is a gerontocracy: of the twenty men who ruled China in 1972, half were very old men—two nearly ninety, two past eighty, six past or nearing

5. She would be precisely what she has become now that the Great Leader is dead and unable to protect her anymore: a non-person.

6. Mao Yuan-hsin, born in the early 1940s, was given a home in Yenan by Mao Tse-tung and Chiang Ch'ing after the death of his father, Mao Tse-min, who was executed in 1943. Since Mao's eldest son, An-ying, died during the Korean War, and his second, An-ch'ing, is mentally ill and confined in an institution in Talien, Mao Yuan-hsin was the Chairman's nearest male heir.

1977 Post Scriptum: Mao Yuan-hsin fell in disgrace too, as soon as Big Uncle passed away. . . .

seventy; and in that small group of patriarchs three or four were senile or chronic invalids. Since the regime knows no retirement or age limit for its higher personnel, there is no honorable and decent choice between absolute power and total disgrace, which explains the keenness and energy with which decrepit, disabled, gouty old men cling to their seats on the Politburo.

Another cause of sclerosis is the fact that the top seven or eight bureaucratic echelons are the more or less exclusive preserve of those who joined the revolutionary movement some forty years ago. What is called in the political jargon "a cadre of '37" (*san-ch'i kan-pu*)—someone who joined the party after the beginning of the war in 1937—has little chance to climb higher than the sixth or seventh level; this hardly encourages the injection of new blood into the system. The rise of younger people like Yao Wen-yuan and Wang Hung-wen[7] remains exceptional and should not mask another significant truth: in 1973, the Tenth Party Congress sanctioned the almost total elimination of young leaders promoted during the Cultural Revolution, completing the cycle that had begun in 1968–69.

The cadres serve as transmission belts between the summit and the base. They have some privileges, of course, but before reproaching them for that, we should consider how unrewarding and dangerous their job is. They are perpetually torn between the leaders and the led. Directives from on high are deliberately ambiguous; in case of failure, the leaders thus have a fall-back position, while those who applied the policy are stranded and unprotected, and can be sacrificed to the rancor of the masses. It is unfair to criticize Maoist bureaucrats for their slowness and inertia: most often nonaction is their best chance of survival. How could they go forward? They must set their compasses on

7. A quite temporary rise: both were purged in 1976, shortly after the death of Mao, in a move that swept away all the last exponents of orthodox Maoism.

the Thought of Mao Tse-tung—a very mobile, shifting, and slippery pole.

Judge for yourself. One should avoid leftism, neither should one fall into rightism (sometimes, as in the case of Lin Piao, leftism is a rightist error), but between those two pitfalls, the cadre will seek in vain for a "middle way"—this being a feudal-Confucian notion. Since the right, the left, and the center are equally fraught with danger, the cadre may be tempted to shut his eyes and follow the successive and contradictory instructions of the Great Leader without a murmur. Another error! "To obey blindly" is a poisonous error invented by Liu Shao-ch'i in pursuit of his unmentionable project of capitalist restoration. In such a situation, the downcast and fearful cadre has his courage renewed by daring new watchwords: one must dare "to swim against the current"; "not be afraid of being in the minority"; "not be afraid of disgrace, even of exclusion from the party." However, before jumping in the water to swim against the current, the cadre cannot but recall that "the current of history is irresistible" and the Communist Party that embodies it is "grandiose and infallible." His resolve weakens; then he is reminded that "rebellion is legitimate." Ready to act now, he gets another cold shower: "in all circumstances, strict Party discipline should be maintained." Whom to believe? "Truth is quite often the position of the minority." This helps, but its value is reduced by another basic axiom: "the minority must always submit to the decisions of the majority." Should decisions be taken by a vote? Not at all, since "respect for majority voting is a bourgeois superstition."

Faced with all this, the cadre who lacks a philosophical turn of mind may feel giddy and be tempted to leave these thorny theoretical problems and tackle more concrete tasks. But these are also booby-trapped. If he wants to interest himself in culture and literature, how can he reconcile "the need to produce more interesting and living works" with "an active repudiation of the vulgar and bourgeois idea of *interesting works* propagated by Liu Shao-ch'i-type crooks"? If he is a soldier, he must "avoid giving priority to professional competence"—a rightist error inherited from Liu Shao-ch'i and P'eng Teh-huai—while guarding himself against the "metaphysical prejudice according to which politics are more important than professional competence," a poisonous theory coming from Lin Piao, in which is manifested the true nature of an apparently-leftist-deviation-which-is-in-fact-rightist-sabotage. Economics, agriculture, and industry are still more dangerously mined fields: one must keep the distinctions clear between phenomena that are identical except in the ideologues' minds. How can one see the difference between "material incentives," the base weapon used by Liu Shao-ch'i to restore capitalism, and "just rewards according to the work done," which is a legitimate and necessary encouragement to the creativity of the masses? This is not of purely academic interest: to tolerate the first is to restore the Liuist policy, to forbid the second could well be a Lin Piaoist sabotage.

The *People's Daily* gives many examples of casuistry to enlighten the minds of the poor confused cadres. Look at this one: in a Production Brigade, the man responsible for cattle obtained extremely good results; thanks to him, the herd increased. The local party branch decided not only to put his name on the honor board but also to give him a sum of money as a reward. Some members of the Brigade now question the decision: is this reward not a "material stimulant" linked to the "primacy of money" advocated by Liu Shao-ch'i? If the words still have their meaning, one would be tempted to say yes; but (in 1972 at least) the official answer of the *People's Daily* was NO; the decision of the local party branch had been quite correct, since far from being a Liu-type "material incentive," this reward was a correct application of the socialist principle of repartition "to each according to his work"; it was beneficial, and encouraged the "positive eagerness" of the workers. Another riddle: members of a Production Brigade took some hay cut on collective ground to feed their private cattle, and the local party secretary bawled them out. Who is right? Paradoxical answer given by the *People's Daily*: the Party secretary was wrong, because in his excessive zeal, he was discouraging a secondary activity (private cattle raising) of the peasants at a time when, for economic reasons, the state was fostering local initiative.

Now that Lin Piao has joined Liu Shao-ch'i in outer darkness, these two antinomian figures can be combined in a single, marvelously complete and Janus-face monster, which on one side corrupted the workers and peasants by giving them material advantages and on the other stifled any initiative by imposing on them a depressing egalitarianism; changed the army into a corps of professional ruffians on one hand, while on the other, and simultaneously, fostered battalions of philosophers in uniform, ideologues who couldn't shoot straight; encouraged frivolous literary activities while being responsible for the drying up of all artistic and literary talents; and so on. To fight such a polyvalent enemy, you need a lot of agility and, above all, ceaseless vigilance. The *People's Daily* may well give you the solution to a certain problem, but it also gives the *opposite* solution to the *same* problem at a *different* time. Maoist truth is essentially fluid and changing; to survive, one cannot miss the train, or the turn. Maoist propaganda may be one of the most monotonous, arid, and indigent creations in the world,[8] but for this reason it is followed by millions with burning interest: their careers, their very lives depend on the changing ideological line, which must be read between the lines and whose message may sometimes be found in the most unexpected and out-of-the-way places. A near-bankrupt businessman does not follow the financial news and the market figures less feverishly than a Chinese cadre peruses the guest list at state functions, burials, and Ping-Pong matches held the day before.

Political ups and downs are also complicated by patronage,

8. Though in this field the prize may well be won by the North Koreans.

one of the most appalling of the feudal legacies burdening Maoist political mores. Each influential person becomes the center of a clique; he has his henchmen, liegemen, and auxiliaries. As a consequence, a disgrace or purge is not a matter limited to isolated individuals: the elimination of a second-rank figure may be the prelude to or early pretext for a larger movement against his powerful protectors. (Remember, for example, how the fall of Wu Han and Teng T'o led to the fall of P'eng Chen and, ultimately, Liu Shao-ch'i.) The downfall of a leader, on the other hand, will invariably bring about that of all his near subordinates: one could fill an entire page simply with the names of the military officers who sank in the wake of Lin Piao.

It would be a mistake to believe that this bureaucratic phenomenon of hierarchies and privileges is a sickness of old age, the result of sclerosis brought about by twenty years of absolute power. Really to understand Maoism, one should not limit one's study to the post-Liberation period; one should go further back. If one studies the Yenan period, for instance, so often described by lyrical illiterates—I use the word here in its technical sense of "Sinologists unable to read Chinese"—as the fraternal and heroic age of the fighting revolution, one can see all the vices of the system, already ripe and well deployed. At the time, in fact, a number of militants were struck with despair when they discovered this, for they had joined Yenan hoping to bring a new world to life and had not expected to find there the despotic and bureaucratic vices of the rotten old world they had abandoned. Yenan was isolated and far away, and few of their shouts were heard, but some echoes reached the outside world, and the best example is shown in the Wang Shih-wei affair.

Wang Shih-wei had been a revolutionary for a long time. His first-hand experience of the Soviet Union and his knowledge of Marxist-Leninist classics (which he had translated) had made him something of an authority in the ideological field, and when he arrived in Yenan, he was given a teaching post in the school for party cadres. At the beginning of 1942, following a pattern that was repeated again in the "Hundred Flowers" of 1956 (truly, there is nothing new under the Maoist sun), the masses were asked to criticize the cadres, and at public meetings the arbitrary and bureaucratic methods were denounced. Yenan intellectuals, believing that the party really wanted to submit itself to this open discussion, started publishing various articles and essays in the Yenan paper, the *Liberation Daily*, hoping that their criticisms might help to cleanse of its vices the system to which they had dedicated their lives. Thus the famous novelist Ting Ling attacked the feudal prejudices that the party cadres still had against women, while the writers Lo Feng and Hsiao Chün and the poet Ai Ch'ing reminded intellectuals of their duty to be the critical conscience of society, and expressed in various ways their disenchantment with the bureaucratic Yenan regime. In this chorus, the voice of Wang Shih-wei was dominant, for his theoretical training enabled him better to diagnose the nature of the disease, and his experience as a revolutionary and a Marxist theorist commanded general esteem. In a series of short articles published in March 1942 under the title "Wild Lilies" ("Yeh pai-ho hua"), he pilloried the emergent ruling class that so desperately followed the model of the old society—arrogant, unmerciful, intolerant of criticism, hungry for privileges—and revealed the abyss that separated ruling and ruled. He ended his last article with these words:

I have heard that a comrade wrote an article on "Egalitarianism and the System of Hierarchical Classes," and that subsequently his "superiors" criticized and attacked him in such a way that he has become half mad. I hope it is only a groundless rumor . . . but it is not impossible. For my part, though I can't say I have as strong nerves as some others do, I think my health is good enough to prevent me from going mad, and therefore I follow that comrade in speaking after him about "egalitarianism and the system of hierarchical classes."

Communism is not synonymous with egalitarianism (in any case we are not now pursuing a Communist revolution): I do not need to write a dissertation on that. And in any case I can affirm it absolutely: there is not one cook here who has the ambition to live on the same footing as his superiors. But the question of hierarchical classes is not so simple. Some deny the existence of hierarchies in Yenan; but their denials are contradicted by reality, because these classes in fact exist. Others say, true, we have a hierarchical system, but it is justified. This second attitude must be looked at more carefully. Those who think that hierarchical classes are justified usually give three kinds of arguments: (1) According to the principle "from each according to his capacities, to each according to his merits," it is normal that those who are burdened with heavier responsibilities should have more favorable treatment. (2) Within the framework of the "three-thirds" system, the government is going to set up a salary system soon, and inevitably those salaries will not be equal. (3) The Soviet Union also has a system of hierarchical classes.

There is a lot to be said about these arguments. On the first: we are right now in the middle of the harsh and difficult process of revolution; everyone is physically exhausted and worn out with suffering, and many of us have had our health permanently impaired; under these circumstances it seems premature to speak about "advantages" and "pleasures." On the contrary, those who shoulder the heaviest responsibilities should especially vow to share the lot of their subordinates (a national virtue that should be fostered anew!) so as to win their true affection and create an unshakable solidarity.... About the second argument: a salary system should keep differentials small. Some favored treatment may be given to people who are not from the Party, but Party members should continue to maintain their great tradition of austere struggle, precisely in order to incite many more people to join us and help us in our enterprise. About the third point: may my bluntness be forgiven, but I would simply ask those "ideological guides," who were all too quick to impose their authority, to keep quiet.[9]

As for me, without being a partisan of egalitarianism, I do not see the need for instituting three classes for clothing and five levels for food; on those points (I enjoy a cadre level for cloth-

9. Wang Shih-wei had been to the Soviet Union and knew only too well what the Russian example was worth.

ing, and I am not compelled to eat canteen food: in my case, it cannot be said that "it's a question of sour grapes"), the directing principle should be to adopt the solutions dictated by need and common sense. However, look what happens: sick comrades do not have a chance to get broth, and young students get only two bowls of thin gruel a day (and when asked if they have enough, those who are Party members must pretend that they have eaten their fill, to give a good example to the others!), while on the other hand we see VIPS in flourishing health and enjoying completely unjustified privileges; such a situation leads subordinates to think that their superiors belong to a different breed of humanity; not only is it difficult to feel affection for them but also, when they think about it, they become uneasy. . . .

In the lines above, I have talked a lot about "affection" and "human warmth"—perhaps as a consequence of my "petty-bourgeois sentimentality"? One will see how I am criticized.[10]

And one saw, indeed. What followed is all too well known.[11] Some weeks later, in answer to this manifestation of independent criticism, Mao Tse-tung struck all thinking heads the sledge-

---

10. Wang Shih-wei, "Yeh pai-ho hua IV" ("Wild Lilies," Part IV), in *Chieh-fang jih-pao* (*Liberation Daily*), Yenan, 22 March 1942.

11. But after all, is it so well known? The whole affair had an enormous effect all over China, but in the West the filters through which information reaches the public at large intercepted it carefully. (One example: I recently had the opportunity to hear a talk given by the illustrious Professor Chesneaux, a most fashionable lecturer for Maoist socialites. He was speaking on the topic "Yenan, the Brotherly Society"(!). Not only did he make no mention of the Wang Shih-wei affair but when one listener ventured to raise the question, there was, for a brief moment, a painful silence. Professor Chesneaux—who was preparing a book on Yenan!—had never heard Wang Shih-wei's name, and thus conveniently chose to drop the whole matter.) Still, a good summary of the Wang Shih-wei affair is given in Merle Goldman, *Literary Dissent in Communist China* (Cambridge, Mass., 1967). See also: C. T. Hsia: *A History of Chinese Modern Fiction* (New Haven & London, 1961). On Wang's execution, see *Chung-kung yen-chiu* (*Research on Chinese Communism*), July 1972, p. 67. The ideological *parti-pris* of these last two sources does not invalidate their generally rigorous and sound historical documentation. Their accuracy was confirmed by Mao Tse-tung himself: in a speech dating from 1962, but made available to us only recently, Mao flatly acknowledged that Wang had been executed and tried hypocritically to wash his hands of this crime by arguing that (1) the security organs acted on their own initiative, and anyway (2) Wang was

hammer blow of his famous "Talks on Arts and Letters," which anesthetized for good intellectual and cultural life in the "liberated areas" before it extended its fatal influence over the rest of China. Dissident intellectuals were sternly purged, and Wang Shih-wei became a scapegoat. For one thing, his prestige as a revolutionary and a Marxist theoretician aggravated his case; for another, his influence in the party cadre school had been resented for some time by his colleague Ch'en Po-ta, who now saw an undreamed-of chance to get rid of his rival. Wang's friends and intimates were compelled to disown him and denounce his "crimes," and Wang himself had to appear several times in public-accusation meetings. But he behaved so courageously, answered calumnies with such calm and pertinence—the last time, supreme sacrilege, he even dared criticize Stalin directly—that the authorities thought best to try his case behind closed doors. He disappeared from view for two years; in 1944 some journalists coming from Chungking managed, after a lot of trouble, to be allowed to see him. They were introduced to a shy and silent man who told them that he was living perfectly happily. When one of them asked him what his present occupation was, he said modestly that he was making matchboxes.

In the spring of 1947, during a Kuomintang offensive, the Communists had to evacuate Yenan in haste. They could not take prisoners with them, but they could not leave such a witness behind either. Wang Shih-wei was shot.

a "secret agent working for the Kuomintang"! See Stuart Schram, ed., *Mao Tse-tung Unrehearsed—Talks and Letters 1956–1971* (London & New York, 1974), pp. 184–85.

6 | Cultural Life

If you look up the history of the First World War, in, for instance, the Encyclopaedia Britannica, *you will find that a respectable amount of the material is drawn from German sources. A British and a German historian would disagree deeply on many things, even on fundamentals, but there would still be that body of, as it were, neutral fact on which neither would seriously challenge the other. It is just this common basis of agreement, with its implication that human beings are all one species of animal, that totalitarianism destroys. Nazi theory indeed specifically denies that such a thing as "the truth" exists. There is, for instance, no such thing as "Science." There is only "German science," "Jewish science," etc.*

The implied objective of this line of thought is a nightmare world in which the Leader, or some ruling clique, controls not only the future but the past. If the Leader says of such and such an event, "It never happened"—well, it never happened. If he says that two and two are five—well, two and two are five. This prospect frightens me much more than bombs—and after our experiences of the last few years, that is not a frivolous statement.

—George Orwell

Basic Principles

Looking only at the surface of things, the evolution of cultural life in the People's Republic of China appears to show periods of severe discipline alternating with relatively "liberal" ones. Freeze and thaw, tension and détente, fat cows and lean cows follow each other in a seasonal rhythm. But every winter some aspect of culture disappears for good, some cultural legacy of the past is gone forever, and every spring there are fewer flowers. In a historical perspective, the cultural policy of Maoism appears remarkably constant: the basic principles were established more than thirty years ago, and the practice since then has not deviated from the orthodox theory set forth at the start by Mao Tse-tung. It would be a mistake to see in the iconoclasm of the Cultural Revolution a kind of accident in the history of the regime: this last aggression against culture was of much larger scope than the others, of course, but in its philosophy it was faithful to the Mao line. It would also be wrong to take the renewal of cultural activities since 1971 (mostly fake, as I shall explain) as a disavowal of previous policy.

The death warrant of Chinese intellectual life was given by Mao Tse-tung in Yenan, in 1942, when he delivered his famous "Talk on Arts and Letters." This clearly expressed resolution to destroy critical intelligence—put into practice at once with the physical elimination of Wang Shih-wei—was applied in ever-widening circles: from the "rectification movement" of 1951–52 to the Hu Feng purge of 1955 to the repression of the "Hundred Flowers" in 1957 to the gigantic purges of the Cultural Revolution. The war against the mind has become larger but has not changed in nature or direction. Between purges, various (practical, technological, even diplomatic) factors will require the reactivation of this or that cultural sector, but these truces are motivated by tactical imperatives and express no change in the regime's cultural policy.

This policy, steadily followed since the Yenan days, has resulted in the near-total extinction of Chinese intellectuals *as such*. There only survive specialized technicians in propaganda, science, and technology; others have been "recycled" in the fields and factories; an irreducible minority of them have committed suicide or been liquidated.

The position of intellectuals in China, which during these last thirty years has been eloquently described and defended by a long series of martyrs—Wang Shih-wei, Hu Feng, Wu Han, and Teng T'o, to name only the most eminent[1]—can best be summarized by this passage from the famous *February Outline*, a document developed under the direction of P'eng Chen in February 1966, in an effort to protect Wu Han against the growing menace of Maoist repression:

One must absolutely maintain the principle according to which the search for truth must begin with facts, and also the principle that all men are equal before the truth. People must be persuaded by rational arguments; one should not act like those academic tyrants who decide everything without debate and misuse their authority to crush their opponents. This ideal must be promoted: to stick resolutely to the truth, always be ready to correct one's mistakes.[2]

To which the Maoist orthodoxy answered in characteristic fashion:

1. The names and personalities of leading dissident intellectuals in the Soviet Union are well known in the West, or at least known well enough to make it hard for the commissars to spread calumnies about them without exposing themselves to indignation and contempt. But as far as China is concerned, the gaps in our information (carefully maintained by "quality" newspapers) leave the field open to those-in-charge-of-propaganda. In his last book, K. S. Karol insinuates coolly that Teng T'o was in fact a mere opportunist, ready to betray his friends to save his own skin: ". . . in 1965, when the writings of Wu Han were criticized, Teng T'o rushed to cast his stone. . . ." Needless to say, Karol does not bring one shred of proof to support this vile calumny. By kicking this man in chains, he adds stupidity to baseness, for he reveals an ignorance of the most elementary sources. In May 1966, the *People's Daily* violently attacked Teng T'o, *precisely because he had dared, even at that time, to defend Wu Han in public*! (See Yü Ch'ang-chiang, "K'an Teng T'o tsen-yang yen-hu Wu Han" [See How Teng T'o Protects Wu Han], in *Jen-min jih-pao* [*People's Daily*], 12 May 1966. One would think that in writing a history of the Cultural Revolution one would at least consult the *People's Daily* for that period, but perhaps this is too much to expect from a journalist.)

2. *Wen-hua ke-ming wu jen hsiao-tsu kuan-yü tang-ch'ien hsüeh-shu t'ao-lun ti hui-pao t'i-kang* (*Outline Report on the Present Academic Discussion Made by the Group of Five in Charge of the Cultural Revolution*), 7 February 1966; see *Hsin Kang yuan*, No. 18, 20 May 1967.

The authors of the *February Outline* have put forward the slogan "all men are equal before the truth." This is a bourgeois slogan. They absolutely deny the fact that truth has a class character; they use this slogan to protect the bourgeois class, to oppose themselves to the proletariat, to Marxism-Leninism and the Thought of Mao Tse-tung. In the struggle between proletariat and bourgeoisie, between Marxist truth and the lies of the bourgeois class and of all oppressive classes, if the east wind does not prevail over the west wind, the west wind will prevail over the east wind, and therefore no equality can exist between them.[3]

This philosophy is, of course, not unique to Maoism: it is inherent in all totalitarian systems of the twentieth century, Stalin's as well as Hitler's. The point is not that for Maoists the distinction is between "Marxist truth" and "bourgeois lie" while for Nazis it was between "German truth" and "Jewish lies" (actually, does not the bourgeoisie play in Maoist China the role assigned to the Jew in Hitler's Germany?); but that on both sides there is a common will to deny that there might be an objective truth, independent of the party's instructions and the orders of the leader, a truth in the light of which those instructions and orders might be submitted to critical examination. Intellectuals by definition having the function of critical examiners, it is easy to understand why the totalitarian state cannot tolerate their existence. For public-relations reasons it will still need a few academics—they can easily be recruited among intellectuals who give up (Kuo Mo-jo is a good specimen of the breed)—but the survival of intellectuals in the original sense of the word, that is, as uncompromising witnesses to truth, is no longer conceivable.[4]

3. "May 16 Circular": *Chungkuo kung-ch'an-tang chung-yang wei-yuan-hui t'ung-chih*, 16 May 1966, published a year later in *Jen-min jih-pao* (*People's Daily*), 17 May 1967.

4. A similar evolution seems to be taking shape in the West. In universities, the commissars of tomorrow question the legitimacy of disinterested research (the crime is to consider that an objective fact is more respectable than all ideologies); any study that cannot serve the dogmas of their propaganda is now condemned for being "irrelevant."

When truth is whatever has been provisionally decreed by the Propaganda Department of the Party's Central Committee, when intellectuals are simply (directly or indirectly) paid employees of the department, it is inevitable that any changes in China's cultural life as a whole are nothing but tactical ups-and-downs with no real significance. The value of an old monument, of a historical document, of a traditional or "revolutionary" play, of a literary or artistic work, even of a sports competition or a new surgical technique, is always and exclusively determined by how useful it will be as a piece of propaganda serving the (variable) "truth" of the moment. Sometimes, even, the regime will try to use them to meet contradictory needs: for example, toward the end of the Cultural Revolution, the destruction of old monuments, which had been organized on a very grand scale for domestic purposes of "revolutionary" pedagogy, had not yet been completed, when a campaign for archaeological diggings was begun and exhibitions were organized showing "historical treasures found during the Cultural Revolution," this to serve the imperatives of a new phase of foreign policy.

The Actual Situation

Reinforce the Party's leadership of the arts—this is the basic guarantee of flourishing socialist artistic creation.

—*People's Daily*, 16 July, 1972

The Cultural Revolution brought all cultural activity in China to a standstill that lasted for several years. Schools were closed, intellectuals were dismissed, pilloried, and deported to the countryside. All scientific, artistic, literary, and cultural periodicals ceased publication. All the books published prior to the Cultural Revolution were taken out of bookshops, which now sold only the works of Mao—wholesale and retail; in complete versions or anthologized; big and small; prose or verse; in Chinese or "Babelian," always and only Mao, in larger and larger quantities. All movies, plays, and operas from before the Cultural Revolution disappeared; all movie studios were closed, except the one studio belonging to the People's Liberation Army, which produced two documentaries in color, showing Mao reviewing the Red Guards in Peking, and the Ninth Party Congress. (These two remarkable *chefs d'oeuvres* have unfortunately vanished: Lin Piao was rather too much in view, not to mention other persons who have fallen out of favor.) A good number of writers, artists, and intellectuals committed suicide—Lao She, Fu Lei, Li Kuang-t'ien, Wu Han, and Chou Hsin-fang among them.[5] The others were silenced. Theaters, movies, radio, and television were taken over, every day all day for years, by Madame Mao's six Revolutionary Model operas. (The case is rather unique: a handful of models that eight hundred million people now know by heart—thanks to the ever-present loudspeakers—but that have not yet generated a single imitation. ...) Needless to say, museums were closed and their personnel sent to the fields. The ancient monuments, especially temples and monasteries, were looted; some were transformed into warehouses, workshops, or garbage dumps, and others were simply razed.

5. In China, suicide has always been essentially a political act—and is now more than ever the highest form of protest against arbitrary power. The suicide of Lao She, who was China's greatest, most universally respected living novelist, is for the Maoist regime a scathing denunciation. His name is never ever mentioned, so enormous does his final crime appear to be. On this burning question, Western Maoists have a rather original line of defense, which has three main points: (1) Lao She did not commit suicide: this is a Taiwan fabrication. (2) His suicide can easily be explained by his bourgeois mentality. (3) In any case, the episode is pointless, so why harp on it?

The news of Lao She's suicide has been solidly documented by many witnesses (Ma Ssu-ts'ung, Jelokhovtsev, Fokkema) and studies (Hu Chin-ch'üan). It has been confirmed to me personally by Han Suyin, whose testimony on such a matter could hardly be questioned. And it was implicitly confirmed by the greenish hue and abrupt silence of various bureaucrats in Peking when I inquired about the health of the great writer.

About the suicide of Wu Han, I am indebted for this important information (given in answer to a question at the end of a public lecture) to Professor Paul Lin, who in this field is an even more reliable source (if that is possible) than Han Suyin.

In the modern world, a great nation cannot go on indefinitely without intellectual activity, especially in science and technology. As we have seen several times before, Maoism is not devoid of suicidal impulses, but at the same time it does respond to basic survival needs. These needs have determined a move back to normal in education and scientific research and in all technical activities; it was a simple question of life and death, and it makes little sense to speak (as some have done) of a "cultural renaissance."

Since the beginning of the 1970s, for various practical reasons, one of the leading factions in the government has been trying to lead China in a daring policy of friendliness and "opening" to the West. To insure the success of, if not simply to lend credibility to this new policy, it was essential to make people forget about the excesses of the Cultural Revolution and to restore the traditional image of a pragmatic, reasonable, courteous, responsible, and deeply cultured China. It is from this angle that one should view China's staging of a "cultural renaissance" intended exclusively for the benefit of foreigners and Overseas Chinese (those last being the best unpaid and official ambassadors of China beyond its frontiers). In every major city of China where foreign visitors come regularly, *one* or *two* monuments have been admirably restored, and a permanent exhibit has been organized to show "archaeological objects found during the Cultural Revolution"—this to give the impression that the Cultural Revolution, far from destroying the Chinese cultural heritage, has enriched it! And let us not forget that many of these monuments—especially temples and monasteries—are open only to foreigners and Overseas Chinese, and forbidden to the common man; the "archaeological exhibits" can be seen only by appointment; and if a tourist perversely escapes from his guides and beyond the circuit of Potemkin monuments he sees only desolation and ruin where famous buildings used to stand.

The Chinese soil is an inexhaustible mine of archaeological treasures *whose sites are very well and precisely known.* In

Peking, for instance, only one Ming imperial tomb out of thirteen has been opened; the environs of Sian are full of unopened Han and T'ang imperial tombs; and in Ma-wang-tui, in the Ch'angsha suburbs, where the opening of a tomb of the early Han period has yielded a prodigious treasure, I was shown the tumuli, still untouched, of four or five other tombs of the same period. Thus, with a government like China's today, strongly centralized and able quickly to mobilize all the labor required, it is always technically possible to order the provinces to produce "archeological discoveries" and to get enough in six months to dazzle the world. The famous (and admirable) exhibition that traveled in Europe, the United States, and Canada was an act of political propaganda, whose aim was to deny and to obliterate the echoes of the Cultural Revolution's savage vandalism.

In the sphere of the arts, it is true that antique shops and art-reproduction workshops are open again (at least in Peking, Canton, Soochow, and Shanghai), but, again, only foreigners are admitted and the prices are set for fat tourist purses. At the To-yun hsüan, in Shanghai, for instance, which *simultaneously* sells cheap Maoist stuff to local customers and reproductions of ancient paintings and calligraphy, this second sector is carefully isolated upstairs, behind locked doors that open only for foreigners.

In publishing the situation is pathetic: a few classical titles —perhaps a dozen or fifteen out of tens of thousands in the whole of Chinese literature—have been symbolically republished, but few copies are printed and they are sold out a month after being issued. A few artistic and literary works of the traditional type have also been published[6]: printed usually in a few *hundred*

---

6. We should note here that special treatment has been given to a classic literary study by Chang Shih-chao. Chang was notorious in the 1920s for the brutal way he repressed student revolutionary agitation when he was Minister of Education in a warlord government. Characteristically, the Maoist regime chose this senile and reactionary swallow to announce its cultural spring. Chang died in 1973, and the People's Republic found it fitting to honor nationally the memory of this obscene symbol of feudal oppression. About Chang, see also above, p. 93.

copies, the bulk of the editions are intended for export (mainly to Hong Kong). In China itself, they can be found almost nowhere except in the bookshops you see in the lobbies of hotels reserved to foreigners. Sometimes a copy can be located in a Chinese bookshop, but then it is kept in a special glass case, locked of course, offered to the curious public somewhat like a two-headed calf pickled in formaldehyde and shown off in a glass bottle. We should note that the price for this kind of book (for a middle-class official it would be two or three months' salary) keeps the proletarian reader safe from its pernicious influence. If you *really* want a copy, you must ask the shop attendant; she goes to the back and discreetly searches, as if it were a pornographic work that could not be left lying around. Nine times out of ten, you are told it is sold out.

Bookshops have completely changed their interior layout: they are now set up like pharmacies, with a counter between the customers and the shelves. On those shelves, which only attendants can reach, only a few dozen titles are displayed, but since the shop must appear to be full with even that scant choice, books are put flat on the shelves, in lines, with the same title endlessly repeated, like sardine cans or tins of peas in a supermarket. The bulk of the stuff is naturally the works of Mao, then the Fathers of Marxist doctrine, and the complete works of Stalin, Kim Il Sung, and Enver Hoxha; children's comics and technical books are also well represented. For the rest, nearly all of Chinese literature—one of the most varied, wealthy, and ancient in the world—has been eliminated. When one thinks that it is impossible today to find, in the capital city of China, just a simple copy of such a basic and popular book as *Three Hundred T'ang Poems*, one is overcome by vertigo and rage. This rage becomes a holy fear when one visits the National Library (Peking Library), where one discovers in the Catalogue Room that *all traces of twentieth-century literary and historic works that do not conform to Maoist orthodoxy have simply vanished.*

It is easy to see that such an atmosphere is not very con-ductive to intellectual life, and in particular to literary produc-tion. Since the end of the Cultural Revolution, about two dozen new titles have been published, mostly collective efforts, short stories written by groups of "soldiers, peasants, and workers." The nature and tone of this production is well summarized in an article from a new Chinese literary monthly: in its first issue, it welcomed contributions from its readers and defined the kind of literature that alone is authorized:

Our publication welcomes all manuscripts which fulfill the following conditions:

A. All novels, essays, articles, works of art which present in a healthy way a revolutionary content. They must: (1) exalt with deep and warm proletarian feelings the great Chairman Mao; exalt the great, glorious and infallible Chinese Communist Party; exalt the great victory of the proletarian revolutionary line of Chairman Mao; (2) following the examples of the Revolu-tionary Model operas, strive with zeal to create peasant and worker heroes; (3) on the theme of the struggle between the two lines, reflect the people's revolutionary struggle, which has lasted for half a century under the leadership of our Party, and, especially, the unbroken revolutionary struggle fought under the aegis of the dictatorship of the proletariat; reflect the unan-imous struggle of the population of our province [Kwangtung, in this case] following the direction given by Chairman Mao, and the unfolding of that struggle in its victorious progression.

B. In artistic and literary theory: we welcome texts that have a mass, revolutionary, and militant character, advocate a simple language and clear lessons, have a lively, vigorous, and original style; we welcome short popularizing essays, with a strong and persuasive force in ideas and analysis on such themes as the study of literary and artistic theories in Marxism-Leninism, the living understanding of the artistic and literary Thought of Mao Tse-tung, the living understanding of the creative experience in the study of the Revolutionary Model operas; we welcome articles that, taking Marxism-Leninism as a guide, study the problems of socialist and artistic literary creation, deepen the denunciation of anti-Marxist points of view and of the revisionist black line in the artistic and literary field, points of view propagated by Liu Shao-ch'i-type swindlers.[7]

In short, as the humorists of *Tel Quel*[8] would say, "Power to the intelligence." Again, what a bitter derision to contrast that drivel with the following luminous and cutting text by Lu Hsün —Lu Hsün, whom everyone is supposed to study but whom nobody, apparently, ever bothers to read:

In Canton, I once quarreled with a "revolutionary" writer (today in Canton, they consider that there is no literature but revolutionary literature, and only phrases like "Forward! Forward! Forward! To death! To death! To death! Revolution! Revolution! Revolution!" are considered revolutionary), making him note that literature and revolution do not easily go together —although in literature there are such things as "literary revolutions." Anybody who wants to have to do with literature must have some free time; when one is fully engaged in revolution, how can one find the leisure to bother with literature? . . . When literature finally appears again, it is only a good long time after the success of a revolution. After the revolutionary victory, there is leisure again. *Then one finds writers who exalt revolution, celebrate the revolution, but this has nothing to do with revolutionary literature. Their celebration and exaltation of revolution is nothing but celebration of those who are in power: what relation can that have with revolution?* However, perhaps at that time writers with more sensitive antennae will be found and they once again will feel dissatisfied with the situation of their time; they will stand up and speak. Before the victory of revolution, revolutionaries approve of writers doing that, but from the moment the revolution succeeds, politicians start to use against writers all the old methods that former oppressors used before, and if the writers go on expressing their dissatisfaction, there is nothing to do but crush them or cut off their heads. Decapitation is still the ideal method, as it has been since the nineteenth

7. *Kwangtung wen-yi* (*Literature and Art of Kwangtung*), No. 1, 1973.

8. A fashionable but narrowly distributed periodical of the Parisian-Maoist intelligentsia.

century, more or less, such is the general trend of universal culture.[9]

Lu Hsün saw the writer as a permanent critic of power—of any power, including revolutionary power, toward which he nourished a healthy skepticism. It is therefore not surprising that Mao Tse-tung reacted vigorously against this conception of the writer's role, and he proclaimed categorically that there could be no place in his regime for the political and social criticism Lu Hsün practiced:

There are comrades without elementary notions of politics, and this brings them to entertain absurd ideas, such as the idea that . . . "we live in a time when critical journalism remains necessary, and we must adopt the Lu Hsün manner." Lu Hsün lived under a regime of obscurantist forces; lacking freedom of speech, he had to use pamphlet and satire to wage his struggle, and in this he was quite right. But for us, in the liberated zones where artists and writers enjoy all the democratic freedoms, the journalistic essay must not be patterned on Lu Hsün's.[10]

Lu Hsün's concept of the writer's role, and his pessimistic lucidity about the writer's chances of survival "after the victory of revolution," prefigure Orwell's apocalyptic vision; but Lu Hsün only experienced an archaic and primitive despotism (the Kuomintang's, which, even for its tortures, had to borrow its trappings from the dusty closets of the old empire), whereas Orwell viewed totalitarianism at first hand, which helped him push his analysis further:

9. Lu Hsün, "Wen-yi yü cheng-chih ti ch'i-t'u" ("The Divergent Ways of Literature and Politics"), in Lu Hsün ch'üan-chi (Peking, 1963), VII, 107–108.

10. Mao Tse-tung, "Tsai Yen-an wen-yi tso-t'an-hui shang ti chiang-hua" ("Intervention on Yenan Talks on Arts and Letters"), in Mao Tse-tung hsüan-chi (Peking, 1961), III, 871–73. Those who still allege that Mao Tse-tung is a warm admirer of Lu Hsün only reveal that they have read neither.

Almost certainly we are moving into an age of totalitarian dictatorships—an age in which freedom of thought will be at first a deadly sin and later on a meaningless abstraction. The autonomous individual is going to be stamped out of existence. But this means that literature, in the form in which we know it, must suffer at least a temporary death. The literature of liberalism is coming to an end and the literature of totalitarianism has not yet appeared and is barely imaginable. As for the writer, he is sitting on a melting iceberg; he is merely an anachronism, a hangover from the bourgeois age, as surely doomed as the hippopotamus. . . . [But] from now onwards the all-important fact for the creative writer is going to be that this is not a writer's world. That does not mean that he cannot help to bring the new society into being, but he can take no part in the process *as a writer*. For *as a writer* he is a liberal, and what is happening is the destruction of liberalism.[11]

The Chinese people remain thirsty for culture. The rapidity with which reprints of classical novels (*The Three Kingdoms, The Water Margin, The Journey to the West, The Dream of the Red Chamber*) disappeared from the bookshops almost the moment they came out bears witness to that thirst, made all the worse by five years of total drought. Nevertheless, the quality of the literary education is declining steadily. Differences among various age groups is startling: Chinese who are now over thirty (meaning those who finished secondary school and then university in the 1950s and early 1960s), though not comparable to prior generations educated under the old regime, still have access to a culture that has become an alien world for the youths who finished school right after the Cultural Revolution. School attendance has greatly and steadily improved since 1949; a larger and larger percentage of children *can* go to school; illiterates are far less numerous than formerly. But if so many more people have access to books, there are a thousand times fewer books. Parallel to the efforts to wipe out illiteracy, other efforts

11. "Inside the Whale," in *Collected Essays, Journalism, and Letters of George Orwell*, I (London 1968; New York, 1971), 525–26.

have been made, no less efficient, to blot out nearly all of the non-Maoist Chinese cultural world; and we come to the paradoxical point where young members of the new ruling elite have less culture than many illiterates or semiliterates under the old regime.[12] The latter were at least familiar with that (not negligible) part of Chinese history and literature made popular in operas and ballads and by traditional storytellers—types of spontaneous popular culture that the regime has eradicated. The most radical reform of writing (the substitution for Chinese characters of a phonetic transcription of them in Roman letters) —a decision of enormous importance for eight hundred million people—is simply decided without any public debate, on the sole basis of a Mao saying. Of course it will take some time before the decision can be effectively carried out; technical problems[13] and all the inertial forces of passive resistance will fend off, but not change, the inevitable conclusion. This reform of writing will allow the Maoist powers to do at one stroke and for good what a hundred Cultural Revolutions with all their autos-da-fé could not do: make all that has been thought, felt, and written in China from antiquity until the present day uncommunicable and unreadable for all future generations of Chinese—with the exception of the books that, having found grace in the eyes of the government, will be adapted as the authorities wish for transposition and publication in alphabetic writing.

The situation is just as dismaying for theater and music. Only one symphonic creation is performed and broadcast (with-

12. In this field, I have assembled a long, dismaying, mind-boggling collection of anecdotes. Visiting Lungmen with officials from the Ministry of Foreign Affairs, I heard one of them ask to which dynasty the Empress Wu Tse-t'ien belonged; elsewhere, another asserted coolly that Ch'ü Yuan was a T'ang poet, and so forth and so on. Each time it was a frisky technocrat with a bright future ahead of him.

13. Not insurmountable, as the Vietnamese precedent shows.

out surcease): the "Yellow River," a concerto for piano and orchestra, which is in fact only a remake of a work written during the war years. In 1972, while on a trip in the provinces, I heard the dean of our group compliment the pianist who had interpreted this mediocre Rachmaninoff pastiche for us (it is brought up-to-date by some bars from the "Internationale") and asked him what other pieces he had in his repertory. The pianist made this disarmingly sober reply: "None."

Chinese traditional opera has been totally eliminated; one must perhaps know its once central place in Chinese life to appreciate the void created by its disappearance. The passion that the Chinese masses had for opera had no counterpart anywhere in the world. No ceremony, no celebration, no solemn or joyful or exceptional circumstance in life was complete without some piece of opera (remember, in *Ah Q*,[14] the disappointment of village by-standers when the hero, condemned to death, forgets to sing his aria when they are leading him to his execution!). The way in which daily speech was filled with expressions and metaphors taken from the stage clearly attested to the hold that theater had over life; a Chinese sociologist has most convincingly described how the Chinese tend to look at human behavior in terms of role-playing and to consider themselves somewhat as actors playing their own existence. As I noted above, the opera was also a mode of cultural popularization for illiterates who, thanks to it, enjoyed a real intimacy with the main figures in various episodes of China's three-thousand-year-old history. And of course it was for that very reason condemned to death: its prestige kept alive the influence of China's past on Chinese feelings and imaginations.

Chinese traditional opera was killed off by stages. First it

14. A reading of *The True Story of Ah Q*, Lu Hsün's masterpiece (1921), remains the best introduction to a real understanding of the human problems of modern and contemporary China. Lu Hsün's pessimistic vision simultaneously shows the urgent necessity of revolution and its essential impossibility. (For an English version of *Ah Q*, see: *Selected Works of Lu Hsün* [Peking, 1956].)

was made aseptic and academic. In the old days Chinese opera houses had a kind of joyful slovenliness, a popular, warm, living atmosphere. The dangerously expert audience booed and applauded with absolutely no inhibition. The Maoist authorities, who fear nothing so much as spontaneous mass happenings (which might always degenerate into uncontrollable avalanches), put the houses in order and started by re-educating the audience: the audience was no longer allowed to roar its enthusiastic *"Hao!"* after each virtuoso piece, but was directed to clap only as the curtain fell, in Western academic fashion. It took some years to reform age-old public habits; when the connoisseurs—and in places like Peking everybody was a connoisseur—showed signs of being overcome by their former intoxication, and when in the pressure cooker of a really good audience the *"Haos"* started rocketing about as they had in the good old days, small red-light panels marked "Silence" would start to blink furiously at the four corners of the auditorium.

After managing to kill life in the audience, the authorities then killed it on the stage. The repertory was weeded out; plays esteemed licentious or reactionary were eliminated; only works that gave moral or heroic lessons remained, and most of those had to be rewritten. But even *these*, playing to newly disciplined audiences, were more than the authorities could bear. Since the Cultural Revolution, *all* the traditional operas have disappeared, and we have only the half-dozen "Revolutionary Model operas on contemporary themes." For nearly eight years now, this artistic, subtle, opera-mad people, which had at its disposal one of the widest theatrical repertories in the world, has been reduced, on Madame Mao's prescription, to the strict regimen of these six feeble Punch and Judy shows, where the only "revolutionary" daring is to maneuver on stage, to languorous saxophonic Khachaturian-like music, platoons of the People's Liberation Army complete with banners and wooden rifles.

Radio, television, and movies all help to give this catastrophic grotesque a nightmarish ubiquity, and its multirepetition every day, all week, months on end, throughout the year, is a saturation that brings on nausea, a screaming boredom. It is another paradox of a regime that prides itself on fostering the "creative spirit of the masses" that it has deliberately killed a folk art *par excellence* and replaced it with an academic formula imposed from on high. Everything is minutely regulated in these miserable stereotyped "operas" to insure a rigorously uniform staging throughout the country, as well as to prevent any kind of local adaptation or improvisation. Nothing could be more rigidly conventional or academic: the play will be the same whether enacted in Shenyang, Canton, or Wuhan, played by professionals, amateurs, soldiers, cripples, children, deaf-mutes, or what have you: everything is identical, every gesture, every detail of décor and costumes—down to the number, color, and placement of the patches on the trousers of this or that "poor peasant." Nothing is left to chance or to the initiative of the directors.

7 Universities

Well, and what was so remarkable about Ch'in Shih-huang? He executed four hundred and sixty scholars. We, we executed forty-six thousand of them! This is what I answered to some democrats: you think you insult us by saying that we are like Ch'in Shih-huang, but you make a mistake, we have passed him a hundred times! You call us Ch'in Shih-huangs, you call us tyrants—we grant readily that we have those qualities; we only deplore that you remain so much below the truth that we have to help you fill out your accusations! [Laughter in the audience.]

—Mao Tse-tung[1]

Having visited some universities in China, it would be easier for me to write about Chinese taxidermy than about higher education. Everywhere I went the authorities persisted in showing me dusty glass cases full of stuffed animals in zoology department galleries, instead of allowing me to see, as I asked to see each time, the Faculties of Arts and Letters at work. For a visit to China's universities[2] follows a quasi-invariable routine, and the answers you get to the usual questions are nearly always the same. In the end, one learns most from the repetition of certain silences, the recurrence of a certain reticence about several points.

1. *Mao Tse-tung ssu-hsiang wan sui* (Peking, 1969), p. 195.
2. The ones I went to were: Peking, Tsinghua, Nan-k'ai (Tientsin), Wuhan, Sun Yat-sen (Canton), Northwest (Sian), and Fu-tan (Shanghai).

For instance, everything that touches on the contents of lectures in the humanities (except in Tsinghua, which is a basically polytechnic college, I always focused on the Department of Chinese Literature) is shrouded in fog: it is hard to get a schedule of lectures, impossible to look at the textbooks or to glance at syllabuses and students' notes, or even simply to get the reading lists that are given to students.

At the beginning of each visit, one is welcomed by a group of five or six people. Among these there will be a Venerable Old Professor, guaranteed authentic, but mute most of the time; and some walk-on extras who also say almost nothing. The introductory briefing is offered by a cadre, who is seldom actually a teacher himself, and, at the end of the visit, it is usually the same cadre who will answer questions. After the welcoming speech, which lasts a quarter of an hour or twenty minutes, we look at stuffed animals, hear "The East Is Red" sung on an electronic computer, pass through hall after hall, down endless corridors to look at transistor batteries, synthetic soap, or whatever else the university produces in the interests of linking University and Work as advocated by the Cultural Revolution. We scrutinize slides of innumerable microscopes and simulate polite interest in the unintelligible swarming patterns.

These dilatory maneuvers easily take two hours; they are not *always*, but they are *sometimes* funny—as in Wuhan, where you can see the museum dedicated to the visit Mao paid to the university in 1958. One is happily surprised to see there, under glass, a dirty old undershirt; this startling specimen of underclothing owes its immortality to a remark made by the Chairman, who saw it on the back of a student in a university workshop and said: "Bravo, there is one who looks like a worker!"

When the visitor has been exhausted by the microscopes and stuffed animals—which on these visits perform the function of the *banderillas* in a *corrida*—and when he is considered ripe for the final cup of tea, he is led back to the briefing hall, where he is allowed to ask some questions—if he has any strength or curiosity left. But at that point should the visitor ask if he might go to a lecture—*any* lecture! in *any* department of the human sciences!—it will be too early or too late; by extraordinary bad luck no lectures are being given that morning or that afternoon; students are on the sports field or studying in their rooms. In the secondary schools, by contrast, authorities always quickly grant this request, so it is somewhat easier to inform oneself about secondary schools; and we should pause a moment to consider them.

Secondary schools in China seem to be functioning more or less normally, but they suffer from a drastic reduction in the length of the time students now spend in them. The old system had three years of lower-middle and three years of higher-middle school; now, in many provinces (the system is still experimental and has not been unified nationally), it has been reduced to two plus two years. Many teachers and parents feel that this is too brief, and it has been suggested that at least one more year should be added (making it three plus two), which has been done in some regions. The most positive innovations brought about by the Cultural Revolution have been in the field of manual work: the schools have their own cultivated fields, their own small factory in which each class learns to handle machinery, and, on top of that, all students periodically do farmwork. The examination system has been little modified, and Chinese pedagogy remains as a rule desperately conservative and traditional: the classes I visited invariably had professors locked into habitual, dogmatic, and peremptory teaching methods, facing passive, respectful, silent pupils. Student participation in school administration is limited to a merely symbolic representation on each institution's Revolutionary Committee. In a big school in Hangchow, for example, the Revolutionary Committee had eleven members: two cadres (one was a former vice-headmaster), four representatives of the Workers-Soldiers Propaganda Team of the Thought of Mao Tse-tung, four teachers, and one pupil. (The Workers-Soldiers Propaganda Teams of the

Thought of Mao Tse-tung were deployed in schools throughout China in the summer of 1968, on the personal order of Mao, to restore discipline and crush the anarcho-revolutionary movements; they are now a permanent feature of all teaching establishments. The members of these teams are changed every year, by rotation, and new ones arrive from factories and barracks. Their main task is to keep the schools on ideological course, and in particular they are responsible for keeping the political-education courses orthodox; they play the role of deans and social assistants, visit the parents, and so forth.)

When the length of secondary studies was shortened, the syllabus was lightened. Now it is composed essentially of: (1) Political theory: this is the most important subject, which has the place that religious courses have in parochial schools in the West. The course is given by a professor, but a member of the Workers-Soldiers Team is present and sees to it that the correct line is followed, without any personal inflections. In practice, most of the course is a scholastic commentary on *People's Daily* editorials and articles in *Red Flag*. (2) Chinese language and literature: this course is 90 per cent modern, 10 per cent classical. Most of the modern material is comprised of Mao's prose, a few ideological articles (Yao Wen-yuan & Co.), and one or two bits of Lu Hsün. The classical-language part (at least in the schools I visited) was devoted entirely to poems by Mao. (His heavy, pedantic verse will thus have a tremendous value in history: it gives a pretext for teaching classical Chinese during these years of obscurantism.) (3) Foreign languages: either English (for most) or Russian (for a few). Here, the books are all too often the unreadable creations of the Cultural Revolution, in which concern for a progressive and practical pedagogy has been sacrificed to ideological purity. These impeccably orthodox texts have been criticized in various articles in *Red Flag* and *People's Daily* because they cannot be used or understood by Chinese children learning their first words of English; teachers themselves admit that the books should be entirely rewritten. But who would dare throw out these anthologies of sacred writ merely because they were unrelated to English-as-spoken? (4) History and geography: I was able to see only one history text (there are no texts distributed nationwide: since the Cultural Revolution, each province experiments with its own), and in it the history of China was reduced to a list of various peasant rebellions that marked the twilight of successive dynasties. (5) Mathematics. (6) Chemistry. (7) Physics. (8) Agriculture (theory and practice). (9) Military training. And (10) Revolutionary culture (Revolutionary Model operas and other artistic activities).

As for extracurricular activities, first we have the Red Guards. These have nothing to do with their homonyms of 1966, but are a youth movement open to all students and include in fact about a third of all school children. They have Boy Scout-like activities: a daily "good deed," getting outdoors twice a week, and so on. Compared to them, the Kung ch'ing t'uan (Young Communist League) seems more aristocratic: the minimum age is fifteen; admission criteria are strict; in each school, only a few students belong to it, and since they have a bright bureaucratic future, they are envied by the others (a paradoxical turn when one remembers that during the Cultural Revolution the true Red Guards compelled the league, which was the nursery for party mandarins, to cease all activities and disappear).

In short, as far as I can judge from having visited classes here and there, though the Cultural Revolution offered new and excellent pedagogical watchwords for secondary schools ("Teaching must wake up the mind, not simply inject knowledge"), these were mostly declarations of intent: the teacher-pupil relationship remains authoritarian and dogmatic. And the main result of the Cultural Revolution is thus to have thinned out the actual content of what is learned by deleting most of the history, language, and literature that are the foundations of culture.

The Cultural Revolution closed all the schools in China on July 13, 1966. Secondary schools stayed closed for four years, but they are apparently all open again now. At the university level things are less promising; out of 500 institutions before the Cultural Revolution, only 196—less than two-fifths—were active in late 1972. Recovery has been haphazard, uneven, and of varying degrees of success.[3] Each university seems to be on its own and does what it can to emerge from its long hibernation. Long gone is the time when Chinese education was a matter for a coherent, centralized, national policy.

For instance, Peking and Tsinghua universities began re-enrolling students in the autumn of 1970, the Hunan Provincial University in late 1971, while the Szechuan and Tsinghai provincial universities and Hunan's medical school and three other institutes got going again only in the spring of 1972. University activities were frequently reduced or existed in theory only—which would explain the authorities' reluctance to let me attend lectures in the universities I visited, or to even let me see others. For example, in Hangchow, I was not allowed to visit the Chekiang Provincial University, and of course the famous Fine Arts Institute has been moved for good, with all its teaching staff and all its students, to the faraway rural market town of Fen-shui. My request to visit the university in Ch'angsha caused a lot of obvious uneasiness; in the end, I was told that the time was not opportune because the students had just left for the fields.

The delays and false starts are not surprising when one realizes the magnitude of the problems Chinese higher education has to face: the problem of recruiting teaching staff, the

3. According to a specialist, "the chaos brought about by the Cultural Revolution in higher learning has deprived the country of eight promotions of graduates in sciences and technology. Instead of giving greater autonomy to China, this loss of one million engineers, doctors, teachers, etc., may well make still more acute the need to import foreign technology." Michael Oksenberg, "The Chinese Political Spectrum," in *Problems of Communism*, March–April 1974, XXIII, 2, 12.

problem of teaching itself (length, content, method), and the problem of students.

Teachers: accused, vilified, harassed by activists of the Cultural Revolution, their time of troubles ended in the summer of 1968 with the arrival of the Workers-Soldiers Propaganda Teams of the Thought of Mao Tse-tung. Professors were then sent in rotating groups to field or factory to re-form their vision of the world by contact with workers and peasants. With them gone, an attempt was made to give their positions to authentic proletarians. But these, after telling of their sufferings before the Liberation and extolling the happiness the new regime had brought them, found they did not have very much to say; they did not want to cling to an academic chair where they felt embarrassed and faintly ridiculous. In the end, the Workers-Soldiers Teams took on the less conspicuous task of being watchdogs: the soldiers keeping order, the workers guarding the orthodox ideology—while little by little the professional chairs were taken back by their (duly re-educated) former incumbents. According to the official figures, 90 per cent of China's teachers have been reinstated. But the fact that they were officially cleared is not enough to solve their problems or erase the memory of their recent traumatic experiences. On the other hand, to rusticate for one or two years, even if it benefits their health, could hardly bring the professors to rethink pedagogical concepts and habits they had developed during their entire careers; to achieve *that* aim, a few seminars in methodology would possibly have been more useful. The official Chinese press now waxes indignant about the overly large number of professors, back from the fields, who have only "put on new shoes to follow old tracks," but was that not to be expected? How does pushing carts and breaking stones help one to discover, as if by magic, new pedagogical principles? But if they still apply their old methods, they do so much less efficiently, since in the meantime they have lost authority over their students and dare not demand anything from them. This is reflected in the official press, which several times has reminded teachers that they must be strict with their students.[4]

As for the aims and content of the teaching, the question about whether to educate "Reds" or "Experts" is an old quarrel. When the Cultural Revolution reaffirmed the priority of "Reds," cut down the length of studies, and forged close links between school and factory, it was not being original: all those Maoist reforms had already been attempted at the time of the Great Leap Forward and had been discarded soon thereafter, experience having shown them to be unrealistic.[5] That is to say, thanks to the Cultural Revolution, Mao was able to return to his old hobby—"revolution in education"—and introduced measures that were tried, and abandoned as unpractical, some fifteen years before. "Revolutions waste a lot of time," says a character in Montherlant.[6] As could be expected, a curve soon appeared in the graph of Chinese educational progress. This time, looping the loop will take longer, for the extremists, far from having been neutralized, harmless, are fighting tenaciously here as elsewhere to retard and sabotage the inevitable "restoration."

4. Those admonitions come from the partisans of technocratic order, who, since the elimination of Ch'en Po-ta and Lin Piao, have measurably strengthened their control of the governmental machine. At the same time the minority extremist faction tries to start a second Cultural Revolution, proposes rebellious slogans to youth, and recently has commended the contesting attitude of some pupils. The teachers, caught in the crossfire, have no idea what direction to take. The fight for power continues at the top, intense as ever, and as long as the issue is in doubt, the lower cadres are paralyzed by fear of backing the wrong horse, unable to take initiative or choose among the contradictory watchwords. They take cover in simply doing nothing.

(Since this note was written, the Maoist radicals fell into disgrace at the end of 1976, and this should clear the way for a certain return to sanity in the field of education and culture.)

5. In 1962 a highly qualified Chinese witness summarized this experience as follows: "The Chinese communists have tried to expand technical education at the speed the Party decided, forcing the professors to turn out graduates in three years instead of four, but as the communist president of Tsinghua University told the Eighth Congress of the People's Representatives: 'It was a fine lesson in waste of time and money.'" Mu Fu-sheng, *The Wilting of the Hundred Flowers* (London, 1962; New York, 1963), p. 195.

6. Porcellio, in *Malatesta*.

There is still no question of making "Expert" prevail over "Red," but at least equality between these two principles is advocated, while the Maoist principle of the "primacy of politics" is now condemned as one of those poisonous thoughts, "apparently leftist but in fact rightist, peddled by Liu Shao-ch'i-type swindlers to sabotage teaching." No one yet dares to attack head-on even such sacred Maoist dogmas as the importance of manual work for intellectuals, but official sources cite schools where 70 or even sometimes 80 per cent of the time is spent on intellectual disciplines. The rule that teaching must be linked to production has also not been directly questioned, but an eloquent recent article by Chou P'ei-yuan pleaded in favor of pure research, reminding readers that progress in science and technology depends, in the last resort, on the development of speculative thought for its own sake, free from practical imperatives or from a productive function (Chou gave as example, among others, the theory of relativity).

The old Chinese examination system, which was swept away by the Cultural Revolution, appears to be now back in full force. Open-book exams, closed-book exams, oral exams, written exams, occasional tests, semester exams, final exams, and even entrance exams—all possible varieties are freely used. In discussions about the examinations, one argument comes out clearly: *If we want to raise the quality of studies, examinations are indispensable*. Here again is the clear intention to return to the old system. Yet it is on this subject that an extremist counteroffensive has centered.

One should perhaps note that the only really important point concerns *entrance* examinations, because the others were never really significant. In higher education in the People's Republic, the rate of failures and wastage *in the course of studies* has always hovered near zero: the students are an elite, rigorously selected and highly motivated, and university authorities are extremely reluctant to fail anybody, this being not only a waste, but an admission of failure and inefficiency on their part. (A friend of mine who taught for a long time at Peking University told me that every time he wanted to fail a dull or incapable student, the authorities compelled him to raise the student's marks. As for failing a student who happened to be an activist or the son of a poor peasant, needless to say this kind of fool-hardiness did not occur to anyone.)

The university cycles, which used to last four or five years, have been shortened to two and three years, and, unlike the situation in secondary schools, no one in a position of responsibility dares openly to criticize the present system. Was it not Mao himself who said, "Two or three years should be enough to train university graduates?" However, they get round that difficulty rather cleverly, they organize general cultural courses for new students which last from six months to a year in preparation for the regular university courses, and this enables them to stay for three and a half or even four years after all. It seems quite clear that the authorities would like to raise the level of higher education and restore true university quality. But to do so is to meet with insoluble contradictions and there is still a wide gap between intentions and facts. For example, to solve the "Red" and "Expert" contradiction, it is not enough to say that students must be both, and despite the instructions from above, which try to maintain a balance between political indoctrination and specific university disciplines, the first still predominates over the second in actual practice.[7]

The professors and cadres who should steer higher teaching back to ways more compatible with the university are, as I have said, too timid to apply the new instructions. One can see why they are reluctant to apply a policy that objectively appears to be "rightist": it is exactly because they applied such a policy so

7. See for instance the program of the Chinese Department of Wuhan University: (1) Marxism; (2) History of the International Communist Movement; (3) History of the Chinese Communist Party; (4) Mao Tse-tung's Poetry; (5) Lu Hsün; (6) Chinese Literature; and (7) Chinese Language. At Peking University, the situation is ever more dismaying; for the main literary works studied in the Chinese literature department are the childish librettos of the Revolutionary Model operas.

docilely that they were pilloried by the Cultural Revolution! Here we find again one of the basic problems of the Chinese regime: the lower echelons, harassed and traumatized by the rapid succession of contradictory campaigns, prefer to wait and see, to keep a policy of prudent inactivity, and this condemns any new political measure (especially if it is more "liberal") to ineffectiveness. In higher education, the long climb back will be all the harder, because the psychological climate is poisoned by fear and defeatism—as is attested by the current sayings such as "teaching is a dangerous job" (*chiao-yü wei-hsien lun*)—though official propaganda tries to counteract it.

Last but not least, there are the students. (Note that since the beginning of the Revolution in Education students are not called "students" (*hsüeh-sheng*) anymore, but "studiers" (*hsüeh-yuan*), on the model of "butcher," "baker," "candlestickmaker." The "studiers" come from among the peasants, workers, and soldiers, and the recruitment process (very complex) has four stages. The candidate must have done two years of manual work in field or factory; his application must be supported by the university. In some cases, when the number of candidates exceeds the number of places, the university may organize entrance examinations to choose amongst them.

This system is a good deal better than the system used in 1970 (right after the Cultural Revolution), when candidates were chosen directly by "the masses" and could not themselves apply to a specific institution. But the system remains tightly political: a candidate who is not the son of a worker or a poor peasant has practically no chance of admission, however brilliant he may be. (*Red Flag* has denounced this extremist error, according to which "the social origins are an absolutely determining factor," and promotes a theoretical tolerance for candidates who, though marked by "a bad social origin," still show "a progressive conception of the world." But, again, few people in responsible positions are ready to apply these more liberal instructions.) Still ruled by the old maxim, "when in doubt, better sin by leftism than by rightism," the cadres in charge of student selection prefer to practice a kind of demagoguery of illiteracy. Did not the Cultural Revolution proclaim the superiority of bridges and dams put up by uneducated workers over those drawn up by engineers, the superiority of village medicine over that practiced by doctors? No wonder that university studies are devalued in the eyes of the people: "Study is useless" (*chiao-yü wu-yung lun*) is another of those maxims that are so common that party organs constantly refute them. Coming from the fields and the factories, students go through university only to go back whence they came: if such is the case, why make the detour? Moreover, for many of them the university is tough: the level of teaching has declined, but it is still too high for many of those new students. (It is so hard to find candidates with an impeccable social pedigree *and* the minimum intellectual preparation that many provincial universities now recruit from the whole country, and not—as used to be the case—exclusively from their province.) And add to this the fact that, as I said above, the universities have preparatory courses for six months to a year, to try to fill up the gaps in the newcomers' culture. The situation is uncomfortable for them; an article in the *People's Daily* described the psychological problems of the unenviable "studiers" who, facing a task for which they are not equipped, live through their university years in a state of "permanent anxiety" (*yi chi erh p'a*).

In summary, we may say that the Cultural Revolution had even worse effects in higher education than elsewhere, but that now the trend is toward normalization, a desire to erase the disastrous consequences of that movement exists here as in other areas of life, yet there are many obstacles to this work of restoration and it may be thwarted at any time.

On the other hand, it would be inconceivable, and undesirable, to go back to the old system. After all, in the late 1960s there was a crisis in universities all over the world, and most of the innovations brought about in China by the Revolution in Education may well be *in principle* less original than appears at first glance: capitalist universities managed in their own way to find solutions that are remarkably similar to those adopted by Maoist ones.[8]

The world over, a new definition of the university must be found. China is heavily handicapped in this essential task by its political dogmas and, even more, by the cumbersome personality of its Supreme Leader, who has very precise and definite ideas about universities and a reckoning to settle with university people.[9] Individual whim takes the place of serious debate among

8. See, for instance, the conclusion of a report in *Newsweek*, 6 November 1972, on the American university:

Students who were once sneered at for dropping out of school are now encouraged to take a year or two off to find themselves. Scores of institutions have revised their curriculums to slice the number of required courses, some have inserted month-long breaks between semesters to allow students to pursue independent study projects; others have developed year-round schedules to save money. Universities may soon be turning out lawyers in five years instead of seven, and graduating doctors in six years instead of the current eight; most important, the standard four years for a baccalaureate degree will certainly be trimmed down to three years. These evolutionary changes may be less provocative than watching students blow up buildings. But to the universities —and to the country—they are a good deal more significant.

9. Mao's mixed suspicion and contempt of intellectuals has never been a secret. (See, for instance, the famous speech he gave in August 1967 to an Albanian military delegation, a translation of which appears in my *Les Habits neufs du Président Mao* [Paris, 1971], pp. 169–77.) The Red Guard press has reproduced some of the juicy little chats where Mao, with his pals, talks to young activists (who took down and later published his words about some of his favorite themes). This, for instance, on the uselessness of university studies:

MAO TSE-TUNG: Except for Marx and Lenin, who went to the university, the others never set foot there. Anyway, Lenin did only one year of law. As for Engels, before he had even finished school, his father sent him to work as accountant in a factory, and that is where he made contact with the world of the workers. Where did Engels get his scientific knowledge? In public libraries, in London, where he stayed for eight years, but he never set foot in a university. Neither did Stalin: he only finished his secondary education in a seminary. Gorki did two years of primary school, even less than Chiang Ch'ing! Chiang Ch'ing, for her part, finished six years of primary school. . . .

YEH CH'UN [Lin Piao's wife]: But Comrade Chiang Ch'ing has always been zealous, and she studied on her own. . . .

MAO: No need to flatter her. Anyway, knowledge is not acquired in schools. As for me, I never studied in military academies, I never studied treatises on strategy. Some people say that in my campaigns

the very people (students and professors) who could be of some use in solving the problems. One sees again how heavily Mao has weighed on China's destiny, and how much his presence has become a paralyzing factor in the life of the country.

I followed the *Three Kingdoms* and *Sun Tzu's Art of War*, but I'll tell you very simply that I've never read *Sun Tzu*. The *Three Kingdoms*, yes, I read that.

LIN PIAO: I remember, back then, you asked me to get you a copy but I never managed to.

MAO: During the Tsun-yi Conference [1935], as I talked with XXX, he asked, "And *Sun Tzu's Art of War*, have you at least read that?" I retorted, "Can you just tell me how many chapters there are in *Sun Tzu*?" He did not know any better than I. I asked what the first chapter was about: he didn't know. It was only later, when I had to write about strategy, that I glanced through *Sun Tzu*. . . .

Who among you is learning English? You must learn English. I had no regular schooling, and this handicapped me in foreign languages. Foreign languages should be started early, when people are very young; they should start learning them in primary school.

T'AN HOU-LAN [a leader of the Red Guards, from the Peking Normal School]: Chairman, now that the Cultural Revolution is over, what must I do? Join the army?

MAO: Six months of military training should be enough. Why have a long military service? In six months you have learned all there is to learn. After that, you should work as a farmer for a year, as a factory worker for two years: that is the true university education!

(Reproduced in *Ming pao*, 20 December 1973; see also a slightly different version in *Mao Tse-tung ssu-hsiang wan sui*, pp. 694–95.)

8 | Here and There

I visited the People's Republic of China for the first time in 1955.
I now return after seventeen years. The difference that strikes
me the most—I speak here of purely visual, intuitive, superficial
impressions, not taking into account the objective achievements
that have been attained in the intervening years, which are certainly considerable—the difference that strikes me the most is
that in 1955 everything seemed new, full of youth and life, and
now everything seems old, run-down, ramshackle. Canton gives
one a feeling of *déjà vu*; it's like another Macao—a significant
comparison for anyone who knows that dirty obsolete old backwater. This impression grows in the north, where the cities
cannot hide their tawdriness behind the luxuriance of tropical
foliage. The buildings that date from after the Liberation of 1949
have not grown old gracefully: ersatz barracks, they become
leprous after a few years. Housing clearly has a much lower
priority than industrial infrastructure; also, the political climate
does not encourage people to smarten up their flats or houses:
better not give rise to neighborly envy; better not live in a way
that might be qualified as "bourgeois"; any individual initiative
to make daily life more pleasant or aggreeable may bring suspicion or cause criticism. The wise man lives in a hovel and
sews patches onto his trousers.

Others will say that the difference between 1955 and 1972
is not so much in what is seen as in who is doing the looking;
in seventeen years one grows older and sourer. But I am struck

159

by the opinion of many Chinese, based on personal experience and deep observation, that the regime was making great strides until 1956–57, only to see its forward dynamism compromised by the Hundred Flowers crisis, and then broken for good by the failure of the Great Leap Forward.

I can listen patiently and courteously when Chinese bureaucrats drone on with the trite sayings of Maoist propaganda: after all, they are only doing their job. But patience begins to fail me when the same old propaganda is served forth by Japanese diplomats or American journalists; the toadying flattery to which they have lowered themselves must sometimes turn the stomach of those they want to please.

A visit, in Sian, to an "art workshop," which makes pictures out of painted silk, plastic, seashells, and ostrich feathers. This petty-bourgeois flim-flam, which under the label of revolutionary and proletarian art is triumphant everywhere to the exclusion of all else, raises interesting philosophical problems.

The aesthetics of politics is a major subject that has yet to be "done." The ability of totalitarian regimes to produce nothing but kitsch is surely the least atrocity of which they are guilty, but it is nevertheless a remarkably sure and constant symptom that aids in the diagnosis of the spiritual vices of those systems. Nazi kitsch, Mussolini kitsch, Stalin kitsch, Mao kitsch are all in the same family; still, they each have specific traits. By studying the specificities (which have little to do with national characteristics), one might begin to discern what goes into each of the variants in the great totalitarian family. Such a work could be simply analytical and descriptive to start with. It would be enough to collect and then subsume under the various major common themes (Cult of the Leader, Denunciation of the Enemy, Happiness of the People, Infallible Teaching of the Party) the expressions developed under each regime in films, poster art, records, decorative art, architecture, sculpture, and so on.

One should not misunderstand the melancholy recollections found here and there on the preceding pages. I would forgive *all* iconoclasms (I would welcome them with enthusiasm!) coming from a political power that was truly *of the people*— revolutionary, creative, opening up the ways of the future. But the present regime in China has destroyed the cultural and human values of the past only to retain its vices: it prolongs in its own interest the habits of feudalism and military bureau-cracy. The psychology and political methods of the few old men who run China today derive directly from the Empire.

In Peking, the only Chinese whom foreigners have a chance to get to know are their own servants. This faithfully repeats the colonialist situation, but now the fault is with the Chinese au-thorities themselves. It is typical that the regime has deliberately re-created all the features of that grotesque and shameful system, with its International Club, its segregated pleasures and shops, its ghetto.

The Papaoshan cemetery is in the country, southwest of Peking. It is here that officials of the regime are supposed to be buried, but the stroller in Papaoshan finds only a waste of broken tombs dating from before the 1960s, on the side of a hill left fallow. Personalities who died more recently were cremated in the Papaoshan crematorium, I suppose, or they were buried in a separate, secret, closed, and guarded graveyard, allowing them to preserve in death the splendid isolation that Power had given them in life. The regime obviously fears to expose its dignitaries' tombs to the fury of the mob: during the Cultural Revolution the mob showed that its anger against bureaucrats did not make exceptions for the dead, and the Papaoshan cemetery (which appears to be abandoned) still bears the marks of that violence. Many steles are pushed over and broken, some painted red or smeared with tar, and pieces of stone are lying about on the ground. This vandalism seems to have expressed blind rage against the ruling class as a whole, all of whose representatives were attacked indiscriminately. Sometimes, in the heart of Peking, one may see similar traces of the Cultural Revolution: in the Forbidden City itself, on the wall of the passage to the second door, the old graffiti dating from 1967–68, which had been carefully painted over, now emerge again, ghostly under the paint. Shouts of anger have crossed time, like Rabelais's frozen words. One can read fragments: "Liberate Kiangsi!" "Fry Sung Teh-xxx in oil!" "Avenge our murdered martyrs!" "Down with Chang xxx!"

W. is a rather high official in a Peking ministry. He must be around forty. He comes from Shanghai, where he was educated by the Jesuits, whence comes his knowledge of French and his sacristan-like demeanor. We met rather often, and I remember especially one long and curious conversation. He started by asking me point-blank: "According to you, what are the best books on China that have been published in Europe recently?"

ME: The number of books published on China every year is enormous, and that's a good thing, because it shows the place that China has begun to fill—at last—in the Western consciousness. Unfortunately there hasn't yet been a single definitive book on the subject: admirers and detractors of the People's Republic usually elaborate on their respective prejudices, and on the basis of a frightening ignorance. But it wouldn't be fair to blame them entirely. If *we* are so ignorant about China today, *you* are the people mainly responsible for it. Example: the Cultural Revolution led to a flood of fancy literature in the West, but it would have been easy to squelch the false rumors by letting people come and see for themselves what was in fact happening. The best work done on the Cultural Revolution is very imperfect: it was written in Hong Kong by people who got most of their information from unfavorable witnesses. They would have liked nothing better than to be able to verify that testimony on the spot, but you never gave them a chance. At best, they can only give their limited and biased version of the facts in good faith, waiting for the day when historians can elaborate a more dispassionate synthesis from all the fragmentary evidence.

w: What do you think of Mrs. Macciocchi's book?[1]

ME: Well, all in all, I prefer Moravia's.[2] Between two jokers, better choose the funny one.

w: I do not know this Moravia you speak of. Why do you say that Mrs. Macciocchi is a joker? Mrs. Macciocchi is a true friend of China.

ME: I don't question the purity of Mrs. Macciocchi's intentions; or at least, not having the honor of knowing her, I'm ready to give her the benefit of the doubt. But I find her book somewhat . . . abstract. She could have written in Europe, without leaving her room, if she had had some issues of *Peking Review* at her disposal; she would have gotten the same results. Her China experience was limited to a visit of a few weeks, and to three dozen interviews. You don't discover by interviewing what people think, what they feel, what makes up the real fabric of their lives. That can only be discovered slowly, over months and years, by *living* with them. I don't believe in the kind of interview she relied on, especially when the words are slowed down, frozen, and formalized by passing through an interpreter, and when . . . when the interviewees are Chinese.

You are Chinese yourself. I don't have to tell you that light-headedness is not a common defect among the Chinese. Your admirable qualities of self-control, thoughtfulness, prudence, and subtlety have as their opposite, if you'll excuse my frankness, a certain self-consciousness and also a (quite terrific) kind of wily cynicism. I have the feeling that often Mrs. Macciocchi, under the impression that she was interviewing comrade Chang San or comrade Li Ssu, was in fact interviewing Ah Q, without

1. Maria A. Macciocchi, *A Daily Life in Revolutionary China* (New York, 1972).

2. Alberto Moravia, *Red Book and the Great Wall*, trans. Ronald Strom (New York, 1968).

knowing his identity. You remember Lu Hsün: 'I was faced with the problem of deciding if Ah Q would become a revolutionary or not. In my mind, so long as there was no revolution in China, Ah Q would not become a revolutionary; but he would become one as soon as the revolution triumphed.' What an interesting episode could be added to *The True Story of Ah Q*! An Italian lady of good works, an ideologist, alights in Weichuang complete with interpreter, Kodak, and notebook. She interviews Ah Q on his revolutionary experience, in the presence, naturally, of Mr. Chao—

w. (*brushing away the preposterous vision*): And Etiemble? What do you think of Etiemble?

me (*somewhat nonplussed, not seeing—or rather, seeing all too well—where he was leading*[3]): Etiemble has always fought for great, just, and necessary ideas—for instance, the need to widen our culture and open it to all the other cultures in the world. He is a humanist and a free man. He is in no one's pay and says what his conscience dictates. Even those who do not agree with some of his ideas should respect the courage with which he swims against the current of fashion and prejudice—

w. (*sternly*): Not so long ago, Etiemble spoke ill of China. Very ill. He slandered China. Well, he's not the only one.

me (*warmly*): Frankly, this notion of "friends who speak well of China" and "enemies who speak ill of China" fills me with dismay and despair. I often get the impression that China can't distinguish its true friends and its true enemies anymore; this encourages and rewards the flatteries of notoriously shady and venal opportunists, and calls "slanderers" people who love China disinterestedly and do not hesitate, at their own risk, to give sincere criticism. The paradox is that these independent critics (whom you think are slanderers) happen quite often to have been the first to see the truth, while those whom you call friends are still blinded by their own servility. Look at the cast of Lin Piao: are there any of those "friends" who were not his enthusiastic supporters, right down to the last day of his career—even a little longer, for those who were less subtle? How can

3. In 1971 Etiemble published in the leftist weekly *Le Nouvel Observateur* a courageous and memorable article on Simon Leys's first book, *Les Habits neufs du Président Mao*, thus breaking the wall of silence that the French intelligentsia had tried to build around this heretical work.

you trust that chorus of obsequious adorers of Power? How can you be taken in by the "fervor" of people like—

w.: We're not taken in by anybody, believe me, and we have better information than you think. To return to our subject: the main thing about any book dealing with China is to see what interests are objectively served by the author.

ME: It's no less important to see objectively the author's competence and the quality of his information. As for the virtuous ignoramuses—

w.: If the intention of the author is to hurt China, then the better his documentation, the more evil his book will be. Everything depends on the spirit in which he uses his information, and on his aims.

ME: That's exactly what I'd like, for you to have a clearer picture of the motivations of those various writers. Those whom you call "detractors of China" may well be those who take the destiny and happiness of your country most to heart. *The Kuomintang accused Lu Hsün of despising China, and the Chinese—*

w.: Since you know so well how the Kuomintang treated the writers who criticized it, I am sure you will appreciate the way we treat those who have attacked us. We let come back to China this or that person who has belittled our socialist state and our Great Proletarian Cultural Revolution: we are ready to give such people another chance; it is by their deeds that we judge them.

Dictionary of idées reçues: applying Flaubert's method, one could compile an enormous volume of the expressions that make up the wooden language of Maoist ideology. The people's struggles are always "fearless" and "victorious." The Albanian, Vietnamese, etc., masses are always "heroic"; the Rumanians, Zambians, etc., are always "fraternal." In his public appearances, Mao always shows a "pink and radiant face," and the sight of him invariably fills onlookers with "feelings of shining love and boundless enthusiasm." The Chinese Communist Party is, of course, "great, glorious, and infallible"; the class enemy, "ever watchful," must be exposed "without pity." The adversary's designs, always "shameful," must be opposed "resolutely"; his crimes are "odious and unforgivable." The successes of the "building-up" of socialism are "prodigious," "immense," "always greater" (in case of failure, one speaks only of "new" or "growing" success). Some articles in Flaubert's *Dictionary* are still valid after a century and could be reprinted unchanged in a Peking version, as for instance: "Feudalism: have no clear idea about it, but fulminate against it. . . ."

Orwell wrote a first-rate essay on how the totalitarian cancer feeds on the corruption of language and secretes the same corruption;[4] he also transposed his ideas in his description of "Newspeak" in *1984*:

The purpose of Newspeak was not only to provide a medium of expression for the world-view and mental habits proper to the devotees of Ingsoc, but to make all other modes of thought impossible. It was intended that when Newspeak had been adopted once and for all and Oldspeak forgotten, a heretical thought—that is, a thought diverging from the principles of Ingsoc—should be literally unthinkable, at least as far as thought is dependent on words. . . . In the Ministry of Truth, the Records Department, in which Winston worked, was called *Recdep*, the Fiction Department was called *Ficdep*, The Teleprogram Department was called *Teledep*, and so on. This was not done solely with the object of saving time. Even in the early decades of the twentieth century, telescoped words and phrases had been one of the characteristic features of political language; and it had been noticed that the tendency to use abbreviations of this kind was most marked in totalitarian countries and totalitarian organizations. Examples were such words as *Nazi, Gestapo, Comintern, Inprecorr, Agitprop*. In the beginning the practice had been adopted instinctively, as it were, but in Newspeak, it was used with a conscious purpose. It was perceived that in thus abbreviating a name one narrowly and subtly altered its meaning, by cutting out most of the associations that would otherwise cling to it. The words *Communist International*, for instance, call up a composite picture of universal human brotherhood, red flags, barricades, Karl Marx, and the Paris Commune. The word

4. "Politics and the English Language," in *Collected Essays, Journalism and Letters of George Orwell* (London, 1968; New York, 1971), IV, 127–40.

Comintern, on the other hand, suggests merely a tightly knit organization and a well-defined body of doctrine. It refers to something as easily recognized, and as limited in purpose, as a chair or a table. *Comintern* is a word that can be uttered almost without taking thought, whereas *Communist International* is a phrase over which one is obliged to linger at least momentarily."[5]

Those who read the Chinese press only occasionally and when not in China may be tempted to dismiss its inept and unreadable Maoist jargon with an amused smile or an ironic shrug. But for those in China who must read it every day, who must endure simultaneously the whole pressure of visual and aural propaganda that illustrates, explains, organizes, that warms up and serves over again and again the same ideological stew, everywhere and all the time (the same slogans are written in gigantic characters on the walls; they are in small print on tickets, calendars, cigarette packs; they are engraved on ashtrays and spittoons, painted on teapots and screens, embroidered on handkerchiefs and towels; loudspeakers moo them in the streets, in the fields, in trains, canteens, factories, latrines, barracks, airplanes, and railway stations), it soon becomes obvious that this gigantic enterprise of cretinizing the most intelligent people on earth is animated, beneath the grotesque exterior, by frighteningly rigorous and coherent intention. The aim is to anesthetize critical intelligence, purge the brain, and inject the cement of official ideology into the emptied skull; once hardened, this will leave no room for the introduction of any new idea, and will oppose its compact, amorphous, and watertight mass to any intellectual operation that would be autonomous or heterodox.

In politics, the citizens of the People's Republic are thus equipped with a mechanical and prefabricated jargon that is a substitute for thought, that excludes the possibility of thinking. The extraordinary effects of this robotization is nowhere better measured than in the writings of dissidents who have tried from

5. *1984* (London, 1948; New York, 1949), pp. 303, 309–10.

the inside to oppose the regime. Their efforts were doomed from the start: they had no intellectual tools to mine the ideological fortress but the cardboard pickaxes that had been provided them by Maoist dialectics.[6]

Broadly speaking one may say that in China people have now at their disposal two levels of languages: one, human and natural, which allows them to speak in their own voice, and which they use to talk about their health, the weather, food, the latest basketball match, and so forth, and another one, mechanical and shrill, to talk about politics. In this way, during one conversation, the person you are talking to may well switch several times from his normal voice to a kind of ideologic ventriloquism, according to the topics. In private life, by the way, ordinary people *never discuss politics*: this is too boring and too dangerous. I have been assured of this countless times by refugees in Hong Kong, and once in China itself by a worker with whom I managed to have a long conversation, while on a trip. Only higher cadres (and their children) discuss such things, rather as financiers in capitalist countries exchange confidences about the stock market.

China's ideological jargon proliferates constantly: the regime believes it can avoid ideological bankruptcy by sheltering in this verbal inflation. The avalanche of new concepts is like a massive issue of plastic tokens serving as intellectual money. The best glossaries of Maoist phraseology are out-of-date a year after

6. One of the most typical and pathetic examples of this phenomenon is probably the book by Lu Yin-t'ao, *Jen-lei ti hu-sheng* (*The Call of Mankind*), a polemical manifesto whose manuscript was smuggled out of China in 1961 and published in Hong Kong in 1967, with an introduction by Hsü Yü. The same remarks apply to nearly all the Red Guard literature and other rebel writings that appeared during the Cultural Revolution.

1976 Post Scriptum: Since I wrote this, a most remarkable political manifesto has appeared in China, written by three young rebels using the pen name of Li Yi-che, *On Democracy and Legality under Socialism* (*Kuan-yü she-hui-chu-yi ti min-chu yü fa-chih*). It should make us question anew the pessimistic views here expressed. (This extraordinary document has been translated and annotated in French, under the title *Chinois, si vous saviez* [Paris, 1976].)

being printed. For the Chinese who have spent time abroad, the terminology is a sealed book; to be able to use it with a minimum of nimbleness, one needs the intensive practice that is given in daily and compulsory doses to all citizens of the People's Republic. Without constant training, how could you juggle with the "one-two-three system," the "one good leading four good/four good leading one good," "one-struggle two-criticism three-reform," "synthesis of two in one and dividing of one in two," "three antis and five antis," "the five and the seven categories of bad elements," "the three red flags," "the one point two plans tactic," the system of "three contracts–one reward" and that of "three freedoms–one contract," the "three-fames principle," the "three-eight work style," "the four together," the "unity-criticism unity," "the five stories," "the Yü-kung spirit," "the Tachai spirit," "the Taching spirit," "the extensive democracy," "the four clean-ups," "the eight-words constitution," "the monsters and demons," "the poisonous weeds," "the comparison–emulation–catching–up–help–overtaking movement," "the three-seven and the three-three system," "the three-prop and two-military," "the three fearless," "the three rightisms," and "the three loyalties". . . . But why copy down a four-hundred-page dictionary?

The reader may have noted in passing that this monstrous gibberish shows a particular liking for numbered abbreviations, which help convert it into a kind of arbitrary and autonomous algebra: any relation that may exist between the language of ideology and the existing reality is purely fortuitous.

I have already mentioned a few examples of those logo-machical contortions that make ordinary language lose its meaning, as for instance the discrimination between "material incentives" (accursed) and "just rewards according to work done" (encouraged), or between "permanent revolution" (a Trotskyist heresy) and "continuous revolution" (a genial and creative development brought to Marxist thought by Mao Tse-tung). The prize should probably go to the feat of legerdemain that changed "left" into "right" at one point in the campaign denouncing Lin

Piao—winning by a hairbreadth over the exhortations of the *People's Daily*, inciting the masses "to rebel . . . without transgressing Party discipline and while respecting the authority of their superiors"!

In reaction against this sophistic emptiness, violent outbursts of literalness will sometimes occur, showing a sudden will to make life coincide with abstract ideological categories. The Red Guards were indignant that "red" could be used to mean "stop" in traffic-control procedures, and during the Cultural Revolution they suggested that signals be inverted; according to them, the revolutionary traffic should stop on the green, and proceed forward on the red. This difficulty was dealt with ingeniously: cars still stop on the red, but they do so (as notices on the reverse of road signs explain) "to respect the revolutionary order."

As could have been expected, the most misused word in the language is "revolutionary." The Maoists put it *everywhere*, its reality being nowhere. "Revolution" has become synonymous with "established order" or "administration." All government organs in the provinces, prefectures, districts, universities, factories, workshops, and stores have simply been baptized "revolutionary committees." There are "revolutionary committees" for restaurateurs, for actors, for taxi drivers. A provincial governor, a prefect, a university president is now "chairman of the revolutionary committee" for the province, prefecture, or university. Their functions and duties have not changed any more than the contents of a suitcase changes when it has been chalked by a customs official: the new name simply means that the given administration has been passed by the Cultural Revolution and can go on working as it had before.

On July 16, every year, all China jumps liturgically into the water to commemorate the bath taken in the Yangtze by Mao Tse-tung on July 16, 1966. The reader will recall that on this occasion the wonderful old man, then in his seventies, crushed all Olympic records. In Peking, at the Summer Palace, the ceremony is performed with the utmost pomp.

The traditional Chinese calendar did not lack for ancient rituals: the custom of eating glutinous rice cakes wrapped in bamboo leaves and of organizing dragon-boat races on the fifth day of the fifth lunar month; looking at the moon while eating moon cakes on the fifteenth day of the eighth month; climbing a hill on the ninth day of the ninth month, and so forth and so on. The origin of some of these practices is lost in antiquity and still puzzle anthropologists, historians, and philosophers. We may wager that two thousand years hence, the ritual bath of July 16 will still be practiced, and that learned theses will be written to try to determine the religious-mythic origins of this peculiar aquatic cult.

State secrets. In theory, except where the contrary is indicated, *everything* is a state secret. This at least is the principle wisely followed by your average man in the street, especially in dealing with foreigners. I think I have said before how in a provincial town passers-by did not answer my requests for information. Sometimes it is funnier: one morning in Peking, I saw teams of workmen putting up banners on Ch'ang-an Avenue, and I asked a soldier on duty what was being prepared. "I do not know exactly," he answered, not compromising himself. Two hundred yards ahead, a large streamer already in place gave me the clue, "Welcome to Prime Minister Trudeau!" and reminded me that the press and radio had already widely announced the news. One could not think of a more deliberately public happening than the visit to Peking of a foreign head of state, but still that good sentry followed the wise principle and faithfully applied the watchword, "everything is secret."

As for written information, foreigners are allowed to read only the national press (two dailies: *People's Daily* and *Kuangming Daily*, plus a periodical, *Red Flag*). All local newspapers and journals are strictly forbidden to them, and so is the military press.[7] Therefore, the foreigner living in Peking is ignorant of movie programs, art exhibits, sports events—in short, of all cultural events and entertainments (except if he learns of one by accident while strolling in the streets), for all such information is printed only in the *Peking Daily,* a local and therefore forbidden newspaper. Sometimes, however, in all innocence, the woman at the market stall where you buy a pound of apples or the cobbler who has repaired your shoes will absent-mindedly give you your goods wrapped in a taboo old newspaper; needless to say, the dirty and crumpled sheets are then smoothed over lovingly by China-watchers, who pass them around with trembling hands, deeply excited, and after being multiphotocopied they end up on the black market in Hong Kong, where various research institutes outbid themselves to get them. The persistence of researchers in collecting the useless tidbits from old papers can be explained only by the equal persistence of the Chinese authorities in forbidding them to be read in the name of the old bureaucratic obsession about "state secrets."

One day, in Hangchow (even now, I cannot forgive myself for this), I took advantage of a little girl's ignorance; this was in a small suburban bookshop where I found a wide choice of forbidden publications: *Arts and Letters of Kwangtung, Arts and Letters of Kwangsi, The Revolution in Education, Arts and Letters of the Liberation Army.* A little girl was looking after the shop; she was alone. She sold me all the papers I wanted, even found me back issues, and wrapped everything in a bundle. I paid (it was quite cheap) and fled with the loot. That evening, the man from the bookstore came to see me in my hotel room, with the girl. (How had he found me? you may ask. Silly ques-

---

7. The armed forces have one daily paper, *Chieh-fang chün pao* (*Liberation Army Daily*), not to be mistaken, as K. S. Karol mistook it (one of his lesser blunders), for *Chieh-fang jih-pao* (*Liberation Daily*), which is a local and civilian Shanghai newspaper; and one periodical, *Chieh-fang chün wen-yi* (*Arts and Letters of the Liberation Army*).

tion. The trace of a foreign traveler in China cannot be lost: he is like a radio satellite on regular orbit, and his course and his coordinates can be fixed in a trice by the "responsible organs.") My visitors were embarrassed and ill at ease, I even more so.

The man put some money on the table. "You must excuse the child," he said. "She is young, she knows nothing. This morning she sold you things that—"

I gave him back my bundle of forbidden papers, and he took it with a sigh of relief and gratitude. We exchanged profuse and mutual excuses. "I should not have—"

"But no, it is my fault—"

"On the contrary—"

They took my collection of state secrets, but left me with a less burdened conscience.

Addresses and telephone numbers, whether of public institutions and organizations or of private persons, are also in the category of state secrets. There is no telephone directory, at least not that foreigners can use, and numbers and addresses that one needs for one's professional contacts are given out individually— stingily, in fact.[8] A number of public buildings have no inscriptions on the outside to identify them: only their majestic appearance and the presence of sentries show that they are official. Which ministry? Better not be too curious.

All things are secret, but some things are more secret than others—things that touch on the army, for example, and on the Supreme Leaders of the Chinese regime. As I said, foreigners are forbidden to read the army newspaper and its cultural periodical. Even more remarkable: foreigners were refused permission to view an exhibit held in Peking of paintings by military artists. As for the regime's leaders, their lives—their deaths!—are

8. In the mid-1960s a story went the rounds in Hong Kong (I was unable to check it, but even if it was an invention it shows nicely the hysteria of information that results naturally from the hysteria of secrecy). An American information organization that bought, for a fortune, a copy of the Tientsin telephone directory discovered later that it had been swindled: the entire directory had been cooked up and printed in Hong Kong.

wrapped in mystery: I have described how in Peking armed sentries are posted on the Chung-nan hai Bridge to insure that no passers-by stop on it: from that bridge it is possible to see part of the lawn near Mao's residence half a mile away. The graves of deceased leaders (never mind those who were liqui-dated) are also protected from the people's curiosity. Even their hobbies are taboo: K'ang Sheng, under the pseudonym of Lu Ch'ih-shui, is a graceful amateur painter (yes, even policemen have their human side), who has had admirable prints of his paintings made by the Jung-pao chai, a Peking studio that has preserved the traditional craft of making woodprint reproductions of fine paintings. I bought one in an art shop and asked the seller, a wily old fox whose experience was obviously not limited to the fine arts, "But who is this Lu Ch'ih-shui?"

"I don't know."

"In Hong Kong, it is rumored that he is K'ang Sheng."

"Eeehhh, yes, well, I've heard people say that. . . ."

By chance, I ran into Madame Z. in the Peking Hotel, the famous Anglo-Saxon novelist who in her latter days has turned herself into the high priestess of Maoism. Her coreligionists do not regard her highly: her tempestuous private life, shining in-telligence, brilliant talents, mordant wit, wide information—all this makes them very uneasy, but they are grateful to her for giving their cult the fame of her name and the audience of her millions of readers.

In her luxurious suite, sipping an exquisite tea (of a variety not found at the grocers I go to), she explains to me what is the true "revolutionary-proletarian line." I listen humbly, sure that I am still trapped in the darkness of feudal thought. After all, she ought to know what she's talking about: for years she has been coming to Peking annually for a long stay. (She skipped her customary visit only once, in 1967–68, when revolution nearly blazed again in China. Her Swiss bank accounts and extravagant life-style might well have gotten her into trouble with disrespect-ful youth, but now that the bureaucracy, supported by the army, seems firmly back in the saddle, she feels in her element again.)

She tells me she has a new book about to be published: "a history of the Chinese Communist Party, which is in fact a biog-raphy of Mao Tse-tung, since—isn't it so?—the history of the party is really the personal development of Mao. . . ." Shades of Li Ta-chao and Ch'en Tu-hsiu, of Ch'ü Ch'iu-pai and Li Li-san, and all of you martyrs of Shanghai and Canton, return again to nothingness!

On the table lies the complete collection of classical novels reprinted in Peking after the Cultural Revolution: *The Water Margin, The Three Kingdoms, The Dream of the Red Chamber, The Journey to the West.* "You see? Cultural life has never been so active here! All these masterpieces of classical literature are reprinted today. . . ." I would have liked to ask her why the books had completely disappeared for seven years and why these new editions could be found almost nowhere but in Hong Kong or in the hands of "public-relations" specialists, and why they remained out of the reach of Chinese readers (they were published in very small print runs), but she speaks so fast and with such authority that I cannot get a word in edgewise.

She goes on to say that she meets many people in Peking, intellectuals, but the two names she gives, Feng Yu-lan, and Hsieh Ping-hsin, are the two intellectuals on duty for all dis-tinguished-guests-coming-from-abroad.

"And Lao She?" I managed this sacrilegious question while she was catching her breath. I remember that in the 1960s she was very proud, and rightly so, of the friendship the great writer had for her.

She takes no offense at my rude question and goes on, quite naturally: "Lao She? What a fool! Why did he stupidly kill him-self? Nobody wanted to harm him, and suddenly he takes fright, for nothing! On the last May Day, Chairman Mao gave a private party for a group of writers!"

Poor Lao She, if he had only known! With his ridiculous suicide, he missed a chance to have tea with the Chairman! Madame Z., for her part, is unlikely ever to commit such a *faux pas.*

N. is an attaché at the Soviet Embassy. He is about thirty, and has been posted in Peking for nearly two years. He is a beefy fellow, subtle as a pachyderm, remarkably unattractive, certainly not a fool: he speaks, heavily and mechanically but fluently, English, Chinese, French, and Spanish. He is a stickler for protocol, more than any Dutchman; one feels that he is full of respect for the diplomatic rites and hierarchies. The perfect parvenu, he is very conscious of the privileges of the bureaucratic caste into which he has been promoted. He came to see me one morning, and since he did not show signs of ever leaving, I had to invite him for lunch.

He and his colleagues at the embassy seem to live in the atmosphere of a besieged fortress. "Here in Peking," he told me in the pathetic tones of a shipwrecked passenger sitting on an ice floe, "we are isolated, more than twelve hundred miles from our nearest frontier!" (How many hours by tank? I nearly asked, remembering the summer of 1968, which I had by chance spent in Czechoslovakia.[9])

During the Cultural Revolution, the Chinese personnel of the Soviet Embassy committed a major blunder: they went on strike. The Russians jumped at the chance to do something they had obviously wanted to do for a long time: they replaced all the Chinese with Soviet citizens, down to the last driver, gardener, and kitchen helper. Now they live, all four hundred of

9. The possibility of a Soviet attack on China remains a real, constant, and pressing menace. The Chinese are intensely conscious of it, and their foreign policy has recently been heavily influenced by it. The West would be wrong to view this skeptically. On this question, at least, it is impossible not to be completely and actively in sympathy with Peking's position.

them, within the walls of the embassy. The ghetto life of foreign diplomats in Peking is not jolly, but before complaining the diplomats should recognize that their life has a certain cosmopolitan charm; imagine what life would be like if one had to live it with *four hundred compatriots, all herded into the same corral!* But such a situation—the mere idea of it makes me shudder— does not seem to affect these Russians: they seem happy, all crammed together in their cozy diplomatic citadel (which, by the way, has a lot of conveniences unknown to Moscow citizens), as sheep under a tree during a storm. They know nothing of Chinese life, they do not wish to; they feel only suspicion and contempt for it. This shows itself in the smallest details: N. does not know which bus lines pass in front of his embassy, and obviously the idea of using public transport has never crossed his mind; and his table manners show a total ignorance of the simplest Chinese daily usages, but where could he have learned them? Certainly not by eating borscht every day at his embassy!

For a long time it was the fashion to deprecate Americans who could not adapt to local conditions in foreign countries where they were posted, but their mixed arrogance and provincialism, which so often isolated them from local realities, are as nothing compared to the massive lack of openness, curiosity, and tact shown by Soviet missions abroad. In China, particularly, Russians acted for a long time like colonialists. Their superior attitude was only confirmed by the servility exhibited by Maoist authorities who gave to the Chinese people this watchword: "In everything, learn from the Soviet big brothers." Mao himself uttered the famous slogan "to lean on one side," defining the unilateral manner in which China would base its development on Soviet aid. A delirious literature then flowered, according to which the Soviet Union was paradise (that incredible toady Kuo Mo-jo deserves special mention here), and any criticism of it was sedition, to be put down mercilessly. In this way, for example, Hsiao Chün, the famous Communist writer from Manchuria, was purged for hinting, however lightly, at the bitterness

of the Chinese in the northeast who had endured the abuses of
the Russian Army and had seen their provinces' industries
systematically looted by the "fraternal ally." No change could
be seen here until the early 1960s, when the Soviet Union failed
brutally to keep its commitments, fulfillment of which was vital
for a then weakened and famished China. Only then did the
Chinese Communist Party acknowledge the obvious facts that
the Chinese people had found out long before.[10]

Today, the Russians try to portray Mao Tse-tung as a new
Genghis Khan; behind every Chinese, they see the ghostly
shadow of the old Mongol invader. The Moscow press does its
best to sustain these gross racist prejudices against the most basic
historical facts: after all, China itself suffered from Mongol
invasions just as much as Russia did![11]

10. Still, it is noteworthy to see that the cult of Stalin is kept faithfully in Maoist China—the selfsame Stalin who so often revealed his suspicion of and hostility to the Chinese revolutionary movement, his scorn for
the person of Mao Tse-tung, and who believed until the last minute in an
impossible Chiang Kai-shek victory.

11. One can measure how deeply these prejudices are rooted and how
successful official propaganda was, when one discovers to one's dismay that
even an upright and free man like Alexander Solzhenitsyn has unconsciously
accepted this view of a new Yellow Peril, and does not seem to realize
that the terrible military threat from his own country hovers permanently
over Chinese borders (see Alexander Solzhenitsyn, *Letter to Soviet Leaders*
[London, 1974], Chapter 2, "War with China," pp. 14–19). Of course, one
understands how the attention of Russian intellectuals has focused on the
frightening neo-Stalin that is Maoism, but it is nonetheless deplorable that
this sometimes brings them to ignore the aggressive stance taken by the
Soviet Union toward China, sometimes even to entertain the illusion that
anti-Chinese spokesmen represent a liberal and progressive force, when in
fact they only prepare the ground for a military intervention similar in
principle to the one that violated Czechoslovak sovereignty. Thus, for
example, Zhores Medvedev speaks of Solzhenitsyn's efforts to gain the
support of Y. V. Andropov: "Andropov was then secretary of the Central
Committee, concerned with international affairs in the Socialist sector. He
was not directly concerned with literary matters, but intellectual circles
considered him as one of the most educated and progressive party figures.
Their assumption was based on the fact that Andropov had directed the
Soviet polemic with the Chinese leadership. Documents from this polemic
were published periodically in the Soviet press, and met with general ap-
proval. Statements issuing from the Central Committee in the course of
the dispute with China were imbued with the spirit of a struggle against the

On the Chinese side, they believe with some reason that Soviet imperialism is simply the successor to tsarist expansionism. *That* Russo-Chinese conflict is dictated by geopolitics and confirmed by the history of three centuries. China has given a spare and convincing version of it: in this domain the Chinese diplomatic communiqués, in complete contrast to their customary unreadable prose, have been prepared with incisive precision; arguments are supported not by quotations from the Maoist holy scriptures but on facts. Having historic truth and justice on their side, they have several times printed the Russian communiqués, side by side with their own refutations—an initiative the Russians have never dared to match.

Russians have had, and still have, excellent Sinologists, but this university elite, though well informed and fully appreciative of Chinese culture, has no political influence[12] and little access to present-day China. As for the Chinese-affairs "technicians," people like N., employed by the state to analyze the present situation in Peking, they are "specialized brutes"; apart from their linguistic competence, they have no humanist education at all, and one can well imagine that if they developed some cultural and human affinities with the Chinese world, they would risk their careers. Not only is it out of the question for them to love China; they are not even asked to understand it. They are supposed to give a "Sinological" justification to the dogmas and a priori thinking of their government, and nothing more is expected of them. Their observations are therefore much less interesting than they might be, because they must fit all their

---

abuses of the personality cult, against arbitrariness, lawlessness, and dogmatism." Zhores Medvedev, *Ten Years after Ivan Denisovich* (London and New York, 1973), p. 46.

12. Some are even persecuted, such as the Sinologist V. Rubin. His crime was to be Jewish and to have asked for a visa to go to Israel. He was stripped of his academic titles and dismissed from his job; as I write this, he has no means of livelihood and is threatened with prosecution.

1976 Post Scriptum: Thanks to the relentless pressure applied on Soviet authorities by Sinologists from all over the world, Rubin has finally been allowed to leave the U.S.S.R.

analyses into a strict ideological mold. It is only in the field of Sino-Soviet relations that what they say has at least reference value; as for Chinese internal politics, they are even less well informed than Western diplomats, since they have less freedom to travel and lack the incomparable listening post of Hong Kong.

On the Lin Piao affair, N. confirms that Lin Piao was not in the Trident that crashed in Mongolia and in which he was supposed to have met his death. The Russians analyzed the remains of the passengers, and they were well equipped to do so: Lin Piao had gone twice to the Soviet Union for extensive medical treatment (in 1939–42 and 1951–53) and they had his precise physical data (such as his dental chart). Of course, one can object that on this affair the testimony of a Soviet citizen is highly suspect, but it remains that the official Chinese version of Lin Piao's death is ludicrously improbable and does not stand up to the simplest analysis. Since it was not appropriate for the regime to admit that Lin Piao had been liquidated, Beria style, in some dark recess of Peking's corridors of power[13] (which could well, of course, have caused the subsequent panicked flight in the famous Trident by some of Lin Piao's relatives and subordinates), the responsible authorities made up this story of his attempted flight to the Soviet Union. Thus they killed two birds with one stone: they conjured away aspects of Maoist political customs that would be unappreciated by the civilized world, and, faithfully following the principle that the memory of a political enemy cannot be vilified enough, they gave Lin Piao the most ignoble and unforgivable end—that of a low traitor—thereby perhaps preventing any show of support or compassion for a man who, when all is said and done,. and as the world knows, served his party and his country heroically on a hundred battlefields. The same logic had been used before to turn Liu Shao-ch'i and Ch'en Po-ta into agents in the pay

13. According to recent and more credible rumors, it seems that he was assassinated in Peitaiho.

of the Kuomintang. But is this surprising? The great Stalinist tradition, which Maoism extols as the model to follow, had depicted Trotsky as a Nazi agent.[14]

I do not remember how it happened, but at one point in my talk with N., I found myself saying: "Well, whatever the ups and downs of present Chinese policy, we must all learn from the Chinese world: if we do not assimilate that great tradition, we cannot pretend to a true world humanism." I am completely convinced of this myself. Yet as I said it I knew there was some provocation in my declaration of faith: I wanted to see how N. would react.

What happened was more than I had hoped for. First he stared at me, incredulous, unbelieving, thinking I was joking. When he realized I was speaking seriously, he launched into a long and passionate harangue: "Do not think that you will ever understand the Chinese! Do not believe that you will ever get to know them! The Chinese are unknowable, the Chinese cannot be understood! You know what? I'll tell you: the fact of the matter is that they are basically immoral! They live for form, for appearance, for 'face,' and not on the level of conscience! The moral, individual, personal conscience, sir! [Deeply moved, he struck his breast, presumed seat of the spiritual faculty to which he was alluding.] Moral individual conscience is the treasure and unique legacy of our Western Christian civilization! I can tell you, sir, there is a thousand times more in common between an illiterate Siberian woodcutter and an American professor, between a French peasant and a Moscow academician, than is between any one of them and his Chinese counterpart! You and I have been nurtured by the same springs [his look became misty and vague]: Greece! Christendom!"

14. Still, it is staggering to see an author as cautious as Alain Peyrefitte swallow hook, line, and sinker the official account of Lin Piao's flight. I suppose that when such a tale is presented to you by Chou En-lai, the sweetest liar in the world, even a graduate from the Ecole Normale Supérieure takes leave of his critical senses. Alain Peyrefitte, *Quand la Chine s'éveillera, le monde tremblera* (Paris, 1974).

At this point—this was during lunch—only an unfortunate natural bashfulness stopped me from crowning him with the soup tureen. I even refrained—it would have been too easy—from asking him how Athenian democracy and the religion of Christ fared in his country. As for speaking about the family ties I happen to have with those poor, unknowable, pagan, and immoral people, I could not: it would have been obscene to allow this Muscovite hippopotamus any further entry into my private life.

We did not see each other again.

As far as we know, all *public* religious activity—Christian, Muslim, or Buddhist worship—has disappeared in China since the Cultural Revolution. Churches, mosques, monasteries, temples have everywhere been looted and then closed. Many have become factories, movie houses, meeting halls; others are simply locked and left derelict. As far as Catholic worship is concerned, one Peking church, the Nant'ang, has been reopened *for foreigners*: they can hear mass every Sunday at half-past nine. Two Chinese priests are in charge, but their workload must be light: except for that weekly mass the church is locked. When I asked one of the priests if it was possible to hear mass during the week, he answered that "Masses can always be arranged by appointment: one should apply at the Protocol Department in the Ministry of Foreign Affairs." Thus, this ministry that arranges all meetings between foreigners and Chinese officials is also competent to arrange their meetings with God. The same priest told me that there were other masses for Chinese parishioners, but that their timetable was indeterminate.[15]

The Sunday mass for foreigners is impeccably managed: liturgical ornaments, candles, Latin prayers, benedictions and

15. Since before the Cultural Revolution, it would appear, part of the faithful kept away from the churches that were open, considering the priests whose ministry had been approved by the government as renegades.

other devotions fallen in disuse in the West, the traditional celebration with the priests' backs to the faithful—everything seems organized to suit the nostalgia of the most die-hard traditionalist, bringing us back to our childhood when the Church in Europe, before *its* Cultural Revolution, did not yet speak of "liturgical renewal," "dialogue," and other "community conscientizations." Still, under this too-perfect mimicry of a quiet provincial parish fifty years ago—with paper flowers and painted plaster Sacred Hearts—there lurks something murky, something perhaps even rather horrible. The show was put on for the first time when an Italian minister, Colombo, visited Peking; I do not think the phenomenon should cause the faithful to rejoice.

At small expense—the candles and incense for Nan-t'ang Church—the Maoist government kills two birds with one stone: it increases the confusion of the Chinese Catholic community, and it blows on the embers of Vatican imaginings, which may well include raising the Papal Standard in the San-li-t'un diplomatic ghetto. After all, why not? Between the Greek colonels' embassy and the Chilean generals' there should be room for a Nuncio, especially if in exchange for this illusory advantage Rome agreed to abandon some of its presence and action (which are really effective) among the fourteen million Chinese on Taiwan.

We have scant information on the present state of the Chinese Catholic Church. Religion seems to have survived only at the family level and to have lost most of its structures. The priests who had the trust and confidence of the faithful have disappeared into labor camps. Those still functioning are suspect and shunned by the faithful. The part of the Church that works with the government has changed in a way that matches theoretically many of the stands taken by the most active part of the Western Church, but it is not followed by the elite of the faithful, who, since they know nothing of the evolution of Catholic theology, see only heresies supported for dubious reasons by the weakest among them—those who are afraid or who are tempted by some small bureaucratic job. In other words, the best of the Church in China may well be suffering and dying now to defend values that have been more or less discarded in Rome. What may happen to this headless Church could be what happened to the small communities of Japanese Catholics, which heroically survived centuries of persecution, in secret and in isolation and with heroic and petrified loyalty, clinging desperately to some remnants of doctrine which had become arbitrary and unintelligible. . . . This is of course only a hypothetical projection based on information which is as scanty as it is doubtful. Please God that my forecast may be wrong. "The worst is not always the most certain."

"The line of the masses."

A Western country was planning a big industrial exhibit in Peking. The Maoist authorities were most cooperative. They asked the organizer, "How many visitors would you like to have?"

"Eh?" asked the other, somewhat taken aback by the bluntness of the question.

"Twenty thousand? Forty thousand? Sixty thousand visitors?"

"We-ell, I think, I dunno, but sixty thousand would be nice. . . ."

His exhibit had precisely sixty thousand visitors.

The Maoist regime has acquired such skill in handling masses, and does it so routinely, that the operators themselves have become quite unconscious of the cynicism underlying their work. They see their job in quantitative, neutral terms and accomplish it with the same unfeeling efficiency as dockers handling bales of cotton.

The Peking common people, who as I have suggested are a noble and witty tribe, have suffered a fate similar to that of Hsiang-tzu the Camel in Lao She's masterpiece. Hsiang-tzu the Camel starts out as a rickshaw boy, a jolly and energetic fellow, but he is beset by misfortune; in the end, vanquished by fate, he abandons his human dignity and in the last chapter we see him completely debased, hired as a standard-bearer in one of those endless funeral processions at which rich Peking families once demonstrated the importance of their deceased—and swelled the ranks with beggars and tramps hired off street corners for the event. The kind of function that the common people fulfill now is of the same order, not at burials but at ceremonies welcoming the arrival of a foreign statesman whom the Maoist authorities wish to impress: the Prime Minister of Somalia, the President of Yemen, the Shah's Empress, Mrs. Bandaranaike, Mobutu Sese Seko, Trudeau, or some other clown from the same circus—the parade is endless. For each of them, the Peking authorities ration exactly the number of participants— a hundred thousand for this one, two hundred thousand for that one, a hundred and fifty thousand for the other—as well as the temperature of the "warm enthusiasm" that must be given. Some foreign critics have deplored the fact that China, a poor country, should waste so much on "public relations," but for Maoist bureaucrats this makes no sense: how much does it cost to put one or two hundred thousand people along the avenues? Here, people are still by far the cheapest commodity, the easiest to replace: they should not be hoarded.

These demonstrations follow an invariable and well-oiled routine. Early in the morning, workers decorate Ch'ang-an Avenue with big cardboard pilasters carrying welcoming messages with the name of the visitor. They tie flags and loudspeakers to lampposts; here and there, portable latrines are put up for the participants, who then begin to arrive by truck and on foot, in orderly columns. They take their appointed places. Colored skirts, scarves, and paper flowers have been issued to schoolgirls (they will give them back later, and they will be used again). Squatting on the pavement, the gigantic crowds wait—one hour, two hours, three hours—in a state of submissive apathy; some play cards. The loudspeakers pour lilting tunes out over the sullen mass. Suddenly, an order: everyone stands up, leaves the pavement in ordered sections, to take up positions in a double row in the middle of the avenue. As an ebb tide leaves crabs on a beach, so this mass movement leaves the plainclothes security agents isolated, now very conspicuous. They are standing at ease, one every twenty yards, hands behind their backs: their job is to make sure that no bona-fide stroller mixes in with the participants—and to keep on the move the few passers-by. Indeed, before and during the passage of the official convoy, it is *forbidden* not to keep moving. A whistle sounds: the crowd, tired and listless a moment before, starts shouting: "Welcome! Welcome!" (*"Je-lieh huan-ying!"*) The schoolgirls jump up and down, waving the scarves and paper flowers, while thirty limousines roar between the two rows and the foreign visitor has for his memory bank the unforgettable sight of a human sea stirred by a tornado of enthusiasm. When the official convoy has passed, another whistle blows; flowers and scarves are lowered, the girls stop jumping. Some short orders: the cohorts, silent again, leave at the command of their leaders. Despite the faultless organization, the crowds are so huge that it takes an hour or two before the avenue can again be used by ordinary traffic.

Thus, once or twice a month, the "creative spontaneity" of the masses finds a chance "to express itself" in "support of the revolutionary diplomacy of Chairman Mao."

People.

The leaders of China manipulate the people cynically, but the people are still the country's only capital. If, despite all the stupid cruelties of politics, China still remains faithful to itself—subtle, human, so supremely civilized—it is due to them. They—the ordinary, the lowly, the anonymous—maintain China, despite the bureaucrats, and allow us not to despair for the future. They have buried twenty dynasties, they will also bury this one. They have not changed. As usual, they are patient; they are not in a hurry: they know so much more than those who rule over them!

The bureaucrats fear them; they understand vaguely that at the end of the play, the people pass judgment on them. Bureaucrats see the people as possible judges and accusers, and this is why they try by all means to build watertight walls between them and us, to dig bottomless ditches, to cut all channels of communication, to forbid any kind of normal human relations. Nevertheless, despite all this and to the bureaucrats' intense disquiet, we still manage—by chance, of course, and stealth—to exchange signs of understanding. Those fleeting moments are precious, for they carry such a load of friendship. But they are also terribly melancholy, reminding us that life, perhaps, could be *different*.

In front of witnesses, Chinese people will usually speak of their happiness in terms borrowed straight from *China Reconstructs*. But in private, it happens that they will confess their sorrows in their own words. V. was an old Asian diplomat whom I saw often. He was leaving Peking after four years, and he wanted to give a little present to his Chinese cook; the cook, whom I had seen every time I visited V., was a man of about forty—competent and devoted, but taciturn and moody. At the beginning, V., who was a nonconformist and who spoke Chinese well, had proposed that instead of eating separately, one in the dining room, one in the kitchen, they should eat together, but this had thrown the cook into such a tremendous nervous fret that V. had given it up. Despite his silence and his nerves, the cook was friendly and very able; a year before, V. had tried to show his gratitude by bringing him a present from abroad, but the cook had not dared to accept it. This time, for a farewell gift he carefully chose an object made in China, which could be accepted more easily. It was a good Chinese fountain pen, and the cook accepted it in his usual laconic way. But on the last evening, some time before saying good-by, the cook came in without being called and sat down at the table where V. was finishing dinner. He seemed to be agitated. Suddenly the dike broke, and the words poured out.

"They have taken my pen! They have taken my pen!" This had been the last straw. "They" were the bureaucrats from the Ministry of Foreign Affairs who were his real and permanent employers. One must grasp the basic fact that personal employees of foreigners in China cannot be hired by their employers: they must be provided by the ministry, and *it is to the ministry that foreigners pay the wages of their servants.* This was another of the cook's grievances against his superiors: from the salary of 120 ¥ which V. paid each month to the Services Department, the latter gave him only 40 ¥—barely enough to feed his wife and six children, who lived in a village forty miles away. He would have liked to have his family with him, but they were forbidden to come to try and find work in town. He could go and visit them only once a month and because he made the trip by bicycle, he could only spend one night with them.[16] The rest of the time he lived in the Services Department dormitory. He had been a farmer, but the authorities had decided to make a cook of him and had given him his present posting. He did not know what his next job would be and did not care, since he felt powerless to change his destiny. His life was devoid of distractions: why go to the movies when it was always the same old program which everyone knows by heart? The only pleasure he had left was tobacco, and he smoked cigarettes with the passion of an addict; for him, as for many others, it was the only diversion in an unvarying daily grind—for to his regular working hours were added endless political-study lessons and education meetings.

In what he said now a very simple image of society recurred, a kind of basic counterpoint to all his observations: society was divided into two groups, "we," and "they," and "they"

16. In fact, he was among the better off: there are workers and employees who can go and see their wives and children only when they get their annual holiday—once *a year.* This is not uncommon in the People's Republic.

were the cadres, party people, and the authorities. His feelings about the party emerged with a naïve freshness in the practical advice he gave about his own embassy: "Watch out for W. and L. They are party men. But M. is a good fellow: *he is not in the party.*"

V. listened, astounded. He had lived for four years in daily commerce with this man, probably the only citizen of the People's Republic with whom he had some intimacy and with whom he felt a real bond of friendship. And here, suddenly, he was seeing this man's *real life*. Without the confiscation of the pen, the cook would have kept his reserve to the last, and V. would have left China without really knowing anything about the one Chinese with whom he could reasonably claim to be acquainted! When they parted, V. asked the cook again: "May I do anything for you? May I write to the ministry to commend your work on the job?"

"No, please don't do that!" he answered. "Before the Cultural Revolution, it could have been useful: now it might bring me problems."

Of course, it is impossible to generalize from one individual case. It is not my intention to let my view of eight hundred million people be colored by what may have been simply the black mood of a single depressed individual. But in his unsophisticated way, V.'s cook had grasped a fundamental intuition about the irreducible antagonism between the workers and the authorities, the former being entirely at the mercy of the latter's exploitation. This is the fruit of a collective experience, and the intuition is expressed with varying degrees of clarity but generally throughout China, in the rich mass of songs, stories, sayings, and proverbs which (especially among the peasants) lampoon the cadres, denounce their privileges, and express the long complaint of the oppressed. The regime is quite aware of the not-so-latent discontent, and tries to fight the menace: its main weapon is the great hoax of the "class struggle," leitmotiv of official propaganda.

In place of the *real* class struggle in China—which in fact

opposes those who are led to leaders, masses to bureaucracy—
party propaganda has substituted a fictive struggle between the
so-called "proletariat" and the so-called "bourgeoisie." "Proletariat" has been redefined to encompass the top as well as the base,
the masses as well as the people, and thus conjures away the
real conflict between oppressors and oppressed. As for the "bourgeoisie," this mythical scarecrow at whom the masses are periodically invited to vent their anger and frustration—in a way that
leaves intact the powers and privileges of their true exploiters
—the "bourgeoisie" is actually comprised of disgraced bureaucrats. The ruling class is torn in a perpetual merciless power
struggle; the winning group always gives the unlucky losers a
"bourgeois-capitalist" label and then abandons them to popular
fury. Thus are two birds killed with one stone: the winners get
rid of its rivals, and popular discontent is allowed to vent itself
safely.

The oppression and exploitation of the Chinese masses is
too real, too deeply felt and universally experienced for the
regime to claim that it does not exist. So the masses are encouraged, *up to a point*, to expose their grievances from time to
time. However, the identification of guilty parties remains the
exclusive preserve of the authorities. And since the struggle for
power goes on endlessly without truce, there is no chance of
running out of scapegoats: yesterday Liu Shao-ch'i and his clique,
today Lin Piao and his lieutenants, tomorrow somebody else.
Since all these targets are members of the ruling class, the masses
recognize readily that they are true oppressors, and lose no time
in vigorously denouncing them. But at this point the authorities
must very carefully guide and control the popular anger and
prevent it from fulfilling its logical development, which would be
to denounce the oppressors *as members of the ruling clique and
the group in power*, because this would mean an accusation not
against individuals but against the bureaucratic class as a whole,
bringing into question the basic principle of the system and
showing for all to see the true nature of the "class struggle"

within the regime. To prevent this danger, the propaganda system must forge a criminal identity so fantastic that it will be impossible to confuse disgraced bureaucrats with their colleagues in power. Thus they become spies in the pay of the U.S.A., Kuomintang agents, spies of the Soviet Union, traitors to their country, minions of feudalism, conspirers for a bourgeois-capitalistic restoration. In short, you stick a false nose on Liu Shao-ch'i so that nobody notices how much he looks like Mao Tse-tung.

The "class struggle" as understood in the Maoist system—that is, the denunciation by the masses of guilty parties who have been singled out for them by the powers that be—is the regime's safety valve, its basic hygiene, a periodic bloodletting that allows it to eliminate the toxins in its organism. For the masses, this ritual exercise gives a very convincing appearance of reality. The violence and the blood that always flows in these operations, the high positions and broad powers that had once been the preserve of the bureaucrats now found guilty—all this seems to show that a true revolution is occurring. In fact, the double cross is perfect, for the essence of the bureaucratic system is the interchangeability of bureaucrats, and no mere change of personnel could alter the nature of the regime. After a while, when the masses realize that "while the bottle may be different, it holds the same purgative,"[17] the people in power have only to throw to the wolves another cartful of "bourgeois," found guilty of a new capitalist "restoration." The great advantage of the "bourgeois" created by the regime over the authentic kind is that while the latter variety is practically extinct in China, the supply of the first exactly matches the demand.

That it should be possible to "fool all of the people all of the time" will be a surprise only for those who do not know the real nature of the totalitarian phenomenon. For a long time it was the fashion for a certain liberal intelligentsia, sympathetic to

17. Sometimes the regime does not even bother to change the bottle, and restores in their former positions the selfsame people who were previously unmasked as "agents of the bourgeois restoration."

Maoism (I myself had such an attitude in the beginning), to quote, apropos of the People's Republic, Dr. Johnson's famous adage, "If the abuse be enormous, nature will rise up and, claiming her original rights, overturn a corrupt political system." But how can this thought of an eighteenth-century man, who in the realm of political corrupt practices knew merely the excesses of absolutist regimes, be applied to that singular twentieth-century phenomenon the totalitarian state, which has no precedent in history?

The future prospects of the Supreme Leader and his heirs remain excellent.[18] Anyone who doubts this should ponder the observation of Albert Speer—an expert on such matters, who after the event very lucidly analyzed his experiences—that during the last war, at the moment when Germany was sinking into its Götterdämmerung, if it had been possible to organize a free referendum among the German population a comfortable majority would have been found in support of Hitler. The Stalinist experience is no less instructive: the last thing that the Soviet masses will forgive Khrushchev is the fact that he tried to topple Stalin from his pedestal. The attempts against the Führer's life, the attempts at de-Stalinization, were all enterprises undertaken by minorities who lacked popular support.

In China, the position of the Supreme Leader is strengthened still further by the consensus among all rival factions to support him while they fight to the death between themselves: Mao is less arbiter of power than its prize or its security. Liu Shao-ch'i protested, to the last breath of his political life, his unswerving loyalty to Mao Tse-tung. As for Lin Piao, even if he really did plot against his master (which remains to be proven), even if he had usurped power, we may be sure that he would have called Mao to witness as warmly as any of his foes do now. The Supreme Leader has come to take the place that was occupied by the emperor in the *ancien régime*: he is the axis around

18. Since the Peking demonstration of 5 April 1976, I am not so sure of this.

which the whole political structure revolves. Take this keystone away, and the whole structure crashes down. To touch it, one needs the courage of a Samson willing to pull the temple down on his own head. It is remarkable that even in the paroxysms of the Cultural Revolution, the groups that went furthest and were most virulent and radical in their rebellion against the bureaucratic order did not dare or knew not how to take that last step, which was *to denounce Mao*. This incapacity to pursue their revolt to its logical conclusion sealed the failure of their efforts.[19]

Are the people happy?

The question is simplistic, but after having come back from China you are asked it all the time. The answer will vary, obviously, according to the prejudices and the subjectivity of the speaker. In any case, observations will usually be concerned more with the genius of a nation, the traditional constants of its psychology, than with the special and temporary effects of this or that political regime.

Some people are naturally morose, and remain so even when they have all the advantages—political, social, and economic. But the Chinese are certainly not such a people. The Chinese faculty of intensely enjoying everything that is available is well expressed in their gastronomy, and everyone knows that the Chinese cuisine is delicious. What many people do not realize is that it is a poor people's food, famine-cooking, and that its infinite inventive resources were stimulated by the need to use

19. At the popular level, at the peasant level, it is significant that in the songs, sayings, proverbs, and stories against bureaucrats, lampoons on Mao are exceptional. The few examples I encountered were almost all expressed in spectacularly obscene language—which in China is certainly not the natural habit of popular speech. The satisfaction of using obscenity here corresponds psychologically to the feeling of sacred awe that grips the profaning individual when he is about to commit sacrilege or break a capital taboo.

everything, to waste nothing, to salvage the most miserable, least appetizing ingredients which richer nations would reject as waste, and turn them into appetizing food. Fish heads, duck's feet, cow and pig stomachs, snakes, offal, tendons and nerves, dog meat and cat meat become prized delicacies. Thus do the Chinese manage to enrich all the events of life, even the most irksome and most barren, and make something savory out of them. This faculty of organizing small islands of happiness, even in seas of the direst hardship, has always roused the wondering admiration of foreign observers. Bertrand Russell, who visited China in 1920, noted this feature and earned a stinging retort from Lu Hsün. About an excursion near the Western Lake, in Hangchow, Russell had written: "I remember one hot day when a party of us were crossing the hills in chairs—the way was rough and very steep, the work for the coolies very severe. At the highest point of our journey, we stopped for ten minutes to let the men rest. Instantly they all sat in a row, brought out their pipes, and began to laugh among themselves as if they had not a care in the world."[20]

To this Lu Hsün replied tartly, and his answer, like everything he wrote, is singularly apt today: "As for Russell, who praises the Chinese after seeing smiling porters at the Western Lake, I do not know exactly what he is driving at. I do know one thing: if the porters had been able not to smile at those whom they had carried, China would have long since been out of its present rut."[21]

Interpreter-guides from the Chinese travel agency are hybrids: halfway between the common people and the officials, they are half-human, half-bureaucrat. Depending on which ele-

20. Bertrand Russell, *The Problem of China* (London, 1926), pp. 200–201.

21. *Lu Hsün ch'üan-chi* (Peking, 1963), I, 316.

ment is dominant, they can be pleasant and instructive company, or they can poison your existence.

Every time that the Peking loneliness weighed too heavily I would take a little trip into the country, in the hope (sometimes fulfilled) of meeting some people and talking a bit. Like all foreigners, in each town the first person I met was invariably the guide from the travel agency who would come to meet me at the airport or train station. During the short taxi ride to the hotel, I had to find out what kind of fellow I was dealing with: a human being with whom pleasant relations would be possible, or a lout to be avoided. It is not always easy in Maoist China to get rid of your keeper, but if you want to do it, *you must do so at once*, before becoming inextricably tangled in a net of various moral obligations: visits to child-care centers, steel mills, sock factories, and agricultural exhibits.

After a while, I developed some simple, quick tests that allowed me to determine quite accurately what kind of person I was dealing with. Since this may have a practical interest for other visitors, I offer my system here (countless variants, equally efficient, may no doubt be devised). You bring the talk around to the harmless and innocent subject of Chinese geography, and ask your guide where he comes from, for example. Then you ask the trap-question: "In your job, you must travel quite a bit. Of all the places you have seen, which do you like best? Where would you most like to live?" Nine times out of ten, the answer is along the lines of, "The place I like best is where I can be most useful to my Country and where I can best Serve the People. Where the Party and the Country send me, there I want to live." In this case, the chances are high that your depraved nature is unworthy of such virtuous company, and the best thing to do, once you get to the hotel, is courteously but firmly to get rid of your guide for the duration of your stay. If, on the other hand (this happens only rarely), you get a daring individualistic answer like, "Well, I would like Tsingtao because the climate is so pleasant there," or, "I like to live in Yangchow because my wife and children live there and I could see them more often," it is a safe bet that your guide is a powerful, original, and independent personality and that you will profit by his further acquaintance.

Since the beginning of this century, the places in China where new ideas start fermenting and revolutionary insurrections begin have been Canton, Shanghai, and Wuhan. After twenty years of Maoism, it was seen during the Cultural Revolution that those three cities had lost none of their revolutionary potential. In them, sooner or later, the Chinese revolution will take fire again.

Again, the "line of the masses": "Cadres and soldiers have always found very difficult to criticize anything that was not first formally denounced by the Party Committee members and the Political Commissars." This candid confession was noted in a broadcast from Radio Heilungkiang, October 27, 1972.

The sight of Chiang Ch'ing reminds one of what one of Koestler's characters says: "One can see what is wrong with the left-wing movement by the ugliness of their women." An ugliness still more significant because it was not natural to her (as photographs taken in the earlier period when she was an actress in Shanghai attest): an acquired, deliberate ugliness, which becomes in some way shrill.

Chou En-lai.
Every time he appears, his fascinating and enigmatic personality reminds me of the King of Ch'i's fighting cock, in Chuang tzu (Chapter xix, 8):

Chi Hsing-tzu was training a fighting-cock for the king.

After ten days the king asked: "Is the cock ready?"

"Not yet," says the trainer. "It is still full of fire and arrogance."

Ten days later the king comes to enquire again.

"It is still not ready. The sight of its rivals still excites it."

Ten days later the same answer: "It has not yet rid itself of its angry stares and excessive ardor."

Ten days later the trainer at last announces: "Now we are ready! The crowing of the other cocks leaves it impassive. Before its foes, it is as if made of wood. Its inner strength is such that its opponents dare not defy it. They take one look and run away."

This is, of course, not the place to analyze Chou's political genius, but I would just like to mention one aspect of his personality that has not been noted by observers: his good taste. Chou is the only member of China's ruling clique who has never taken advantage of his position to have his poems published.[22] Think about it: it shows uncommon strength of character.

Of course the Maoist bureaucracy has a number of brilliant, witty men. Unfortunately, to have the right to be themselves, they must have reached at least the rank of vice-minister. At the level on which Kissinger meets people when he goes to Peking, the quality of political discourse must be dazzling, in complete contrast to the wooden jargon served up by the cardboard characters at lower levels in the hierarchy. But to what degree does the excitement that foreign politicians experience in China reflect a truth about the People's Republic? In the scales of China's destiny, which weighs heavier: the visionary wisdom of a few men at the top or the sterilizing stupidity of a bureaucratic *apparat* that is dull, dogmatic, mediocre, arrogant, neurotic,

22. I trust that the single inconspicuous piece that appeared in the anthology *Shih hsuan* (Peking, 1957) is an isolated accident, not enough to spoil an otherwise impeccable record.

frozen in conformism, terrified of initiative, and unable to transmit to the base the visions of the summit without disfiguring them? The stupidity of middle and lower bureaucrats is obviously not peculiar to the Chinese, but in China as in the other so-called "socialist" countries, the tragedy is that they hold extraordinary power over the people they administer; their stupidity has a vast and murderous potential out of all proportion to what their counterparts in other countries could even dream of. This leaden mantle of the middle and lower cadres weighs upon the shoulders of the people, crushes their creative genius, stifles their traditional qualities of initiative and inventiveness. It is one of the gravest problems of the regime.

Exoticism is not dead. At the turn of the century, during his dreamy Asiatic dilly-dallying, Pierre Loti was entranced by the sight of pale blobs, exquisitely fringed with purple, in the dark arch of a yamen; they turned out to be a string of cut-off human hands; the little girls, or boys, whom he bought here and there to while away the spleen of an Oriental night amused him with their chatter of lovebirds and their painted faces reminiscent of dwarfs painted on folding screens. Today, if we are to believe a recent article in *Le Monde*, the aesthetes of *Tel Quel* seem to have found again in China the exquisite secrets of Madame Chrysanthème's patron. We know that the campaign against Confucius and Lin Piao has already caused blood to flow: a friend, an English Sinologist returning from Nanking, told me he saw the names of the first batch of people executed in this campaign posted on the walls there, and similar reports have reached us from Canton and Wuhan, while in Peking wall posters told of massacres in Kiangsi. But Roland Barthes, confronted with such posters, would no doubt see only calligraphy "with a grand lyrical movement, elegant, willowy," and the enigma of those graceful hieroglyphics would not bother him much—now that he has discovered how ridiculous we are "when we think that our intellectual task is always to try to find a meaning." Also for him, the very name of the purge taking place under cover of an anti-Confucian campaign, "in Chinese, Pilin-Pikong,[23] tinkles like a happy bell, and the campaign expresses itself in newly invented games: a cartoon, a poem, a skit by children, during which suddenly, between two dances, a little girl, all made-up, strikes down the ghost of Lin Piao; the political Text (but only that) causes these tiny 'happenings.' "[24] Lu Hsün made the point: "Our much vaunted Chinese civilization is nothing but a banquet of human flesh prepared for the rich and the powerful, and China is merely the kitchen where that meal is cooked up. Those who praise us can be excused only in as much as they do not know what they are talking about, such as these foreigners whose high status and comfortable life has rendered them absolutely blind and obtuse."

Central to the crisis of modern China is the question of how to face the outside world. The faction which we may call conservative, idealist, reactionary, integrist, xenophobic, obscurantist—yesterday the Manchu aristocracy, the Empress Tz'u-hsi, the Boxers; today the Maoist extremists—advocates sealing up the empire and avoiding all foreign contacts, ignoring the very existence of the outside world, so as to keep its vision of Chinese order pure, intact, and unchanging. The faction we may call realist, cultured, liberal, progressive—yesterday the reformist intellectuals; today the pragmatic technocrats around Chou En-lai—proposes, on the contrary, to insure China's survival in the modern world, to learn from the latter and at least to borrow its weapons. For them, the famous slogan of Chang Chih-tung (1837–1909), "to put Western technology in the service of

23. This movement is so vast and complex in its overt manifestations, and even more in its covert developments, that I cannot adequately deal with it here; see my article "The Grandmaster's Checkmate," in *Far Eastern Economic Review*, January 1975.

24. Roland Barthes, "Alors, la Chine," in *Le Monde*, 24 May 1974.

Chinese genius,"[25] is still relevant. But the conservatives object as pertinently as they did a century ago that it is impossible to divorce substance and function: if the Western function is adopted, the Chinese substance will be inevitably and irremediably affected.

But when they refuse to face the reality of the external world, the integrists deprive China of its rightful place on the modern scene. Worse, they expose it once again to the danger of becoming a helpless victim of imperialist aggression. When this last becomes too threatening a possibility, the reformists are called to the helm, but they soon overshoot the mark and foreign technology begins to corrode the substance of Chinese national ideology, shaking the empire to its foundations, justifying the worst fears of the conservatives, under whose pressure all open doors are now slammed shut.

This dramatic debate will not quickly end.

Why Maoism? What makes such a phenomenon possible? A text of Lu Hsün—one of his most despairing pages—gives a possible answer to this haunting question.

... It has never been granted to the Chinese people that they are human beings; at best, they have been raised to the level of slaves, and this is still the case today. In the past, they were often lower than slaves. The Chinese masses are neutral; in time of war they do not know what faction they belong to, and in fact they belong to any faction. Come the rebels: considering the people as being the government's, they loot and murder. Comes the regular army: instead of recognizing its own, it loots and murders too, as if the people belonged to the rebels. At this point, the only wish of the population is to find a Master, a Master who would deign to accept them as his people—no, not even that—who would deign

25. I translate freely the famous "*chung hsüeh wei t'i, hsi hsüeh wei yung.*" A more literal translation would be, "Take Chinese culture as basis and Western culture as instrument." Or, "Chinese culture as substance, Western culture as function."

to accept them as his cattle. The people would be ready to eat grass if necessary; all they ask is that the Master point out in what direction they must trot.

As long as someone is willing to make decisions for them, they will extol all the enslaving regulations imposed on them as "infinite imperial favor. . . ."

. . . As a rule, after each period of anarchy, when chaos reaches its climax, some personality appears—more powerful, more clever, more cunning (sometimes a foreigner)—to unify the empire and grant it some measure of order. He gives laws, edicts, regulations: how to raise a labor force, how to pay taxes, how to prostrate oneself before him, how to sing his praises. And since these laws do not change, everyone is happy and the empire is again at peace.

. . . In the end, the simplest and most adequate way of describing the history of China would be to distinguish between two types of periods: (1) the periods when the people wish in vain to enjoy a stable slave condition; and (2) the periods when the people manage to enjoy a stable slave condition. The alternation of these two states is what our old scholars called "the cycle of chaos and order."[26]

Western ideologues now use Maoist China just as the eighteenth-century philosophers used Confucian China: as a myth, an abstract ideal projection, a utopia which allows them to denounce everything that is bad in the West without taking the trouble to think for themselves. We stifle in the miasma of industrial civilization, our cities rot, our roads are blocked by the insane proliferation of cars, et cetera. So they hurry to celebrate the People's Republic, where pollution, delinquency, and traffic problems are nonexistent. One might as well praise an amputee because his feet aren't dirty.

This starry-eyed admiration for all that is done, or not done, in China, with no effort at critical scrutiny—is it really the best service one can render a despotism that already has too much of a propensity to believe in its own infallibility ("Long live the great, glorious and always infallible Chinese Communist

26. *"Teng-hsia man-pi"* (*"Random Thoughts under the Lamp"*), in *Lu Hsün ch'üan-chi,* I, 311–12.

Party!")? Would it not be more useful to call: "Stop! Watch out!" when one sees China rushing headlong into deadends that the West, to its cost, has already explored? If China is still relatively free of pollution and traffic problems, it is not for lack of trying. It does not yet have the industrial means to poison the urban air as efficiently as we do, but it is certainly going in that direction, choosing ancient cities, filled with art, and historical landmarks as sites for industries that could have worked just as well—and probably better—elsewhere. Thus, southeastern Peking is already polluted by a steel complex. And in Soochow, the guides proudly repeat this cliché to visitors: "The countless pagodas of our city have given way to a forest of smokestacks!" The Maoist government, made up of old men with a nineteenth-century psychology in such matters, would be ashamed of its backwardness if it did not manage to pollute *at least* two or three of China's most venerable cultural metropolises. Western capitals, under the stupid and inhuman pressure of a motor traffic we are unable (or unwilling) to control, have destroyed their beauty to widen their streets and make parking space. They did better in Peking: whole neighborhoods were razed to make vast macadam wastes that in the future will furnish the arena for automotive madness. Right now, the emptiness is dotted with bicycles and donkey carts—making the destruction more odious still, since it was pointless.

The Maoist fashions that prevail in the West today in some intellectual circles are remarkably similar in their dynamic to the passion for all *chinoiserie* in the eighteenth century. It is a new exoticism based, like the earlier ones, on ignorance and imagination. With the best intention in the world it shows, unconsciously, an immense contempt for the Chinese, for their humanity, their real life, their language, their culture, their past and their present. As in the eighteenth century China is far away; this very distance, which allowed Boucher to paint fancy mandarins for the adornment of Paris drawing rooms, now allows philosophers to give Maoism whatever shape they fancy. Examples can be found by the hundred, and I take one at random —in today's paper: ". . . Sartre himself acknowledges that Marxism is not scientific—it was the Russians' mistake to believe that it was, and *to the credit of the Chinese that they questioned it.*"27 I would like to be shown *even one* Chinese text where this healthy doubt is expressed. In return, I could easily dump on the head of the fellow who wrote such nonsense several garbage-truckfuls of Chinese prose—the writings of the Great Teacher Himself, to start with, where it is insisted, page after page, that Marxism has all the virtues of a science. With the same quiet and assured contempt for obvious facts, various pilgrims try to make the West believe that Maoist China has veered somewhat from Stalinism. Obviously their enthusiasm for Mao does not go so far as reading his works,28 while their ignorance of Chinese excuses them from seeing to what use the thoughts of Stalin are put (*often on the same level of importance as those of Mao Tse-tung himself*) in Peking's ideological publications. One may

27. B. Poirot-Delpech, in *Le Monde*, 24 May 1974.
28. Where they may come on passages such as this one:

Wishing the best to Stalin is not a formal custom or convention; by sending him our best wishes, we tell him that we support him, that we support his enterprises, that we support the victory of socialism, that we support the direction he points out to all mankind, that we support him as our intimate friend. Most of mankind around the globe is suffering; only by following the way shown by Stalin, by accepting the help of Stalin, can mankind free itself from suffering. . . . Stalin is the tried and true friend of the Liberation of the Chinese people; the respectful love the Chinese people feel for Stalin, the friendship they feel for the Soviet Union, are totally sincere, and anyone who would try to create misunderstandings about this would be wasting his time and his work." (*Mao Tse-tung hsüan-chi* [Peking, 1958], II, 651–52.)

The final Maoist verdict on Stalin was given in a well-known joint article in the *People's Daily* and *Red Flag*, "On the Question of Stalin" ("Kuan-yü Ssu-ta-lin wen-t'i," 3 October 1963), which concluded: "Stalin's achievements are considerable, his errors are venial. . . . Stalin's whole life was the life of a great Marxist-Leninist, a great proletarian revolutionary. . . . Stalin's writings are immortal Marxist-Leninist works, and make an everlasting contribution to the international communist movement."

excuse them from not measuring the yardage that the Chinese translation of Stalin's *Complete Works* takes up in the bookstores, and such like. But it is hard to understand how their political myopia has kept them from seeing those thousands of portraits of Stalin that grace all of China's government buildings, including the famous monster effigy that adorns the west angle of T'ien-an men in Peking! In fact I see no country (North Korea possibly excepted) that can pride itself more than China on its faithfulness to the letter as well as the spirit of Stalinism. The Peking mandarins show a rather touching steadfastness in still honoring the Little Father of the peoples, when one thinks of all the dirty tricks he played on them when he was alive!

But why go on in this vein? As Schiller said: "*Mit der Dummheit kämpfen Götter selbst vergebens....*"

Professor C. is Chinese; he left his country some twenty-five years ago to pursue a brilliant academic career in the West. I met him again by chance in Peking, where he was making a short visit. During our conversation, we got to talking about the attitude of Overseas Chinese intellectuals toward Maoist power. Many of them had expressed their hostility to the Peking regime as long as its future was in doubt; they fell silent when it consolidated its power; and, finally, after Nixon's visit, they started to form a rather impressive choir singing the praises of Maoism. Professor C. took up their defense with a warmth that suggested a certain degree of self-justification, but his argument was not devoid of interest, and here it is in rough outline:

In the West, political power and ideological authority do not always coincide. In their allegiance to the temporal authorities and to the church, for example, individuals may be torn between contradictory demands; in these conflicts individual conscience in the end has to decide. Since the beginning of modern history—the end of the Middle Ages—Europe has had a plurality of political systems and religious confessions; rebels and heretics, when hunted in one state, could take refuge in the next, and go on according to their convictions. These factors have permitted and fostered liberal ideals and individualism among intellectuals. In China, on the contrary, since the first imperial unification under the Ch'in, twenty-two hundred years ago, the political, ideological, and cultural worlds have always coincided, and they make up a monolithic whole. Beyond that whole, there was no alternative for the individual conscience: to reject the "orthodoxy in power" (cheng-t'ung) meant not only to exclude oneself from society, but also to turn one's back on civilization, to reject the human condition. To adopt that course, one had to be ready to live alone in forests or deserts, with wild beasts as one's companions. Dynasties followed upon each other, but the orthodoxy remained: it was from that permanence that each dynasty drew its legitimacy. The only periods when China was without an orthodoxy were the dangerous, chaotic gaps that might occur between two dynasties, when the country sank into lawlessness and violence, until from the turmoil a power emerged that restored the neglected orthodoxy and became the nucleus around which the empire could be made whole again. Chinese scholars are conditioned by two thousand years of history not only to support the ruling orthodoxy, sole barrier against the injustice of lawlessness and disorder, but also to watch for its coming, to welcome it and rejoice in its accession after the darkness of each interregnum.

Anyone who criticized Hitler was immediately accused by his supporters of being anti-German. To attack Mussolini was to show your hatred of Italy. And one had to hate Russia, of course, to resist the charisma of that genius Stalin. This confusionism is typically fascist, and it is practiced actively by Maoists today. According to them, to attack Mao is to attack China and the Chinese people; inversely, a true love of China cannot be shown except through the worship of Mao. The aim is obviously to ward off the dangerous idea that it is precisely a love of China that could and should inspire a critical review of Maoism.

The trick is not new. Those who are called "China-haters" today should not worry too much, for they are in good company. Their dean is Lu Hsün, who in his time was called exactly that by Kuomintang-paid hacks. For them, the attacks of this great patriot and brave man against the Nanking government were "treasonable acts against the country," while his essays on politics and ethics as well as his fiction (especially *Ah Q*) expressed "a visceral hatred of the Chinese people."[29]

It is really very difficult in China to do something new: history has a precedent for everything. Even the queerest excesses of Maoism do not escape this rule, as the precedent of Chu Yuan-chang shows. Chu Yuan-chang, the founder of the Ming dynasty, was a talented statesman, but he was also a brutal tyrant who terrorized the intellectual life of the entire country. He had an abiding hatred for Confucianism, especially its more democratic brand as represented by Mencius (Mencius vindicated tyrannicide and put the interest of the people above that of the ruler). Not only did he want to have the philosopher's effigy in the great temple of Confucius destroyed but he had more than a hundred passages of Mencius censored. At the same time, he fancied himself a political philosopher. His works reveal a self-made man—an odd mixture of trite sayings, clichés, truisms, with here and there a dazzling, sharp, original remark. His principal thoughts were condensed in a digest called *Ming ta kao* (*Great Ming Edict*), and its reading was compulsory for all subjects of the empire: each family had to have a copy. Since (the fourteenth century) the Chinese population was then around

29. One can find a very good sample of these insults in Su Hsüeh-lin's *Wo lun Lu Hsün* (Taipei, 1971), a book whose announced purpose is to expose the "Sinophobia" of Lu Hsün!

eighty million, the *Ming ta kao* remained for a long time one of the most wdely distributed books in the world.[30]

This enormous distribution did not prevent its almost complete disappearance. Today the *Ming ta kao* is a very rare curiosity, eagerly sought by bibliophiles. The first edition of the *Little Red Book*—that is, the one with a foreword by Lin Piao —has reached the same level only a few years after being published.

Other precedents are offered by more recent history. The Red Guards and the ideology of the Cultural Revolution were strangely prefigured by the Fascist movement of the Blue Shirts that developed in Kuomintang China during the 1930s.[31] The Blue Shirts were a paramilitary movement which demanded of its members that they place above everything else their personal and unconditional allegiance to the Supreme Leader. In cultural matters, the movement flaunted its contempt for the humanities and for traditional education, which maintained and spread the habits and prejudices of a decadent, parasitic elite. They advocated that in schools the students, instead of "wasting their time over dead books trying to become bureaucrats," should engage in directly productive work: a quarter of their time should be given to agricultural and other manual work. Before graduating from high school or the university, all students should be compelled to work for a year in farms, factories, or shops. Engineering students should spend half their day in factory work in order to overcome the traditional contempt which they, as

30. Since then, of course, the *Little Red Book* has beaten all the records: according to a dispatch by the New China News Agency of January 1969, 740 million copies have been printed, including the translations in foreign languages. However, the ideal achieved by Chu Yuan-chang, to have a copy of his *Thoughts* in *every* home in the country, has been matched 100 per cent for Mao only in one prefecture of Tsinghai province.

On this parallel between Chu and Mao, see the interview granted a few years ago by the brilliant scholar Yu Ying-shih to *Ming Pao Monthly*, April 1974.

31. See L. E. Eastman, "Fascism in Kuomintang China: The Blue Shirts," in *China Quarterly*, January–March 1972.

intellectuals, had for manual labor, and in order for themselves to become productive citizens.[32] The Blue Shirts had a very radical economic program and advocated agrarian collectivization. Xenophobes and anti-imperialists, they were the spearhead of the fight against the Japanese, murdering collaborators, and so forth. (Because of this, the Japanese paid special attention to that movement, and a large part of the presently available sources on the Blue Shirts, apart from their own publications, is comprised of secret reports of the Japanese intelligence services.) The movement fought against the "pernicious influence of the West," root of the moral and cultural bankruptcy of modern China, and groups of commandos raided movie houses and dancing halls, pouring acid on patrons dressed in Western clothes. The Blue Shirts hated liberalism and its "corrupting license," believing that "individualism" and "cosmopolitan dissipation" must be eliminated, by violence if necessary. The movement *praised Ch'in Shih-huang*, who had burned books and killed scholars for the good of the country, and it declared unceasing war against corrupt bureaucrats. As was written in a lead article in one of their periodicals (*She-hui hsin-wen* [*Social News*]): "The only way to get rid of the bureaucratic organization is to create a mass-violence organization, taking the people as its supreme principle."

The case of Chu Yuan-chang brings us back to two fundamental questions that were touched on above: the isolation of China and the phenomenon of its monolithic orthodoxy.

Professor C.'s argument about this one-way orthodoxy needs some modulations. It is true that the Chinese universe has always appeared as an organic whole, but it is only since the Ming that this civilization of the organic whole became totalitarian. Under

32. See Yü Wen-wei, "What Kind of Education the Chinese Nation Needs Today" (*"Chung-hua min-tsu hsien-tsai hsü-yao he chung chiao-yü"*), *The Future* (*Ch-ien-t'u*), 7 July 1933.

the Han, the T'ang, and the Sung, China's authoritarian regimes were not despotic; a wide and fruitful margin of expression was allowed to minority or opposition groups, and because of that, it was inconceivable that the *honnête homme* should not take part in politics: a saying such as "The destiny of the empire is my personal responsibility" (*yi t'ien-hsia wei chi jen*) could serve as the motto of the entire scholar elite (whereas anybody who would have dared utter it under the Ming would have been guilty of the capital crime of high treason!). Statesmen sometimes fell out of favor and were exiled to far-flung border provinces, but they continued to do official tasks and to receive their salaries. Promotion or removal depended not on the whim of the ruler (whose powers were severely restricted by the very complexity of the governmental and administrative structure) but, rather, on the contradictory actions of various political factions. (In the time of Su Tung-p'o and Wang An-shih, conservatives and progressives succeeded each other in power in a way not far removed from the alternation of power in a two-party democracy.) With the Ming, this all changed drastically. The emperor took on absolute power and he exercised it not through ministers and the traditional high administration, but through his eunuchs and private servants. A career in politics, which for two thousand years (practically since the time of Confucius!) had been the privilege and responsibility of the scholar elite, became a cesspool from which honest men recoiled in disgust, a den of cutthroats from which they fled in fear. At the same time, the rigid control over public opinion exercised by the Ming regime condemned intellectual life to dogmatism, paralysis, and sterility. The only original thinkers of the period were active at the risk of their lives. As a corollary, and crowning their totalitarian enterprise, the Ming then cut off the Chinese empire from all external contacts. (The famous sea expeditions of Cheng Ho were ventures of empty prestige, with no cultural or economic significance, and cannot be compared to the flourishing maritime activities of the Sung.)

The image of China that the West received—of a static, sclerotic, hermetically sealed empire—reflects the state of affairs created by the Ming and perpetuated by the Ch'ing (the latter were barbarians with no political traditions, who painstakingly modeled their governmental administration on what they thought was the traditional Chinese model, whereas it was only a Ming perversion of it). This image does not in the least fit the reality of China under the Han, the T'ang, the Sung, even the Yuan. China's powers of invention, evolution, and adaptation, its creative genius, its political, cultural, and economic vitality, were both the result and the cause of a civilization that was essentially open, even frankly cosmopolitan.[33] If the start of the industrial revolution in Europe had coincided with one of those times when China was wide open to the outside world—which was its normal historical situation—China would never have been outdistanced in the modern "race to progress." The multiple, dense net of cultural and, even more important, economic ties that linked it with other countries would have kept it informed of the changes taking place. The pressure of these new developments would have been enough to generate similar or superior developments in China, long before the West acquired the decisive superiority in technology that was to bring about the tragedies of the nineteenth and twentieth centuries.

In fact, because of this fatal historical accident—the establishment of the isolationist and totalitarian Ming system, made worse by the new lease of life that the Manchus offered—China confronted the modern world blind and paralyzed, with the worst possible political heritage. A fair evaluation of the Maoist regime should take into account the heavy burden of this past. The totalitarian cancer, the organized cretinization, the dictatorship of illiterates,[34] the crass ignorance of the external

33. As a quick example: Ch'ang-an, the T'ang capital, which was at that time the largest city in the world, had not less than *two thousand* foreign-trading firms within its walls!

34. How else can we call those ideological authorities who (for in-

world together with a pathetic inferiority complex toward it[35]— those traits are not the natural features of the most civilized people on earth. To understand how Maoism could temporarily lead them into a rut so unworthy of their calling and their genius, it would no doubt be necessary to retrace the historical events by which the nation was so incredibly derailed.

Post Scriptum: I wrote most of the foregoing in 1972–73. I hesitated for a long time before having it published. Meanwhile, I returned to China again, and this helped me to bring my notes up to date on a few minor points.

This book is at the opposite pole from the one I would wish to write—and one day hope I can write.

If the Maoist bureaucrats could only shed some of the pessimism, suspicion, and contempt with which they look down on those over whom they rule, and if they would only take a risk and let us live, truly live, among the people, I cannot believe that the experience would furnish such negative impressions as mine here. Not that the daily life of the Chinese people is such a picnic—far from it—but at least its inexhaustible humanity would be enough to wash the sterile sarcasm from these pages.

July 1974

---

stance) gravely contrast the progressive genius of P. Degeyter (the composer of the "Internationale") with the decadent and corrupt scribblings of Debussy, "who expresses in music the historical transition from free trade to monopolistic capitalism"? (*Hung-ch'i*, No. 3, 1974.) Chiang Ch'ing, who ruled for ten years over China's intellectual and artistic life, once felt herself that the ruling elite's lack of culture was causing problems; she once enjoined a group of writers who paid a call on her to study closely the universal literary masterpieces so as to raise the level of their art, and proposed as models *The Count of Monte Cristo* and *Gone with the Wind* . . .

35. How else can we understand the attitude of the Peking mandarins, solemnly mobilizing eight hundred million people to denounce a puny charlatan like Antonioni?

A Short
Critical Bibliography

Need I remind the reader that this is not an objective book? Objectivity needs detachment—or indifference—and I feel incapable of either where China is concerned. But do we expect a witness to be objective? It is enough if he is sincere: impartiality is for the judge—in this case, the historian—who will pass judgment after hearing all the contradictory evidence. That in this matter serene and well-informed judges can be found is attested by the evidence of three books that are compulsory reading for anyone who is interested in modern and contemporary China:

Bianco, Lucien. *Origins of the Chinese Revolution.* Palo Alto: Stanford University Press, 1971.

Guillermaz, Jacques. *A History of the Chinese Communist Party*: I, *1921–1949*, London: Methuen, 1972; New York: Random House, 1972 and II: *The Chinese Communist Party in Power*: *1949–1976*, Boulder: Westview Press, 1976.

The reader who wants to go further in his research will find excellent bibliographies in these three books. I might also remind him of the gripping classic by Harold R. Isaacs, *The Tragedy of the Chinese Revolution* (Palo Alto: Stanford University Press, 1951).

On the Cultural Revolution, my book entitled *Les Habits neufs du Président Mao* (Paris: Champ Libre, 1971) [*The Chairman's New Clothes* (London: Allison and Busby, 1977)] gives a handy general survey; some deplore its verbal excesses; it has the advantage of being based on direct and irrefutable Chinese evidence. On the same subject, Pierre Illiez's *Chine rouge, page blanche* (Paris: Julliard, 1973) is a meticulous study that can be consulted with profit. In English, Stanley Karnow's *Mao and China* (New York: Viking, 1972) remains one of the most lucid and readable accounts of this chaotic period.

While we do not lack foreign witnesses, Chinese witnesses are very rare, and this adds worth to that admirable, irreplaceable book by Mu Fu-sheng, *The Wilting of the Hundred Flowers* (New York: Frederick A. Praeger, 1962). On the question of thought control and thought reform, one must read Bao Ruo-wang (Jean Pasqualini and Rudolph Chelminski), *Prisoner of Mao* (New York: Coward McCann & Geoghegan, 1973). No one will ever understand what the Cultural Revolution actually meant for the Chinese, or what a tragedy Maoism became for China, without reading Ken Ling's *Revenge of Heaven* (New York: Putnam, 1972).

Taken neat, the whimsy and rambling pages of *this* book might be deleterious; taken along with some Maoist texts, their effect may well be tonic. Which Maoist readings should be particularly recommended? At the elementary level, I would suggest the periodicals: *Peking Review, China, China Reconstructs*; a joint subscription to those is cheaper than buying the weighty volumes by Macciocchi, K. S. Karol, Daubier, *et al.*, and gives the same contents, plus pictures and minus mistakes. (The Peking publications, at least, do not take Ta-ku K'ou for a man!) For style and legibility these periodicals can be compared to the articles on China in *Le Monde*, though in the realm of humor and pure fantasy they cannot measure up to some of the essays in *Tel Quel*.

Now if one wants to climb higher and reach the level of intelligence, one should refer essentially to the three authors I mentioned in the foreword: Han Suyin, Edgar Snow (*opera omnia*), and John King Fairbank, "The New China and the American Connection," in *Foreign Affairs*, Vol. 51, No. 1 (October, 1972). They are not without defects: the first is cynical, the second naïve, and the third too much of a diplomat,[1] but they are each uncommon personalities in their fields (literature, journalism, scholarship) with superior information at their disposal. In the West, Maoism has no more convincing advocates, because (unlike the other members of that flock) they know whereof they speak—even if they do not say all they know.

1. Diplomacy does not always pay. Though Fairbank has written, "the Maoist revolution is, on the whole, the best thing that has happened to the Chinese people in many centuries," the Peking mandarins are not grateful—at least if I am to believe the sharp comments made about him by Assistant Minister Chang Wen-chin during a private evening party that I had the pleasure to attend. The crime of the great American scholar had been to describe new China in historical perspective! (Unreconstructed Sinologists . . .) For Peking, flattery is not enough: it must be done in the style and with the terminology of the New China News Agency. Below that level, everything is calumny.

Index